Hal Ashby and the Making of *Harold and Maude*

Hal Ashby
and the Making of
Harold and Maude

James A. Davidson

McFarland & Company, Inc., Publishers
Jefferson, North Carolina

LIBRARY OF CONGRESS CATALOGUING-IN-PUBLICATION DATA

Names: Davidson, James A., 1958– author.
Title: Hal Ashby and the making of Harold and Maude /
James A. Davidson.
Description: Jefferson, N.C. : McFarland & Company, Inc.,
Publishers, 2016. | Includes bibliographical references and index.
Identifiers: LCCN 2016000166 | ISBN 9781476663210
(softcover : acid free paper) ∞
Subjects: LCSH: Harold and Maude (Motion picture) |
Ashby, Hal—Criticism and interpretation.
Classification: LCC PN1997.H2595 D37 2016 |
DDC 791.43/72—dc23
LC record available at http://lccn.loc.gov/2016000166

BRITISH LIBRARY CATALOGUING DATA ARE AVAILABLE

ISBN (print) 978-1-4766-6321-0
ISBN (ebook) 978-1-4766-2385-6

© 2016 James A. Davidson. All rights reserved

No part of this book may be reproduced or transmitted in any form or by any means, electronic or mechanical, including photocopying or recording, or by any information storage and retrieval system, without permission in writing from the publisher.

Front cover: Ruth Gordon as Maude and
Bud Cort as Harold in *Harold and Maude*, 1971 (Paramount
Pictures/Photofest); background images © 2016 iStock

Printed in the United States of America

*McFarland & Company, Inc., Publishers
Box 611, Jefferson, North Carolina 28640*
www.mcfarlandpub.com

Table of Contents

Acknowledgments	vii
Preface	1
Introduction	5
Cast of Filmmakers	9
1. The Chauffeur, the Pool Boy and the Screenwriter	13
2. The *Harold and Maude* Script	26
3. Selling the Script	39
4. The Accidental Director	50
5. The Kid Stays in the Picture	60
6. The Most Difficult Part of Making a Film	68
7. I Feel I Could Make This Film About as Funny as the Vietnam War	82
8. Bay Area Bound	90
9. The Rosecourt	105
10. The Motorcycle Cop, the Ambulance and the Railcar	118
11. Cat Stevens	133
12. Editing the Film	143
13. Dropping a Bomb and Rising from the Ashes	157
14. After *Harold and Maude*: Hal Ashby	168
15. After *Harold and Maude*: The Rest of the Cast and Crew	179
16. The Legacy of *Harold and Maude*	189
Chapter Notes	197
Bibliography	205
Index	207

Acknowledgments

This book could not have been written without the existence of the Academy of Motion Picture Arts & Sciences' Margaret Herrick Library in Los Angeles. This library holds production files related to the making of many of Hollywood's greatest films, and is available to researchers. I must say a big thank you to Jenny Romero and her staff there, including Faye Thompson, for being extraordinarily helpful to me when I was researching the documentation in the Hal Ashby files related to *Harold and Maude*. My thanks also goes to the staff at the Western Railway Museum in Rio Vista, California, for a special tour of the *Harold and Maude* railcar and relating some stories about how it was used in the making of the movie. I also visited the UCLA Library Special Collections to research the papers of Colin Higgins, and the staff there was very helpful and gave their full attention to all my requests as I looked through scripts, notes, film ideas scribbled on paper, newspaper articles and other memorabilia, trying to get inside the head of the man who had dreamed up the original script.

My wife and I visited many of the filming locations in the San Francisco Bay Area, and it was a great help to me to get the feeling and sense of the film's world in the light of everyday reality. I should thank those on the Internet and in various forums who offered clues to the locations that were used.

Nick Dawson was of special assistance to me in writing this book. Early on, he sent me the chapter notes that he had prepared for his biography *Being Hal Ashby: Life of a Hollywood Rebel*, and they were invaluable to me in fleshing out the story of the film in detail. I also offer my thanks to Amy Scott and Christine Bebbe, who were beginning work on their Ashby documentary around the same time that I was starting to work on my book. They gave encouragement and assistance at various points in the project. Tiwanna Ellerbe of the Bud Cort Fan

Acknowledgments

Club was also of great help to me and allowed me to use a photo of Bud that she had taken.

Contacting and speaking with people directly involved in the film was difficult, but Jeff Wexler was a particular help to me. *Harold and Maude* was Jeff's first film; he was a production assistant who was on hand for virtually all of the filming, so the answers that he gave to all my questions were invaluable. Pamela Bebermeyer, Ruth Gordon's stunt double, also took time out to speak with me and answer questions, as did actor Edward Vasgerdsian. Ellen Geer was very gracious in responding to my questions, and I owe her a great debt of gratitude for taking the time to respond to me. Tom Skerritt also took time out of his busy schedule to speak with me about his experiences on the film, and to remember Hal Ashby and Robert Altman, two men whom he worked with early in his career and whom he considered mentors. I should also thank the many others associated with the film who took the time through the years to give interviews in magazines, newspapers and film periodicals, all of which were a tremendous assistance in charting the making of this unique film.

Ron Mandelbaum and his brother, Howard, of Photofest in New York took extensive time to speak with me about my project and to give me advice and assistance on finding the best pictures to use for the book.

On a personal level, I must thank Rhonda Knudson, who opened her home in Manhattan Beach to me while I was doing my research in Los Angeles. Rhonda had recently lost her beloved husband Vern when I first visited in early 2014, and it must have been a very difficult time for her, but she nonetheless welcomed me into her home.

My greatest support in writing this book came from my wife Donna. She was at various times a research assistant, cheerleader, sounding board and critic, always encouraging me, always helping me to keep moving along, and never saying a discouraging word. I love her more than I can express in mere words, and know full well that this book would not have been possible without her.

Preface

Not too surprisingly, as the decade of the 1970s wore on, the term "cult film" was increasingly applied to the movie *Harold and Maude*. Webster's Dictionary defines the term "cult" as "a misplaced or excessive admiration for a particular person or thing." In the case of *Harold and Maude*, the admiration that many people felt was probably not misplaced, but may have been a bit excessive. As the love for the film grew, *Harold and Maude* was on the verge of moving beyond the stage of just being a "cult" film to becoming a genuine box office success. By the 1980s when the film was finally recognized as a moneymaker for the studio and a success for the filmmakers, it began to fall more into the category of beloved classic than oddball "cult" film.

So ... why a book about *Harold and Maude*, a movie made and released over 40 years ago?

The genesis of this book started about three years ago, when I re-watched the movie with my wife and son after it had been released on Blu-ray. We all enjoyed it very much, and I thought to myself how funny it was that a film so old, a film so steeped in the ideas of the flower power generation, had not really aged very much. It was still watchable, still enjoyable. Even my son (then 21), who had grown up in the video game era, liked it very much. Shortly thereafter, when I was casting around for an idea for a movie to write about, *Harold and Maude* came to mind.

I had always wanted to write something about Hal Ashby, a director I have admired since his glory days in the 1970s. I saw *The Last Detail*, *Harold and Maude* and *Shampoo* in a little over a year in the 1974–75 period, at which point I realized that these three great films were directed by the same man, a man that I had heard very little about. As the years went by, Ashby remained something of a mystery to me, even after his death in 1988. I wrote one short article about Ashby in

1999 for *Images Film Journal*, but I knew that I wanted to write more about him. Even after Nick Dawson's groundbreaking biography *Being Hal Ashby: Life of a Hollywood Rebel* came out in 2009, I stayed committed to my idea.

Harold and Maude seemed like a great film to undertake to write about, because it is beloved by so many people. Those that I have discussed the film with speak of it in terms that are so personal, deep and meaningful, that I knew it would be a good subject. Furthermore, there were a lot of things about the movie that I wanted to find out for myself. So, with the idea that this book would be a story about the film with a cast of characters as well as a beginning, middle and end, I set out on "the road to find out" about *Harold and Maude*.

My journey began in Los Angeles at the Academy of Motion Picture Arts & Sciences' Margaret Herrick Library, where I studied the production files related to the film in the Hal Ashby collection. This included memos, letters, casting notes, budgets, camera reports and other documentation related to the production. Particularly interesting were the letters and correspondence exchanged between Ashby and Paramount production chief Robert Evans, including the most memorable December 1, 1970, letter detailed in Chapter 7 of this book. My wife and I also visited the Western Railway Museum in Rio Vista, California, and the staff there graciously agreed to help us when I told them that I was writing a book about *Harold and Maude*. They gave us a special tour of the railcar seen in the movie and told us some wonderful stories about its use in the film.

After writing much of this book, I found that Colin Higgins, the man who had originally dreamed up the characters of Harold and Maude, remained mostly a mystery to me. Fortunately, I discovered that his papers were in the Special Collections department of the UCLA Library, and I was able to go through scripts, notes, film ideas scribbled on paper, newspaper articles, brochures and other memorabilia that he had saved from this period. This was very helpful to me in trying to get inside the head of the man who had created characters that were so memorable to so many people. I was also able to finally put my finger on one thing that had eluded me so far, the genesis of the philosophy that Higgins used in filling out the fascinating and compelling character of Maude.

To really understand the making of a film, it is best to actually

Preface

walk in the shoes of the people who were there so many years ago. As a result, my wife and I visited many of the filming locations in the San Francisco Bay Area, and this was a great help to me in getting the feeling and sense of the film's world in the light of everyday reality. In addition, I tried to contact and speak with people involved in the making of *Harold and Maude*, although unfortunately many of the major players have passed away.

Finally, I researched and consulted as many books, periodicals and articles as I could to piece together what went on behind the scenes during the making of this amazing film. There were many resources in this area to draw upon and what began to emerge was the story of a film that could only have been made in the time and place of early 1970s Hollywood. The film industry had been shaken by years of changes until, in the mid– to late 1960s, an era emerged that we now call the "New Hollywood," an era that seemed to welcome new talent with a slant and point of view favoring the youth of America. Never before had such an unlikely scenario taken place as this one, in which a pool boy working at the home of a Hollywood producer managed to sell his first full-length script to one of the major Hollywood studios. The film was rushed into production in order to take advantage of the current popularity of youth-oriented pictures, and so with a director at the helm who had been described as an "acid freak," the making of *Harold and Maude* was quickly underway. It was shot entirely on location in the San Francisco Bay Area.

When the film finally made its way into movie theaters, it was almost completely rejected by audiences. But that was not the end of *Harold and Maude*. Rising from the ashes, it continued to play and play and play, going through several major re-releases, until finally, a decade after it was made, it started showing a profit. With a story this unbelievable, someone would have to ask, "Why write a book about *Harold and Maude*?" The only response I can think of is ... why *not*? It's fascinating. I hope you enjoy reading it as much as I have enjoyed researching and writing it.

Introduction

In December of 1971 I was 13 years old, living with my parents and sister in St. Louis, Missouri. One night, my parents went out to see a movie, and when they came home, I asked my mother what they had seen.
"*Harold and Maude*," she said. I asked what it was about.
"Well, it was about a very young man, almost still a teenager, really, who falls in love with a woman almost 80 years old."
That set me back! I mean, my grandma was an 80-year-old woman and, while she was a sweet old lady, I couldn't imagine anyone being in love with her but an 80-year-old man.
In 1974, when Paramount re-released *Harold and Maude* after it had begun to build its reputation as a cult favorite, I got to see it. I loved it. Despite the subject matter, there was something so captivating and fresh about the movie that it never left my mind. It became one of my favorite films and the next summer, when I saw *Shampoo*, I noticed that it had been directed by Hal Ashby, director of *Harold and Maude*. I saw *Harold and Maude* again in 1976, and have seen it many times since.
In 1981, I moved to the San Francisco Bay Area and, as I drove past the Golden Gate Cemetery in San Bruno or went to the Cliff House and noticed the Sutro Bath ruins on the cliffs below, I thought to myself, "That must have been where they filmed *Harold and Maude*." But it wasn't until years later that I finally began to truly investigate the film, where it was made, and the circumstances under which it was made. After noticing that people on the Internet were still fascinated with this film years and years later, I decided that I had to learn more. And to share what I had learned.

Introduction

Nineteen seventy-one was the beginning of what would be a transition in American life. The rage and tumult of America in the late 1960s had come to a head in late 1969 and 1970 with the Woodstock Music Festival, the moon landing and the Kent State University shootings. A country that had been divided by the Vietnam War and differences over racism, sexism and inequality was hoping to turn the corner and begin a healing process. In January, Charles Manson and three of his female followers were convicted of brutally murdering actress Sharon Tate and several others in the summer of 1969. In July, Doors lead singer Jim Morrison was found dead in a Paris bathtub. And in August, 40,000 people attended George Harrison's Concert for Bangladesh in New York in an effort to raise money for the country that had been stricken by famine and drought.

In Washington, D.C., President Richard Nixon installed a secret taping system in the White House Oval Office in February, so that all of his conversations would be recorded for posterity. In June, the *New York Times* began to publish excerpts from secret White House documents known as the Pentagon Papers that had been leaked to the press by former Pentagon insider Daniel Ellsberg; they detailed the years of cover-ups and lies that the U.S. government had engaged in during the Vietnam War. Finally the American public knew the extent to which they had been misled by their own leaders. Inevitably, the combination of these two events—along with Richard Nixon's paranoia—sowed the seeds of the Watergate scandal that would dominate the news for three years to come.

And in the San Francisco Bay Area and Hollywood, a movie was being made that was called *Harold and Maude*. It was an unusual love story, to say the least, between a young boy and an old woman. Perhaps it reflected the dazed and confused state in which America found itself during that time. Though *Harold and Maude* made barely a ripple upon its first release, it would become one of the longest-running and most beloved in the history of filmmaking.

In looking back on the making of *Harold and Maude* with 40 years of hindsight, we can see what a surprise it was that the film got made at all. Here is the story of an unusual movie made under the most unusual of circumstances. The first-time writer responsible for the script had been working as a pool boy for one of the producers before the script was sold. The director was a film editor until only recently.

Introduction

And the leading lady, at 74 years old, didn't even know how to drive a car well enough to do her own driving!

This is the story of *Harold and Maude*, the story of 1971, the year it was made and released, and the story of a movie that—no matter what—would not die.

Cast of Filmmakers

Hal Ashby: The 41-year-old director of *Harold and Maude* had won an Academy Award for film editing in 1968. *Harold and Maude* was his second directorial effort. He went on to a Best Director Oscar nomination for directing *Coming Home* (1978). He died of pancreatic cancer a decade later, at age 59.

Colin Higgins: Higgins was a UCLA grad student who, at age 28, went to work for a Hollywood producer and his wife as a pool boy and driver for their children. They helped him sell his script for *Harold and Maude* to Paramount. Higgins went on to write and direct several more films including the massive hit *Nine to Five* (1980) before succumbing to AIDS in 1988 at the age of 47.

Ruth Gordon: The first lady of American theater, Gordon was 74 when she made *Harold and Maude*. She had won an Academy Award in 1969 for *Rosemary's Baby*. Gordon went on to star and co-star in a number of other films before passing away in 1985 at the age of 88.

Bud Cort: Cort got his start in stand-up comedy in New York and was cast in Robert Altman's films *MASH* and *Brewster McCloud*. He won the part of Harold over several other actors. Still acting in the new millennium, he appeared in 2004 in Wes Anderson's *The Life Aquatic with Steve Zissou*.

Cat Stevens: Singer-songwriter Stevens, tremendously popular in the early 1970s, contributed two original songs and a number of other pre-recorded favorites to the *Harold and Maude* soundtrack. A convert to Islam in 1978, he is now known as Yusuf Islam and has recently resumed his recording career.

Robert Evans: A former actor, Evans was made head of production at Paramount in 1967. He was in charge at the studio until the mid–1970s, during which time he purchased the script for *Harold and Maude* and put it into production.

Cast of Filmmakers

Peter Bart: Evans' second-in-command and a longtime film executive, he brought the *Harold and Maude* script to Evans' attention. A former journalist, Bart was also a fan of director Hal Ashby and recommended to Evans that Ashby direct *Harold and Maude*.

Charles B. Mulvehill: A production coordinator for the Mirisch Company, Mulvehill came to work for Hal Ashby and ended up co-producer on *Harold and Maude*, as well as working on many of Ashby's other films. He produced *The Godfather III* in 1990.

Mildred Lewis: Wife of Hollywood producer Edward Lewis, Mildred hired Colin Higgins to clean the pool and drive her daughter Susan to and from school. When she read Colin's script, she and her husband arranged for the sale of the script to Paramount for development as a feature film.

Vivian Pickles: Stage-trained actress Pickles had appeared in several films that impressed Hal Ashby, and he cast her as the stuffy Mrs. Chasen, Harold's mother.

Charles Tyner: Tyner played a sadistic prison guard in *Cool Hand Luke*. Ashby cast him over several other notable actors to play the part of Harold's Uncle Victor, a general who tries to induct Harold into the military.

Eric Christmas: Veteran character actor Christmas played the flummoxed priest and he is hilarious as he is repeatedly shocked by Harold and Maude.

G. Wood: Wood played the psychiatrist who unsuccessfully tries to treat Harold. Wood had been in *MASH* as Brigadier General Hammond and again played that role in several episodes of the TV series; he and Gary "Radar" Burghoff were the only actors to reprise their *MASH* characters on TV.

Cyril Cusack: The respected Irish actor played the sculptor, Glaucus. Unfortunately, most of his scenes were cut from the final edit of the film.

Marjorie Eaton: Eaton played Maude's neighbor, Madame Arouet. Both of Eaton's scenes were cut from the film, so she did not receive an on-screen credit.

William Lucking: Cast as the motorcycle cop who hassles Harold and Maude, Lucking suffered an injury on the first day of filming and was out of the picture. He recently appeared on the TV series *Sons of Anarchy*.

Cast of Filmmakers

Tom Skerritt: A friend of Hal Ashby's, Skerritt took over for Lucking when he was sidelined with his injury and played the motorcycle cop. He was credited as "M. Borman." Skerritt has had a long and successful TV and film acting career.

Ellen Geer: The daughter of famed actor Will Geer, she was cast as Sunshine Dore, Harold's last computer date. She taught acting at UCLA for many years.

Shari Summers: The actress who played Harold's second computer date, Edith Fern, married producer Charles B. Mulvehill shortly after filming wrapped.

Judy Engles: Bud Cort's former comedy partner, she played Harold's first computer date, Candy Gulf.

Michael D. Haller: *Harold and Maude*'s production designer, Haller came up with many of the key ideas that made the movie unique. He passed away in 1998.

1

The Chauffeur, the Pool Boy and the Screenwriter

In the fall of 1968, the University of California, Los Angeles campus was quiet. Located in the city's suburban Westwood district, it was largely a middle-class commuter school that had, for the most part, not been involved in the campus unrest of the late 1960s. It was unlike Berkeley to the north and Columbia on the East Coast in that revolutionaries and agitators had not taken over the campus. The most exciting thing that had recently happened was a second straight national basketball championship that had been won by John Wooden's Bruins squad the previous spring.

Like crosstown rival USC, UCLA was becoming well-known for its Theater Arts Department. In 1961, it was renamed the UCLA College of Fine Arts. For its first two years the department offered undergraduate study across three divisions: theater, motion pictures and radio. Developed in cooperation with the Academy of Motion Picture Arts and Sciences, Hollywood's four major radio broadcasting networks and the Associated Committee on Television, this arrangement marked the first time a leading university had brought together these distinct subjects under a single administration. It has a number of distinguished alumni to its credit; recent UCLA graduate Francis Ford Coppola had already started to make his mark on the film world by the time Colin Higgins enrolled in the Master of Fine Arts (MFA) screenwriting program in the fall of 1968.[1]

Higgins was 27, a few years older than most of the other graduate students in screenwriting at UCLA. Six feet tall and handsome, with wavy brown hair and blue eyes, Higgins had been around the world and had already had many experiences that his fellow students could only dream about. To those who knew him, his personality seemed to vacillate; sometimes he could be outgoing and friendly, and at other times he was inwardly drawn and shy. It was clear to anyone who met him that Colin Higgins had a brilliant mind and a great sense of humor, and that on practically every level he had a lot going for him. But he also hid a secret that many like him had to keep hidden during the more conservative era of the 1960s: Colin Higgins was a homosexual.

Like many students, Higgins was just scraping by and needed a place to live. One day in Melnitz Hall, the home of UCLA's Theater Arts Department, he saw on a bulletin board an ad which seemed to him as if a life preserver was being thrown to him by someone out of the blue. The note, placed by a woman named Mildred Lewis, was fairly simple: She needed someone to clean the pool at her nearby Bel Air home, sweep the tennis courts and drive her daughter to and from school. In exchange for this, there would be a place to live in the cottage at the back of the Lewis home. All he needed was a clean driver's license and the ability to sweep and clean, and he was home free.

It would seem like a menial job for someone as extraordinarily talented as Colin Higgins, but fortunately for him, Mildred was the wife of a Hollywood producer named Edward Lewis. Higgins didn't know it at the time, but when he answered that ad and got the job, it set in motion a series of events that resulted in his screenplay being bought by a major motion picture studio and made into a film on which he, Colin Higgins, served as producer. Even beyond that, it would result in the making of *Harold and Maude*, which would become known as one of the greatest cult films in the history of the cinema, and a movie that would launch the careers of many talented people.

Colin Higgins was born on July 28, 1941, in Nouméa, New Caledonia, a French territory near Australia, to an Australian mother and American father. He was the second eldest of six brothers, and his life as a boy was a constant whirlwind of activity. Like many people with numerous siblings, Colin could only imagine what life would be like as an only child. When he was later asked if his life growing up had been

1. The Chauffeur, the Pool Boy and the Screenwriter

anything like that of the only child that he had dreamed up, Harold Chasen, Higgins could only chuckle. Colin's father, an American working for Pan Am Airlines, enlisted in the Army following the attack on Pearl Harbor and so was gone for much of Colin's early childhood. After the war began, the Higgins family moved from New Caledonia to Sydney, Australia, where they lived for the duration of the war. In 1946, the family moved to Oakland, California, where Colin attended school. The Higginses returned to Sydney in 1950, residing in the suburb of Hunters Hill until 1958 and then returning to California. Colin, meanwhile, remained in Australia after the family moved in order to finish high school at St. Anthony's College, Robertson, N.S.W. He passed the state's Leaving Certificate examination with honors.[2]

All this moving back and forth, as well as the mixed citizenry of his parents, left Higgins with something of a feeling of being constantly out of place. In a short essay he wrote on his life growing up, he noted, "I spent most of my childhood in Australia—an American boy in British exile—and so I fell under the heavy influence of Queen and Commonwealth." The phrase "exile" is interesting, as it expresses how out of place he felt as a child and young man, feelings that both Harold and Maude could easily identify with. He finished the essay by noting that in 1959, "I returned home to the States—an American citizen with a solid British heritage."[3] Always identifying himself as an American (despite being born on foreign soil), Higgins would sometimes feel like a stranger in his own homeland.

As a youth, Higgins was a frequent and avid reader. He noted that at "the predominantly British-oriented boarding schools I went to, I was given the usual stiff quota of Shakespeare *et al.* but the novels I remember reading with pleasure are *Treasure Island, Coral Island* and *The 39 Steps.*" These choices are not surprising for a boy who liked fantasy and action stories, and who would come to particularly love and admire the films of Alfred Hitchcock. (Hitch had his first great international success with his movie adaptation of John Buchan's *The 39 Steps* in 1935.) Higgins noted that he also had a "mania" for detective stories, particularly Sherlock Holmes, as well as British prisoner of war stories such as *The Great Escape* (memorably produced by United Artists in 1963, directed by John Sturges and starring Steve McQueen and Richard Attenborough).[4]

After rejoining his family in Menlo Park, California, in 1959, Higgins attended nearby Stanford University for a year, but eventually he lost his scholarship when he decided to become an actor. He hitchhiked to New York and hung around the Actors Studio. When he could find no other work, he took a job as a page at the ABC television studios. After Higgins spent another year at Stanford, the Vietnam War started heating up and he faced the possibility of being drafted. So in 1962 Higgins enlisted in the U.S. Army where he graduated in Army journalism and, in Oxford, Mississippi, covered the first days at college of James Meredith, the first black student to break the color barrier there. Higgins was eventually sent to Germany, where he honed his writing skills working for *Stars and Stripes*, and served as feature editor of the 8th division newspaper *Arrow*.

After Higgins was discharged from the Army in 1965, he spent six months in Paris, studying at the Sorbonne, before returning to Stanford University. He was awarded a Bachelor of Arts in Creative Writing in 1967. While at college he supported himself as an actor, playing in small theater productions in the Bay Area. After graduation, he briefly worked as a merchant seaman, but ended up hitch-hiking to Montreal in the summer of 1967 to attend the Exposition and World's Fair going on in the city at that time.

Higgins' attendance at "Expo '67," as it became known, was something of a turning point in his life. The event was one of the most successful World's Fairs of the 20th century, with many countries participating and millions of people attending during the six months that the fair was open. Higgins spent many days at the Expo pavilions, repeatedly watching films such as *Kaleidoscope* by Morley Markson and *We Are Young* by Francis Thompson and Czech avant-garde filmmaker Alexander Hammid. These experimental, creative and imaginative films were sometimes shown in large formats and on multiple screens, and opened Higgins' eyes to the technical and artistic possibilities of film.[5] Ultimately inspired to go deeper than just acting or even writing, Higgins left Montreal intent on becoming a filmmaker. Returning to California, he enrolled in the fall of 1968 in the Master of Fine Arts program in screenwriting at UCLA.

Higgins had lived an ambitious and restless lifestyle up to this point, traveling constantly and trying his hand at various endeavors in order to quench his thirst for adventure and new experiences. His tenure at UCLA would be the culmination of this period. In the UCLA

1. The Chauffeur, the Pool Boy and the Screenwriter

screenwriting program, the students needed to write and produce three films, the third of which would serve as the student's thesis in order to attain his or her Master's degree. Higgins' first film *Opus One*, a satire on student films, was bought by Filmways, a highly successful film and television production company. Included in Filmways' "Genesis I" program, *Opus One* was shown at theaters and colleges; additionally, the script of the film was published in a book called *Films on Campus* by Thomas Fensch. Higgins' second film *Retreat* was an anti-war statement and won the Long Beach Film Festival Grand Prize and was again bought by Filmways for inclusion in "Genesis II." During his three years at UCLA he also continued acting, being voted Best Actor of the Year in 1969 by the UCLA Student Theatrical Society and appearing with Jack Lemmon in the Garson Kanin production of *Idiot's Delight* at the Ahmanson Theatre in Los Angeles.[6]

But despite all this success, Colin Higgins was still just another college graduate student. He was far past the point of being financially assisted by his parents, and so was looking around for a part-time job and a place to live. Both of these problems were solved the day he saw Mildred Lewis' ad at Melnitz Hall. When he met with Mildred, he impressed her as being reliable and serious, and got the job over several other candidates. At the time, Colin Higgins believed he had just found a position that would help him with his finances and living arrangements as a UCLA graduate student; he had no idea what kind of life-changing circumstances he had gotten himself into, because he had no idea that Edward Lewis was a Hollywood producer who had worked with the likes of Kirk Douglas and produced the epic film *Spartacus*.

———

Edward Lewis had come to Hollywood after serving in World War II and, like Higgins, began his career writing screenplays, at first with limited success. In 1949 he produced *The Lovable Cheat*, his own screen version of a story by Balzac, and another film, *The Admiral Was a Lady*. Lewis formed a television production company in 1951 and went east to produce *The Faye Emerson Show*, the first television series to be filmed for national distribution. In addition to this, his other early TV producing efforts included the *China Smith* series and 50 episodes of *Schlitz Playhouse of Stars*. The industry practice of using individual episodes of an anthology series as pilots for new series originated with *Schlitz Playhouse.*

In 1956, Lewis was signed to a writer-producer contract for Kirk Douglas' Bryna Productions, and within two years he had been elevated to the position of Bryna's vice-president. By now, Lewis was married to Mildred Inez (whom he and others called "Millie"), who was also acting as his producing partner. Millie introduced her husband to Howard Fast's novel *Spartacus* and Lewis, impressed with it, suggested it to Kirk Douglas for development by Bryna Productions. Part of the interesting backstory of *Spartacus* is that when a screenwriting deal with writer Howard Fast did not work out, Lewis and Kirk Douglas decided to hire blacklisted screenwriter Dalton Trumbo to write the script. Lewis was to front for Trumbo, taking the screenwriting credit and passing payments along to Trumbo under the table. But Lewis became increasingly embarrassed at receiving praise for a script he had not written, and finally all parties concerned decided to go out on a limb and give screen credit to Trumbo, in spite of the industry's unspoken blacklist. Years later, Trumbo would thank Lewis for being "the man who gave me my name back." As the years went on, Lewis had the distinction of producing more of Trumbo's screenplays than anyone else, including *Lonely Are the Brave* (1962), *The Fixer* (1968), *The Horsemen* (1971), *Executive Action* (1973) and *The Last Sunset* (1961).[7]

Edward and Millie lived near the UCLA campus in an opulent Bel Air home at 214 St. Pierre Road, complete with swimming pool and tennis court. The couple also had a ten-year-old daughter named Susan, and a big part of Colin's job was to drive her to and from school, so that Millie wouldn't be burdened with the task. One day in 1969, while driving Susan to school, Colin began telling her the story of the new script that he was writing for his "Project 3," the last and most important film that he would make at UCLA. In a June 7, 2001, interview, Susan recalled that "every day on our way to school, he would tell me where he was in creating the story, and he'd ask me for advice. You know, treat me like I was very adult. And at some point, I came home and I told my mom about it. Because it was just an amazing, just a great story."[8]

Higgins originally envisioned the story for his third film script at UCLA as a play (which eventually came to fruition after the film was

1. The Chauffeur, the Pool Boy and the Screenwriter

completed) but ultimately he wrote the story as a screenplay, tentatively entitled *Harold and Maude—A Love Story for Our Time*. It was, in some ways, a sort of a "girl next door" love story, except that the "girl" that Higgins' 19-year-old protagonist falls in love with is 79 years old. In 1979, during an American Film Institute seminar, Higgins told the audience that he modeled Maude on three woman: his grandmother; a woman that he had known in Australia who lived an avant-garde and somewhat "artsy" lifestyle; and a woman that he had met in America who, despite being a concentration camp survivor, kept a positive and upbeat outlook on the world. These three characters melded in Higgins' mind and came together in his script as the amazing and indomitable Dame Marjorie "Maude" Chardin, with whom Harold (and eventually legions of filmgoers) would eventually fall in love.[9]

Higgins' first draft begins the same way all the others would; that is, with the scene in which Harold hangs himself for his mother's benefit. About this time, something happened that allowed Higgins to imagine the sequence as it would be on film, and would allow him to model this opening on that of one of his idols: Alfred Hitchcock. While working on a film that was being made by some other students, Higgins found an L.A. facility that would rent him a camera dolly that would allow him to move the camera from nine inches off the floor to as high as nine feet.[10] Higgins envisioned an opening shot for his film that would follow Harold's feet as he enters the room, then continue to follow them as he steps up on a chair, then follows them as he steps off the chair and hangs himself, his feet dangling in space. The camera would then continue up over Harold's shoulder as his mother enters the room and finally notices him hanging there. This inexpensive dolly allowed Colin to envision this complicated shot and gave him a way that he could pull it off.

The first draft of the 20-minute film also included the dinner scene with Mrs. Chasen and her friends; the scene in which Harold commits suicide in Mrs. Chasen's bathroom; several discussions with the psychiatrist; and two scenes of Harold viewing a junkyard. There is an additional scene in this draft (which never appeared in later drafts) in which Harold commits a fake suicide by apparently blowing himself up in his room. Harold eventually meets Maude at the first funeral he is shown attending, the outdoor funeral, and they quickly get to know one another, going to the flower farm and sitting in front of the fire in

Maude's apartment. After they have fallen in love, Harold returns home to tell his mother he is marrying Maude, but on her 85th birthday (not her 80th, as it would be in later drafts), Maude takes sleeping pills and is rushed to the hospital where she dies. The last scene is a replay of the first scene in which Harold appears to hang himself as his mother comes into the room admonishing him to be on time for dinner. But in the final sequence of shots, quick cuts from a long shot to a closeup, we see that Harold has actually committed suicide this time and the film ends on a closeup of Harold's impassive, dead face.

———

In Higgins' "Project 3 Proposal," he outlined his intentions for his final film at UCLA. He wanted to "work with professional actors of some name value under the new SAG rulings ... to devise and execute complicated dolly and crane shots (springing from a desire to try my hand at Hitchcockian ropewalking)" and finally to "bring the film to work print completion for $1500."[11] These goals seemed somewhat modest, but we can see, even with Higgins' coy reference to "Hitchcockian ropewalking" (referring to Hitchcock's 1948 film *Rope*, in which the Master of Suspense used long ten-minute takes to make the film appear to be one long shot), that his goals were actually pretty lofty.

After hearing from her daughter about the script that Higgins was writing, Millie said she would like to see for herself what was so extraordinary about it. When Millie read the work in progress, she knew right away that it was something special. She told Colin he was "crazy to blow this great idea on a 20-minute job," and Higgins undertook to rewrite the short script into something that could be turned into a feature. In a new thesis proposal, Higgins told his professors, Louis C. Stoumen, Roger MacDougall and Department Chair John Boehm, that he wanted to expand his script to feature length so that "I will have something to market when I leave the University."[12] Higgins also intended to enter the script in the prestigious Samuel Goldwyn Creative Writing Awards offered to UCLA students.

In expanding his script, Higgins had to add many characters and scenes and expand existing scenes that he already had completed. He added a sculptor who is a friend of Maude's; the sculptor's name is Conrad in the early versions of the script, Glaucus in the later versions.

1. The Chauffeur, the Pool Boy and the Screenwriter

The sculptor served the useful function of helping Harold and Maude with tools and implements when they decide to steal and replant the little dying tree. Higgins also added a neighbor of Maude's, a foreign woman named Madame Arouet, whose only role seems to be to work in her garden. It appears that Higgins wanted the characters of Glaucus and Madame Arouet to be somewhat complimentary, but also to stand in opposition to each other. Madame Arouet represents a desire to till the soil and work with nature, while Glaucus is a somewhat frustrated individual who seems to represent the futility of man working with tools (for instance, Glaucus' penchant for chiseling sculptures out of ice which melt as soon as he is finished with them). Mrs. Chasen, meanwhile, is given a brother, a one-star general named Victor Ball who keeps Harold out of the draft because his sister has asked him to, but who eventually advises her on induction. A priest is added to the mix as the logical person who officiates at the funerals that Harold attends. Finally, Higgins decided to add three computer dates to the story, each of whom Harold successfully chases away before the date goes very far.

But most significantly, Higgins decided that at the end of the script, Harold would choose life instead of following Maude into death via suicide. Because of this, he would need one crucial thing that would make or break his script: He had to find for the character of Maude a philosophy, a point of view which would be so compelling, so captivating, that Harold and the audience would fall completely in love with her and the way she looks at life. This would, in the end, save Harold and send him out into the world ready to live and love again. And in the tumultuous times and place that he lived, he didn't have to look very far to find what he was looking for.

Higgins faced a daunting task as he lengthened his script and expanded and deepened the characters. Most notably, he had to explain what it was about meeting Maude, this woman on the verge of becoming an octogenarian, which would be so life-changing for his young hero, Harold Chasen. As he wrote, Higgins' notes indicate that he seemed to want to understand exactly who Maude was and where she had come from in order to be able to clearly show the way that she would influence Harold. This included sketching out a timeline of

Maude's life, from her birth in Vienna around 1890, to her marriage to her first husband, Eric, in the 1910s (Eric dies six months later in a "house fall"), to her years with Frederick in the 1930s and her period of "Resistance & Concentration Camp" in the 1940s. Higgins' notes indicate that 1945 was the year that Maude came to America. He also noted that her family was wealthy. Like Higgins himself, Maude had parents from two different countries: Her mother was English and her father Austrian.

But first and foremost, Higgins knew that Maude had to actually reflect a compelling philosophical stance that she could convey to Harold during the course of the story in order to change his life. Around the time Higgins was expanding the script, the winter of 1970, he read an article in the January 13, 1970, issue of *Look* magazine that seems to have had a profound influence on him. Written by John Poppy, it was entitled "Why We Need a New Religion." Higgins highlighted the section article where Poppy wrote: "We need a religion that is life-oriented enough to deal with death.... [A] new religion would honor those who live in harmony with the earth instead of trying to subjugate it."[13] In mulling over what this "new religion" could be, a religion that would allow all to live in harmony with the Earth, Higgins seems to have finally found the philosophical outlook that he could apply to Maude that would allow her to truly enlighten and encourage Harold to embrace life, not reject it. And he found it in what was going on in the world around him at that time, the dawn of the new decade of the 1970s.

In the late 1960s, a new subculture began to emerge out of the counterculture revolution that had taken place during the "Summer of Love" and the tumultuous years that followed. The 1967 stage production *Hair: The American Tribal Love-Rock Musical* predicted the coming of a new age and at the time, it did seem to many that a change was coming in the way people thought about themselves. Experiments with psychedelic and hallucinogenic drugs, as well as acid rock music, were opening the eyes of many young people to the power that could be harnessed inside them. These thoughts and feelings began to emerge with a new appreciation for concepts like astrology, harmonic convergence and reincarnation. Groups began to form around the concept of spiritual training in order to reach a deeper consciousness within oneself, utilizing methods such as meditation and other personalized tech-

1. The Chauffeur, the Pool Boy and the Screenwriter

niques that stressed finding inner truth. Concepts such as Transcendental Meditation, EST and Yoga all emerged from this period as popular teaching techniques for spiritual and personal enlightenment. As silly as it seems, this new way of thinking even reached the public consciousness in something as banal as a television commercial, as in the extraordinarily popular 1971 TV ad campaign for Coca-Cola in which a group of young people stood on a scenic mountainside, holding hands and singing about how they'd like to teach the world to sing.

Higgins knew that Maude would have to express this New Age thinking in a way that would connect with his audience and give her the status of a visionary leader who helps Harold find himself (and by extension, also helps audience members interested in self-growth). But as he pondered this, he wondered what philosophy would best express this to the audience. He seems to have found what he was looking for when he came upon a philosophy that had gained popularity at the time in the wake of the New Age movement: It was called Theosophy, and a close look at its tenets indicates that Higgins may have based much of what Maude said and believed on its notions and ideas.

The term Theosophy is derived from the Greek word theos (or "god") and Sophia (or "wisdom"). It is sometimes referred to simply as "divine wisdom." An occult movement that had its origins in antiquity, Theosophy underwent a revival with the formation of the Theosophical Society in New York in 1875.

Is this the "real" Maude? Helena P. Blavatsky founded the modern Theosophy movement and wrote several of its integral texts. Like Maude, she came to America from Europe later in her life. She died in 1891.

23

A unity of religion, science and philosophy, the contemporary theosophical movement was led by Helena Petrovna Blavatsky (1831–1891). Blavatsky, like Maude, was born into an aristocratic family of European descent before relocating to America. As a leading thinker of the Theosophical movement, she wrote *Isis Unveiled* and *The Secret Doctrine*, along with other works recognized as classic expositions of Theosophical doctrine.

The basic goals of Theosophy are included in the so-called Three Objects: to form a nucleus of universal brotherhood of humanity, without distinction of race, creed, sex, caste or color; to encourage the study of comparative religion, philosophy and science; and to investigate unexplained laws of nature and the powers latent in human beings.[14] The Theosophical Society also suggested that the uninitiated can best understand the philosophy by comprehending the concept that there "is one infinite life, without beginning or end; no such thing as dead matter exists in nature. Every atom is a spark of the one Life. The divine unity behind all manifestation, commonly called spirit and matter, which some call God ... is so infinitely beyond comprehension that we can only stand in mute awe and refuse to insult its majesty by attempting to describe it. The most reverent conception for us is that which comes from Oriental teachings: absolute compassion."[15]

Higgins had gone so far as to acquire a number of pamphlets on Theosophy in order to study and utilize this philosophy that had been seized on by New Age theorists as an answer to many of the compelling questions asked by American youth. As he familiarized himself with these ideas, he noted, "Man is flowing with and participating in nature and its processes. That's self-evident—Man is part of nature.... Man is the only creature aware of his own mortality but incapable of facing it—hence fear. The awesome and agonizing loneliness of death." Ultimately, though, he would only succeed if he related such Theosophical concepts to the story of Harold and Maude and what happened to them after they met. He wrote to himself that Harold "faces the terrifying insignificance and aloneness in the cosmos. No faith," while Maude believes that "if life has no meaning then she creates her own meaning. Has faith. Like a child she sees everything with an unvarnished sense of wonder." Completing the thought, Higgins wrote that, in Maude's world, "the universe is not hostile—it's indifferent. Maude accepts this and carries her own light off into the darkness."[16]

1. The Chauffeur, the Pool Boy and the Screenwriter

Maude realizes that, as Victor Hugo said, we are "all under sentence of death but with a sort of indefinite reprieve." Furthermore, about death, she believed as the Theosophists did that the body "is a house to be rid of" and that "the only thing you own is your body.... Society tries to make someone everyone. But each human is unique, unprecedented, unrepeatable. Respect that individuality. Hold onto your face."[17] In the new, extended version of the script, Maude spoke new lines such as "Greet the dawn with the breath of fire!" and "We don't own anything. It's a transitory world. We come on the earth with nothing, and we go out with nothing, so isn't 'ownership' a little absurd?"[18] These lines clearly reflect the philosophical wisdom of Theosophy. With these new ideas in place, it was easy for Higgins to craft sequences like the one between Harold and Maude in the daisy field, and to forge the relationship between the older woman and the younger man as if it was one between a teacher and a student, between a giver of knowledge and a seeker of truth.

Now when Harold met Maude, he would end up choosing life over death and would want to live and not follow her into death through the ultimate act of suicide. His script had come a long way, with a completed story, a wide variety of characters and a resolution that made sense.

His script was finished, but there still was a long way to go before the cameras would roll.

2

The *Harold and Maude* Script

Higgins' script ended up 110 pages long and a world away from the 20-minute student film that he had first envisioned. New parts were added and scenes extended, and considerable character development now took place. But like every version that Higgins had done, the opening remained the same: the extended camera shot in which we follow Harold's feet as he hangs himself. In the script, we see a door open and a pair of feet enter the room. The feet belong to Harold Parker Chasen, a morose 21-year-old who lives with his wealthy, widowed mother. The camera follows Harold's feet behind the opening credits as he crosses the room, puts on a record, takes down a window shade cord, steps up onto a chair and finally steps off the chair with his feet dangling in the air, appearing to have hung himself. The camera pans around to show a woman of about 45, whom we learn is Harold's mother, enter the room and glance over at him. Her response is not what we expect: "I suppose you think this is very funny, Harold!" Mrs. Chasen says, before making a phone call to her hair stylist. She turns, reminds Harold that dinner is at eight and leaves the room, unimpressed. Harold is left hanging.

At dinner, Mrs. Chasen entertains guests with a story of Harold's late father, who disappeared on a trip to Paris and was found by the French police floating naked down the Seine River. Based on this story, Harold's father appears to have been something of a free spirit and, we can assume, probably found himself in conflict with his wife's rigid views about normal societal behavior. Mrs. Chasen then speaks condescendingly to Harold, as if he was still a child who had to be reminded to eat his vegetables. Later that night, as Mrs. Chasen is getting ready for bed, she enters her bathroom, only to find that Harold appears to

2. The Harold and Maude *Script*

have gruesomely slashed himself to death in the tub. Mrs. Chasen appears more visibly upset by this bit of "amateur theatrics," storming out of the bathroom claiming that she has had enough. Harold grins slyly, happy that this time he got a real reaction out of her. There is a cut to a scene in the office of Harold's psychiatrist. (Originally he was named Dr. Schidler but in the movie he is referred to only as "the psychiatrist.") In the script this scene, in which they discuss Harold's fake suicides, is intercut with a shot of construction demolition, which was apparently meant to serve as a counterpoint to the banal talk between doctor and patient. The finished film, for the most part, did away with this technique except for the one scene in which Harold and Maude picnic at a construction site.

In the next scene, Mrs. Chasen goes into a pool house as she prepares to go for a swim. She glances through a window that looks into the underwater area of the pool and sees Harold, floating face down in the water, apparently drowned. She ignores him and closes the window blinds. The story then cuts back to the psychiatrist office, as Harold says that he is worried that his fake suicides are not having the effect on his mother that they used to have. When the doctor asks if Harold has any other pastimes, Harold tells him about going to watch the machines working in a junkyard, and there is a quick cut to an auto demolition yard. When the psychiatrist presses Harold about other pastimes, Harold tells him that he enjoys attending funerals, and there is a quick cut to Harold attending a funeral at a cemetery. Off in the distance, Harold gets a first glimpse of the woman he and the audience will come to know as Maude, who is sitting under a tree eating a piece of fruit, apparently having a picnic.

Harold arrives home driving a hearse, just as two of his mother's friends are leaving. After wondering why Harold would buy such a "monstrosity," his mother tells him that she wants him to see her brother, Harold's Uncle Victor Ball, a one-star general who was "General Bradley's right hand man." In the ensuing scene, Uncle Victor, a "bluff, hearty, totally military man," encourages Harold to consider joining the Army to help him grow up and he encourages Harold to be more like American patriot Nathan Hale, who was captured by the British during the Revolutionary War and hung, uttering his famous line, "I only regret that I have but one life to give for my country." The general's admiration for Hale is ironic, particularly since Harold conducted his own mock hanging in the first scene of the film and continues to give various lives during his subsequent fake suicides. Mrs. Chasen also wants Harold to mature, and after his meeting with Uncle Victor she tells him that it is time for him to get married and begin to accept some adult responsibilities.

Next, in an extended scene at a church funeral, Harold meets Maude for the first time. Both acknowledge that they don't know the deceased, and that they attend funerals as a pastime. Maude says that she heard that the deceased was 80, which seems to her to be the right age to die. She makes the telling comment, "I mean, 75 is too early, but at 85, well, you're just marking time and you may as well look over the horizon." On the way out of the church, Maude borrows Harold's pen and draws smiles on the faces of the statues of four saints in the church foyer. Outside, Maude offers Harold a ride, but Harold says that he has his own car. After Maude drives off, the priest comes up to Harold asking who that old woman was, since she just drove off in his car. It appears that, in addition to attending funerals of people that she doesn't know, Maude also has a pastime of stealing cars.

In the Chasen den, Mrs. Chasen tells Harold she has signed him up for computer dating and fills out the information form for Harold, ultimately including her own opinions, not Harold's, on the form. Harold draws a pistol and, after contemplating shooting his mother, he ends up performing another mock suicide.

At another funeral, Maude whispers to Harold during the solemn graveside service, causing a disturbance. Afterwards she picks up Harold in his own car, which she has stolen. After he mentions this fact, Maude lets Harold drive her to her apartment and they begin to get to know each other.

In another scene with the psychiatrist, Harold says that he "burned down the chemistry building" at his old school and resists memories of his father. Next there is a scene in Harold's room at night, showing some of the things that he uses to commit his mock suicides. Harold also has a dummy of his own severed head on a dish, which he puts on a dummy of his body. When he can't affix the head correctly, he goes into the closet to look for something. Mrs. Chasen enters the room to inform Harold that his first computer date will be arriving the next day and to warn him to be on his best behavior. She speaks to the dummy, not noticing it is not Harold, only commenting that he looks "a little

2. *The* Harold and Maude *Script*

When Bud Cort was screen-tested at Ashby's home in December 1970, it was clear to everyone present that he was the right choice to play Harold. Eventually even Colin Higgins was won over. He is shown here with Ruth Gordon.

pale." Harold stands in his closet listening to his mother, wielding a cleaver.

Harold's first computer date, Candy Gulf, arrives at the Chasen home as expected. She is talking pleasantly with Mrs. Chasen when Harold goes out into the yard and appears to set himself on fire. Candy runs off in terror, making Harold's first date a short one.

Harold goes back to Maude's and meets her neighbor Madame Arouet, a worldly-wise woman from southern France who tends to the garden behind Maude's apartment. Madame Arouet directs Harold to the studio of Glaucus, the sculptor, for whom Maude is posing in the nude. Harold and Maude return to Maude's home for some oat straw tea, where Harold is shown some of Maude's odd paintings. One, "The Rape of Rome," depicts Leda and the Swan. He also sees a provocative sculpture, which he fondles suggestively when Maude is not looking. Maude tells Harold that she will turn eighty years old next

Saturday, then introduces him to the "odorifics," a machine that reproduces smells. Harold is drawn to this woman who seems to live life for all that its worth and believes in "greeting the dawn with a breath of fire!"

In a series of shots, Harold and Maude spend more time together, and Harold begins to be drawn towards Maude as he learns her views of life. First they picnic at a junkyard, then they take a walk through a vegetable field and a flower farm and daisy field, where Maude tells Harold her philosophy (Theosophy) of life. She is determined to embrace every moment that life has to offer and to make the most out of what every day brings. Maude believes fully in individualism, as she points out to Harold that many people are like "this" (and holds up a daisy) "but let themselves be treated like *this*" (as she gestures to the wide daisy field). Maude also believes in self-determinism, in making her own decisions about how she lives and, eventually, about how she dies. This view stands largely in opposition to Harold's feelings at the beginning of the film, when he seemed to believe that he was fated to live out a dreary life under the thumb of his mother and her claustrophobic society.

Although Maude's penchant for stealing cars at first puts Harold off, she says she is only "reminding people not to get too attached to material things," an attitude that Higgins doesn't necessarily seem to endorse, but primarily plays for comic effect. So when Maude is driving and she and Harold discover a little tree that is being choked by automobile smog and needs to be replanted in nature, she has no problem concocting a scheme to steal it from public property. After deftly avoiding the police, they return to Glaucus' studio to discuss strategies for the best way to liberate the little tree but find that Glaucus has fallen asleep as his ice sculpture melts. Back at Maude's apartment, Maude tells Harold about her past as a little girl growing up in Vienna. There she fell in love with a man named Frederick, "a doctor at the University, and in the government ... but that was all before," she adds mysteriously. The story of what happened to Maude and Frederick is never resolved in either the script or the film, but we can assume from Maude's melancholy attitude while discussing him that it did not end well. Finally, trying to shake off her mood, she moves to the piano and plays a song for Harold. When he says he does not play music, she gives him a banjo and encourages him to learn.

2. The Harold and Maude Script

Next we see Harold at home, trying to learn the banjo. Mrs. Chasen shows Harold the new sports car she has bought him to replace his hearse, but Harold has other things in mind. He gets a welding gun and modifies the sports car to look like a hearse. Harold and Maude go to Glaucus to get some tools for stealing the tree. In the next scene they are driving with the tree when a motorcycle cop—a classic authority figure—stops them to find out what they are doing. Maude escapes from the cop, driving donuts around him, and then she and Harold plant the tree in the woods. Again they are spotted by the cop, who stops them and tells them that they are in trouble. While his back is turned, Maude jumps on his motorcycle and she and Harold make their escape, returning to Glaucus to tell him what has happened. At Maude's apartment, Harold and Maude get high, and Harold relates to Maude the story of his first "death": While at boarding school, he caused a huge explosion in the chemistry building and was thought dead; he sneaked out and returned home, only to observe his mother being told by the police of his demise. His mother fainted away melodramatically at hearing the news, and Harold decided at that point that he preferred being dead; from then on he began re-enacting this moment over and over again via his mock suicides. Maude listens sympathetically, but she encourages Harold not to give in to despair and tells him to embrace life and live it fully.

Harold meets his second computer date, Edith Fern. Harold shows her and his mother how he has modified the sports car to look like a hearse. Edith runs off in terror when Harold pulls out a butcher knife and appears to cut his hand off as he sits chatting with her pleasantly.

In the next scene, Harold and Maude are lying on a blanket having a picnic; they are clearly growing closer. They sit on a beach at sunset holding hands, and as Harold glances down at Maude's arm he notices a tattooed number, indicating that she has likely been in a concentration camp. Maude is still optimistic and not bitter about life, despite all that she has been through.

When Harold's next computer date, an actress named Sunshine Dore, arrives, Harold demonstrates for her the process of performing the Oriental art of Hari Kari. Sunshine actually plays along, picking up the fake dagger from the prone Harold and stabbing herself, but as Mrs. Chasen arrives with drinks, all she can say upon seeing the apparently dead Sunshine is "Harold ... that was your last date!" Mrs. Chasen quickly sends Harold to see his Uncle Victor, who tells Harold that he is to be inducted into the Army, which will make a man out of him. Harold goes to see Maude, who is working in her garden with Madame Arouet, and they concoct a plan. While Harold is discussing the Army with Uncle Victor at a reservoir, Maude appears as a protestor for peace. Harold pretends to go berserk with hatred for her. Much to the chagrin of Uncle Victor, Harold chases her and during a struggle she eventually falls into the churning waters of the dam. The plan to deceive Uncle Victor has worked and Harold is dismissed from the Army for being mentally unfit.

Harold and Maude happily get together afterwards and talk about how they have pulled off the charade. They go to an arcade at a beach boardwalk and sit together on a pier holding hands, as fireworks go off. Harold gives Maude a small token he has made at the arcade that says "Harold loves Maude." The next morning, at Maude's apartment, it appears that she and Harold have spent the night together making love. Harold returns home to tell his mother that he is planning on marrying Maude, and he shows her Maude's picture. Harold's mother is shocked and goes to the psychiatrist. In a montage, Uncle Victor, the psychiatrist and the priest all express outrage that Harold is planning on marrying a woman "old enough to be [his] grandmother!" Back at the Chasen home, Harold and his mother talk about his plans to marry Maude, Mrs. Chasen expressing outrage that Harold would pick a woman so inappropriate for him.

On Maude's 80th birthday, Harold prepares a celebration for her at her apartment. He gives her a ring and tells her that he wants to marry her. But Maude has a surprise: As she has turned 80 years old, she feels that she has lived long enough, and earlier in the evening took sleeping pills. She tells Harold she will be "gone by midnight." Harold reacts with outrage and calls an ambulance. In the ambulance, Harold tells Maude that she must go on living because he now loves her, and Maude replies: "Oh, that's wonderful, Harold. Go ... and love some more..." They rush Maude to the hospital and Harold argues with an intern and the admitting nurse about Maude's insurance. After a long night of waiting, we see that it is too late, as a doctor tells a distraught Harold that Maude didn't make it. Harold drives his car wildly away from the hospital and towards the ocean edge. We see the car fly off a cliff and fall to the ground, smashing into total destruction. But then

2. The Harold and Maude Script

the camera tilts up and we see Harold standing on the cliff edge, holding the banjo. He walks off into the distance, plucking the banjo strings as the credits roll.[1]

Colin Higgins' *Harold and Maude* script was certainly extraordinary, particularly given the fact that it was essentially the work of a first-time screenwriter. At a time when youth "alienation" films were either blaming the older generation for all the ills in the world or criticizing the youth of America for being a bunch of drug-crazed, out-of-control "hippies," Higgins decided to take a different approach. Although Harold feels alienated by his mother and her generation's preoccupation with social status, material success and monetary achievement, Higgins suggests that by reaching out to an even older generation—represented here by the venerable Maude—the younger generation might be able to find some of the answers they seek. It was a completely new approach to the "generation gap" problem that faced the youth of the late 1960s: Look to an even older generation that, having endured the catastrophic horrors of the early part of the twentieth century, can now live life with a deeper meaning and a true appreciation for the changes that living brings.

With her yellow umbrella symbolizing both her zest for life and her desire to fight for change, Maude's philosophical approach shows Harold a way to embrace the living while accepting life's sorrows. Maude's umbrella represents the past for her, but the words she speaks were particularly relevant during the late 1960s and early '70s, a time of great political and personal change in America: "Oh, that's just a relic. I found it when I was packing to come to America. It used to be my defense on picket lines and rallies and political meetings—being dragged off by police or attacked by thugs of the opposition." And although Maude admits she is no longer fighting the way she used to, she is still fighting "but now in my small, individual way."[2] In this sense, *Harold and Maude* was slightly ahead of its time, and this may explain why it became more and more popular as the 1970s wore on and the ideas of New Age philosophy took hold. As Maude encourages Harold (and by extension the entire younger generation) to be less concerned with fighting for larger political issues than to look inward and embrace personal change and growth, she is advocating for a cultural shift from the radical years of the 1960s to the "Me Generation" of the 1970s. These words struck a resonant chord with audiences as time went by, resulting in the increasing popularity of the film.

In Higgins' script, Harold is attending a funeral when he first glimpses Maude, off in the distance having what Higgins describes as a "happy picnic." Maude seems to appear out of the blue, and she is introduced in a mythic, almost biblical way, as if she has stepped out of the Garden of Eden. Because Maude dies towards the film's end, and dies off-screen, she in a sense just "disappears" from Harold's life as suddenly and abruptly as she first appeared. In this way, Maude functions for Harold a bit like a fairy godmother or some other figure from myth, who only appears in Harold's life in order to instruct him on the value of living and loving. Maude may be seen on some levels as not even a "real" person, but a charmed figure who comes into Harold's life to spread a message (remember that Mrs. Chasen never actually meets her, and Uncle Victor only briefly glimpses her). In the end, Harold has loved Maude and has lost her, but now she has given him a chance to be reborn alive and find love again.

Harold is certainly traumatized by his past when the film begins. Lacking a father figure and clearly resenting his dominating mother, Harold is in some ways a variation of the character of the psychotic Norman Bates in *Psycho* (Harold's second fake suicide is a bathroom murder as in *Psycho*). Harold's fake drowning suicide recalls *Sunset Blvd.* and the pool murder of Joe Gillis, another young man under the control and influence of an older woman: his killer, the crazy Norma Desmond. Rejecting his mother's world and finding only the unsatisfactory alternatives represented by the triad of Uncle Victor, the priest and the psychiatrist, Harold has embraced a form of nihilism in which he believes in nothing except for the possibility of death and the relief it will bring from the burden of life. As a homosexual man who had to hide his sexual orientation in the repressive 1950s and early '60s, Higgins certainly empathized with both Harold and Maude as outsiders in a world that has, by and large, rejected them. But instead of embracing Harold's feelings of loss and disillusionment, Higgins has these two characters meet, and as a result Harold's entire view of the world changes.

Some of the best films of the hippie era were what we might call

2. The Harold and Maude Script

"road" films, in which the characters travel from place to place without settling down. *Easy Rider* and *Bonnie and Clyde* certain qualify as road films and even less significant "New Hollywood" films such as Francis Ford Coppola's *The Rain People* as fall into this category. These films represent the ennui and dissatisfaction of late 1960s youth as both a metaphysical as well as a physical journey, a movement from place to place, a restless search for inner truth. In addition, these films express a distrust and contempt for the institutions that had dominated American life for many years. In *The Rain People*, for instance, James Caan's character, college football player "Killer" Gannon, is injured in a game and has a plate put in his head, rendering him slightly stupid. The college heartlessly gives him a job raking leaves and finally cuts him loose to hitch-hike aimlessly around the country with a thousand dollars in his pocket. An institution such as a college, formerly something to be admired and trusted, is now regarded with suspicion and distrust, as American youth realized they had been duped by their government, which was sending them to fight a war in Vietnam that we couldn't win, a war that was also unjust.

Higgins, who had traveled across America and Canada through most of the 1960s, trying various jobs and going to several institutions of higher learning, must have identified with the characters in these films. However, when it came time for him to write a movie, he did not make *Harold and Maude* a road film. The characters don't travel aimlessly anywhere outside of the realm of where they live their day-to-day lives, but they still appear to be on a journey of self-discovery, very much looking to find out what it means to be a fully realized person capable of commitment and love. In *Harold and Maude* institutions such as marriage and the church are viewed with suspicion but they are not fully rejected; it is clear that these institutions are worthwhile but only once one fully understands themselves and their place in society. In this sense, *Harold and Maude* becomes a road film without the road. Its final message, to "go out and love some more," is in the end not as downbeat as many of the films of its time; it is a worthwhile and effective message, somewhat optimistic, and almost certainly why the film became so deeply loved over the years.

The scene in which Harold and Maude sit looking out at the bay holding hands is one of the script's greatest moments. At the point at which Harold is beginning to fall in love with Maude, he glances down and sees the tattoo on her arm; at this moment, Maude says "Dreyfus once wrote that on Devil's Island he would see the most glorious birds. Many years later in Brittany he realized they had only been sea gulls. To me they will always be glorious birds."[3] The reference is to Alfred Dreyfus, a Jewish French artillery officer convicted of treason and imprisoned on Devil's Island in 1895, only to eventually be exonerated and pardoned when it appeared the charges against him were based on anti–Semitism. Maude's reference to Dreyfus at the moment Harold realizes she was in a concentration camp is apt, because he now realizes that she has suffered from unjust imprisonment and possibly even anti–Semitism. The film never makes clear whether or not Maude is Jewish, or if she was just rounded up by the Nazis for her political activism; Higgins' notes seem to indicate that the latter is the case: In an early version of the script, Harold tells Maude that when it appears he is going to have to go in the army, she will help him just like she "did against the Gestapo." In fact, if Maude is not Jewish, it makes her imprisonment even more poignant, because she was confined not out of prejudice but to quell her anti-authoritarian spirit. Yet, despite all the hardship of her life, Maude does not wallow in self-pity or regret; instead, she continues to optimistically believe that those seagulls Dreyfus saw were "glorious birds."

Higgins described the *Harold and Maude* story not only to Susan Lewis and her mother, but to many people, in part to get their opinions and in part to help him flesh out ideas. One of them was an aspiring actress named Sandra Lowell, whom he met during the winter of 1970. Faced with the difficult task of typing the lengthy script on a manual typewriter as he tried to get it into a final version to submit to the Goldwyn awards and knowing that Lowell was out of work, he called her on February 9 and offered to hire her to come over and help him type the script. Lowell agreed to help Colin but, somewhat to his surprise, she offered to do the work without pay. Shortly thereafter, she arrived at the Lewis home and began to type the script as Colin dictated his additions to her. Everything went along fine for a couple of days, but eventually Lowell grew bored and started to try to make contributions and suggestions, all of which Colin rejected. He became frustrated with the slow progress they were making, as Lowell's contributions did not help at all and only slowed the process of getting the script in shape.

Somewhat frustrated by Higgins' rebuffs, Lowell at one point told him, "You never use anything I suggest." Eventually Higgins began doing most of the typing, as Lowell lolled on his bed, playing with her hair and making small talk. Whether she was looking for something more from the attractive young man is not known (something that, as a gay man, he was not interested in giving her) but after Higgins refused the idea of using a song that she had scribbled out, Lowell decided that she had had enough and would not be coming back. Somewhat relieved at her departure, Higgins carried on with the typing on his own, finishing the job the best that he could. After completing the draft, he took what he had to a professional typist and paid $50 to have it retyped, and completed the script in time to submit it for the Goldwyn awards.[4]

As winter turned to spring, even after the script was submitted to the competition (it came in third), Higgins continued to refine his work and shape the characters. A friend named Tom wrote comments on one of the scripts that Colin gave him, telling Higgins that he thought it was unlikely that Harold would call the motorcycle cop that stops him and Maude a "pig" since Harold is "not a revolutionary or a hippie."[5] Higgins heeded the advice and changed the line. However, on some other things, Higgins stuck to his guns. A friend named Jim commented on a script dated April 10 that, although overall he liked the script and felt it had "great potential," that "the whole concentration camp number seemed to be placed for affect only. I found nothing up to this point to give a clue that this was her history." Furthermore, Jim commented, the ice sculptor "appears to have no valid function in the piece except as a holder of tools."[6] Higgins left these parts of the script as they were, showing that he was confident in his work. (The sculptor *was* later largely cut from the film, indicating that Jim may have had a valid point. While the concentration camp number on Maude's arm did remain, some have also criticized it as being an unnecessary and superfluous addition.)

Over a year of hard, painstaking work had resulted in a script that showed tremendous promise. Friends and associates of Higgins such as Barbara Sammeth, Ross Brown and Bob Kosberg all praised it, telling

Higgins that it they had no doubt that it could be made into a great film. At this point Higgins was contemplating his next move: Should he try to raise money and produce *Harold and Maude* himself? He felt that he would need approximately $750,000. Yet he had no idea where that money would come from.

3

Selling the Script

Edward Lewis placed great faith in the opinion of his wife. Mildred had already recommended *Spartacus* to him, and it had turned out to be a major success. In 1982, she would share producer credit with her husband on the successful Costa-Gavras thriller *Missing*, starring Jack Lemmon and Sissy Spacek. "Ed was constantly pushing scripts at me," she told James Rogers in 2001, so when she read Higgins' script, she knew right away it was destined to be more than a student film. Furthermore, Millie felt that Higgins "was so modest, he was so un-pushy," and this lack of aggression on Higgins' part worked in his favor with the couple, who were tired of typical Hollywood types who were trying to get their scripts made into films. (Ed Lewis, at the time working on the John Frankenheimer film *The Horsemen*, even invited Colin to come to the studio to watch the famed director work, but Higgins never took him up on his offer despite his obvious interest.) Once Millie read *Harold and Maude*, she loved it. "I thought, 'My God, this can't possibly be used for a class thesis; it's much too good.' And from there, I told Ed about it and put him to work at what he does best—promoting—and somehow between all this, *Harold and Maude* evolved," Mildred said in the 2001 interview with Rogers.[1]

Instead of shopping the script around to anyone and everyone, the savvy Ed Lewis decided to take it to Paramount. "Paramount was the first and only studio I gave the script," said Lewis, who sent it to his good friend Peter Bart, the studio's assistant head of production. "I figured Bart would dig it," Lewis said in 1974. "I also felt the script was very commercial. So did Paramount."[2] Creating a sense of urgency about the script, Lewis told Bart and his boss, Robert Evans, that the script was very hot and they had to read it overnight and say yes or no, or it would go to another studio.

Although it was Hollywood's oldest and most venerable studio,

Hal Ashby and the Making of *Harold and Maude*

Paramount Pictures was on many levels a logical choice for a project as daring as *Harold and Maude*. Paramount was founded in May 1914 by W.W. Hodkinson. Sometimes known as "The Man Who Invented Hollywood," Hodkinson was born in 1881 and opened his first movie theaters in Ogden, Utah (birthplace of future *Harold and Maude* director Hal Ashby), in 1907. He expanded his theater chain into Salt Lake City and then to Los Angeles and San Francisco, becoming one of the West Coast's leading film distributors. Paramount was founded first and foremost as a film distribution company, not a production company, and it handled exclusive rights agreements with Adolph Zukor's Famous Players as well as Jesse Lasky's Feature Play Company. Hodkinson's significance to Paramount's history also includes his doodling of the mountaintop image that eventually became Paramount's logo.

After Zukor and Lasky's companies merged in June 1916, forming Famous Players-Lasky, they acquired Paramount, and Hodkinson was summarily fired from the company he started, with Zukor assuming the role of studio head. Like many early Hollywood moguls, Zukor was Jewish and European, born in Hungary, but at age 16 he had moved to America and become involved in the garment business. After these humble beginnings, he had great success as a fur designer, eventually amassing substantial wealth and entering the film business in the early twentieth century. His film career began when he invested in a partnership to build movie theaters, but by 1912 Zukor was also on the production side, forming Famous Players in order to bring successful stage plays to the screen.

Construction of the newly formed Paramount Pictures began in 1917 on Melrose Avenue, with the studio moving to its current location on Gower Street in 1926 and constructing the famous iron gates for which the studio would be known. The same year, Paramount acquired the Balaban and Katz movie chain and made Barney Balaban the studio president, while partner Sam Katz became president of The Publix theaters group. Paramount's early successes included *The Sheik* with heartthrob Rudolph Valentino and *Wings*, the first Academy Award winner for Best Picture.

Like most of the major studios, Paramount survived and thrived through the Depression years, boasting stars such as Mae West and W.C. Fields and directors like Cecil B. DeMille. Boasting a somewhat European style, Paramount even briefly hired German-American direc-

3. Selling the Script

tor Ernst Lubitsch as its head of production in 1935; he was fired after a year on the job and returned to directing. The studio was later home to such luminaries as Billy Wilder, who made the scorching Hollywood expose *Sunset Blvd.* there in 1950, and Higgins' idol Alfred Hitchcock, who directed some of his best films of the 1950s for Paramount, including *Rear Window* and *Vertigo*.

Like other studios, Paramount found the road rocky after the 1948 Justice Department decree that ordered the studios to divest themselves of their movie chains. Paramount sold off its Balaban and Katz theaters in 1949. Paramount was taken over by a corporate giant, Gulf+Western, in 1966. Gulf+Western was headed by the Austrian-born Charlie Bluhdorn, an industrialist and self-made man who had purchased a small Michigan auto parts company in the 1950s and turned it into a massive Wall Street success and corporate conglomerate. Bluhdorn was hardnosed, energetic, ambitious and a workaholic who hoped to turn Paramount into a filmmaking mecca.

A decade earlier, there probably would not have been a chance for a script such as *Harold and Maude* to be sold by an independent producer to a major studio. But the timing of the year 1970 was exactly perfect for Colin Higgins to realize his dream. For one thing, by the late 1960s the movie industry had lost a huge share of its audience, primarily to television. "The movie industry was more on its ass than any time in its history, literally almost wiped off the face of the earth," Peter Bart said about this period in Hollywood history. Moviegoing had peaked during World War II and the early postwar years, but had fallen continually since that time, dropping from a box office attendance of 78.2 million a week in 1946 to a low of 15.8 million a week in 1971, the year that *Harold and Maude* was released.[3] As in most industries during a time of crisis, studio executives were in a panic to bring people back into the theaters, and were doing anything they could to accomplish this goal, even if it meant substantially relaxing industry restrictions on sex and violence.

Furthermore, Hollywood studios had undergone a huge shakeup in the previous 15 years, changing from a studio system dominated by an assembly line approach to filmmaking to a much more free form environment in which themes of youth, violence and antiestablishment were utilized. Beginning in 1967, when *The Graduate* and *Bonnie and Clyde* were the big hits, the traditional approach to moviemaking changed. Established directors like Hitchcock, John Ford, Billy Wilder and Howard Hawks now seemed to miss the mark with younger audiences, who preferred more avant-garde films made by newcomer directors such as Mike Nichols and Arthur Penn, influenced by European directors like Godard and Truffaut.

Following the success of Nichols' *The Graduate*, Hollywood was awash in films that tried to cash in on the formula of the older vs. the younger generation. Films such as *The Trip, The Happening, Cactus Flower, Head* and *I Love You, Alice B. Toklas* tried to duplicate the success that Nichols had with his film, mostly to no avail. Paramount had tried themselves to capitalize on this trend with the Otto Preminger film *Skidoo*, released in late 1968. Audiences, however, were embarrassed at the sight of an aging Jackie Gleason taking an LSD trip while his wife, played by Carol Channing, cavorted with a number of crazy hippies and flower children. The film was a horrific bomb and eventually the studios realized that many of these more superficial treatments of the very real generation gap problem were only alienating their audiences further.

The two biggest hits of 1969 had been *Midnight Cowboy*, a film about two offbeat losers trying to get by in New York City, and *Easy Rider*, a road film in which two hippies take a trip across the country encountering girls, drugs and anger at their long hair and counterculture lifestyle. These films were made on real locations, not in studios, and were shot by young directors, with actors who often came from outside of the established Hollywood system. Parts of *Easy Rider* were even filmed with a 16mm camera while the "actors" wandered around New Orleans, high on LSD. In the early days of this "New Hollywood" era, studio executives, particularly the young, savvy ones such as Robert Evans, seized the moment and brought in filmmaking talent from unconventional sources. Thus, when Peter Bart called the flamboyant Evans about Higgins' exciting new script, Evans was willing to listen.

Evans, whose real name was Robert J. Shapera, had arrived in Hollywood in the 1950s as an actor but, realizing his shortcomings, quickly turned to a role behind the camera. In a surprise move, new Paramount chief Bluhdorn named Evans head of production in 1967 following Paramount's takeover by Gulf+Western. Evans' tenure at Paramount began somewhat inauspiciously, but hits such as the 1968 releases *Rosemary's Baby* and *The Odd Couple* improved his standing.[4] By the time

3. Selling the Script

he received a copy of the *Harold and Maude* script, Evans, not yet 40 years old, was looking to cash in on the wave of "New Hollywood" films and was willing to gamble on an unknown.

The spring of 1970 was an uncertain time for many young people in America. The anti-war movement, going strong since 1967, had begun to lose some steam. Then on April 30, President Richard Nixon made a televised announcement that U.S. forces in Vietnam would be making an incursion into Cambodia in an attempt to root out Viet Cong and other forces sympathetic to the north that were being harbored in the supposedly neutral neighboring country. Legend has it that Nixon came to this decision after a viewing of the film *Patton*, during which George C. Scott's performance as the title character stirred up patriotic feelings within the president and convinced him that America could still prevail in Vietnam.

The result of this announcement was a sudden resurgence in anti-war protests on American college campuses. Young people vented their outrage and frustration at Nixon's decision in increasingly violent demonstrations, which culminated on May 4 when four students were shot dead during an anti-war rally by National Guardsmen at Kent State University. This event shocked and further divided the country, not just over the issue of America's involvement in the Vietnam War, but of the entire divide between young and older Americans. It was in the context of these highly contentious events that Robert Evans received from Ed Lewis the script called *Harold and Maude* by an unknown young writer.

After reading the script, Evans was interested in the film and wanted to consider it, but Ed Lewis—always the promoter and wheeler dealer—drove a hard bargain, threatening to take the script to another studio if Evans hesitated to make a decision. In his biography *The Kid Stays in the Picture: A Notorious Life*, Evans recalled thinking, "I can just see me telling Bluhdorn the story. He'll take his glasses off, squint and state eloquently: 'I want to vomit!'"[5] Evans knew that buying a script like this, from an unknown writer with such a highly usual storyline, was extremely risky and that he was potentially jeopardizing his position at Paramount by taking such a chance.

To Evans' credit, he decided to take that chance, but he was smart enough to know that he could not possibly be straightforward with the studio about the kind of film in which they would be making a substantial investment. In the best Hollywood tradition, he decided that the solution was very simple: lie. In 2002, he told John Hiscock of the *London Daily Telegraph*, "We made *Harold and Maude* because we lied and didn't tell them what the story was. How do you tell the front office that you want to tell a story about an 18-year-old boy falling in love with an 80-year-old woman..."[6]

Evans decided not to call Ed's bluff about taking the script to another studio. Evans knew there was a big downside to the project, but the possible upside of snaring another *Easy Rider* or *Midnight Cowboy* was too much for him. The deal was made quickly and negotiations were concluded over the course of one weekend; Evans agreed to purchase the script and put the film in production. He even agreed that he would consider having Higgins direct, despite the fact that Higgins was a total novice who had never made anything more than a 16mm college film.

What is almost more surprising is the fact that when Lewis first brought the news to Higgins about the Paramount deal, the young writer had second thoughts about signing on the dotted line. Seemingly afraid that his film would be co-opted and changed to the point that it would no longer his vision, Higgins sat on the couch in the Lewises' living room and told Ed and Millie that he was afraid he was "selling out." He knew there was a chance that Paramount could alter *Harold and Maude* in the way that Hollywood had butchered other youth films, or even that Evans could just decide to throw the script in the dustbin and never actually put it into production. Maybe, he wondered out loud, he should just try to find the backing to produce the film himself. Eventually, however, common sense prevailed: The opportunity to receive major studio funding and the perks that went with it was too much, and Higgins agreed to the deal as long as Paramount was willing to consider letting him direct.

Colin and Mildred made their partnership legal by forming a production company, Lewis-Higgins Productions, Inc., with the expressed task of producing *Harold and Maude*. On May 26, 1970, a contract was signed between Lewis-Higgins Productions and Paramount Studios. Higgins was contracted to receive $100,000 for his original

3. Selling the Script

screenplay and for his additional services as screenwriter during the production of the film. He would receive a quarter of his fee on the signing of the memo, a quarter on the first day of principal photography, a quarter on the completion of principal photography and the final quarter on the completion of the finished film. Additionally, Higgins would receive up to $100,000 out of deferred profits if the film made money.[7]

Mildred Lewis would serve as the film's executive producer, a somewhat nominal title that did not allow for much participation in its production. As producer—a more significant role that would concern itself with the budget, as well as looking out for the studio's interests in the film—Paramount initially hired Howard Jaffe. Jaffe came from a show business family that included his father, Leo, a top executive for Columbia Pictures, and his brother, Stanley, who had recently had success at Paramount with the 1969 film *Goodbye, Columbus* and who would soon be named studio president. Jaffe was assigned to the project despite the fact that he had very little hands-on film production experience. As a matter of fact, none of the three principals involved in the picture at this point (Jaffe, Lewis and Higgins) had much experience.

Higgins had presented Paramount with a script that was an unusual love story, to say the least, one that would have to be handled with deftness and style. The Paramount brass was doubtful that the UCLA grad student could pull it off, having never before directed anything more than a student film. As Evans told Peter Bart: "It's gonna get me fired, you know—an unknown director, a pool boy writer, two impossible-to-cast parts. It's gonna give Marty Davis [a Gulf+Western executive, second to Bluhdorn in the company's pecking order] the shot he's been waiting for—straitjacket time."[8] Evans was canny enough not to flatly turn down Higgins' request to direct and risk losing the script, so he included a clause that would give the novice up to $7500 to shoot test footage in order to evaluate whether he would be up to the task of directing the film. This would placate Higgins temporarily, while giving Evans an out in the likely event that he decided on a more experienced director.

Having sold his first feature-length script to a major studio, and having the possibility of directing dangled in front of him, Higgins was high as a kite. He quickly began making wish lists of actors. For Harold, Richard Dreyfuss, John Rubinstein, Brad David, Bob Random and even Jeff Bridges (though Higgins noted to himself that Bridges was "too tall"). For Maude, Jean Arthur, Lillian Gish, Helen Hayes, Marlene Dietrich, Mildred Dunnock and, in a moment of inspiration, Ruth Gordon. For Harold's mother, he considered Cloris Leachman, Louise Latham, Nina Foch, Constance Towers and Diana Webster; for Uncle Victor, Jack Albertson, Carroll O'Conner, Roger Bowen, Pat McCormick and Ernest Borgnine. For the role of Sunshine Dore, Higgins considered future stars Penny Marshall, Diane Keaton, Teri Garr and Talia Coppola (later Talia Shire).

But first, the novice filmmaker was hit out of the blue by something that he never expected, something that a more experienced Hollywood type probably could have avoided. In June, just as he was preparing for his directorial test, he had a call from Sandra Lowell, his one-time volunteer typist. And at his moment of greatest triumph, his world was suddenly turned upside down.

Lowell told Colin that she was "very hurt" that he had not told her about the news of the sale to Paramount or the fact that they were beginning to think about casting the film. She went on to say that Higgins "had promised her the role of Sunshine Dore" and that if she did not get it, she was going to demand co-screenplay credit as well as 50 percent of the money that he was receiving. Colin was stunned and "absolutely astounded at her demands and her attitude." He told her that he remembered nothing about promising her the part of Sunshine, only that he might have agreed that she would be good for the part. Higgins did tell her that she was welcome to come down and audition for the part, which Lowell eventually did.[9]

When Lowell did not land the part of Sunshine or of Edith Fern (she auditioned for both), she called Colin in a state of emotional upset. Angered at not being cast in the film, she demanded a screen credit, saying that she would settle for an "additional material by" credit. She also wanted 20 percent of the money that Colin was getting for the screenplay, which would have eventually worked out to be over $20,000. After trying to reason with her, Colin told her that she could not get any kind of screenplay credit because her contribution had been absolutely nothing of any originality. As far as money goes, he told her that he was planning to offer her a gift for her help but so far he had received no actual cash from the studio so that he had no money to give her.

A few days later, Lowell met with Higgins at Paramount to further discuss the matter. She agreed that she would not ask for screen credit but that she wanted at least $1000 or she would get a lawyer. Higgins felt that he had no legal obligation to her at all but that he would "pay her $200 for the secretarial help that she gave" him back in February. Lowell refused, at which time Higgins told her he would not be offering her any money in the future and that she would be "creating an embarrassing nuisance of herself" if she took the matter further. Lowell left at that point, saying that she would speak with her lawyer.[10]

This awkward situation was no doubt in part caused by Higgins' lack of experience in situations in which he was dealing with people, particularly where large amounts of money and fame were at stake. Higgins should have been on guard about Lowell's intentions when he first met her; even though they didn't know each other well, she admitted to him that she was out of work but was seeing lawyers with the intent of suing her former employers. For someone with experience, this would have been a red flag; and when she offered to do secretarial work with no pay, he should have realized that something was up.

The matter was eventually settled with minimal difficulty. Lowell did hire a lawyer, Ludwig H. Gerber, who contacted Higgins by letter in September. When Higgins did not respond, Gerber contacted Evans directly on October 17, stating that he was seeking a "peaceable settlement" for Lowell's claims, or that he would "have no alternative but to institute appropriate litigation."[11] Evans quickly settled the matter out of court. Higgins learned an important lesson about keeping his work to himself and not letting strangers into his inner circle.

Somewhat more humorous was an article that Higgins found in the tabloid *The National Enquirer*. Headlined "19-Year-Old Weds Woman, 80," it was the story of Gus Stifflemire, who married octogenarian Henrietta on May 23 in Grove Hill, Alabama. The article included a picture of the loving couple and noted that Stifflemire, an "unemployed shirt factory worker with an 11th grade education, shares his wife's Social Security check as well as her cottage." It quoted the groom as saying, "A heap of folks want to make fun of us ... but I tell 'em to go ahead and make all the fun they please. Life's too short not to do what you want."[12] This was no doubt a somewhat simplified version of Maude's zesty philosophy of life and living. Having now found an example of a real Harold and Maude, Higgins knew that in this crazy world almost anything was possible, and that the story they were getting ready to put on the screen should not be too much for anybody to believe.

With other distractions put aside, Higgins began to focus on his directorial test for *Harold and Maude*. The tests would be shot at Columbia Studios, where sets were available, from June 30 to July 3. As the role of Maude was so crucial and so difficult to cast, Higgins decided to forego any scenes with Maude and instead focus on scenes between Harold and his mother and with some of the computer dates. He elected to shoot scene 114, where Harold meets Edith Fern; scene 121, the date with Sunshine Dore; and scene 45, in which Mrs. Chasen fills out the computer dating form while Harold shoots himself in the head.

In mid–June, Higgins held auditions for the actors who would be in the test scenes. He auditioned Penny Marshall, Nancy Priddy, Ellen Godfrey, Flora Plumb, Julie Payne and, of course, Sandra Lowell, for the parts of Sunshine and Edith. For Mrs. Chasen, Higgins auditioned, among others, Margaret Muse, Marian Walters and Louise Latham; Latham had played the integral part of Marnie's mother in the 1964 film *Marnie*, directed by Higgins' idol, Alfred Hitchcock. For Harold, he auditioned John Rubinstein, Bob Chicatelli, Jack LaRue, Jr., Bob Morton, Jack Bender, Hank Jones and a then-unknown John Ritter.

Higgins finally settled on a young unknown actor, Bob Bacalupi, for the part of Harold. For Mrs. Chasen, he chose 43-year-old Nan Martin, a character actress who had done a great deal of television work in the 1960s, including stints on *Twilight Zone*, *Perry Mason* and *Mannix*. Martin had also done some feature film work, recently appearing in Paramount's *Goodbye Columbus* as Mrs. Patimkin, mother to Ali MacGraw's Brenda.

Having learned in film school about the film ratio (the ratio of film shot vs. film used in the final production), Higgins thought he would

3. Selling the Script

impress Paramount with such knowledge by showing that he could work quickly. In the end, though, this turned out to be the classic situation in which a little knowledge is a bad thing, and having this information worked against him. He later admitted that what he should have done was focus on one scene and make it very good, instead of trying to show that he could work quickly and efficiently. It's also possible that Evans had no intention of giving Higgins the job to begin with, and was just humoring him. Whatever the case, the directorial test turned out to be a thumbs-down for Colin Higgins, and he had to accept that, for the time being at least, his first professional job in film would be as a screenwriter only.

Higgins recalled the circumstances of his directorial test for *Harold and Maude* in the fall 1972 edition of *Film Quarterly*:

> So I made the test, with a different cast but with a professional group of people. We shot it on the stages at Columbia for two days: three scenes, $7,500. They saw the test and they decided that they would prefer another director.... I don't think they really wanted me to direct the film in the first place. I was going to make a half-million dollar film and they wanted to make a million-and-a-half dollar film. They didn't think I could handle it. The test itself isn't that bad, but I should have spent the two days doing one scene instead of three. I wanted to show them how quick I was.[13]

Higgins' impression that he was being set up to fail ended up to be true, as Evans decided that he would look for a more experienced director. Higgins was disappointed, but in the end that decision would be the best thing possible for the finished film. Hal Ashby was about to come aboard.

4

The Accidental Director

Hal Ashby, the studio's eventual choice to direct *Harold and Maude*, had a wispy beard, thick glasses and prematurely gray hair that he had grown long. Thin and gaunt, dressed in his trademark jeans and t-shirt, Ashby looked like a zonked-out, aged hippie, like something out of a Cheech and Chong comedy sketch; not exactly a typical Hollywood director type. He was a mass of contradictions; Jane Fonda later commented about Ashby, "He appeared to be very laid-back but in reality was wired and tough as a bull."[1] While Ashby's penchant to worry about little details helped him as a director, his inclination to stress out could sometimes be a problem, as on the day that he was shooting his first feature film and a doctor had to be called in to make sure the director hadn't suffered a heart attack. It turned out to be just a case of nerves.

Ashby was born in Ogden, Utah, on September 2, 1929. Nick Dawson's excellent biography *Being Hal Ashby: Life of a Hollywood Rebel* details Ashby's tumultuous childhood in great detail and should be a reference guide for anyone interested in the director's life. His mother Eileen was a strict Mormon, and after she and her husband James had two children, she convinced him to go on a two-and-a-half year Mormon mission to South Africa, beginning in 1916. When he returned in 1919, James bought out the Uintah Dairy Company, where he had previously worked and, according to Dawson, "over the next ten years, he turned it into a mini-empire"[2] which included delivery routes, a grocery store and lunch stand. The Ashbys had another child in 1925 and finally William Hal Ashby, the last of their four children, was born in 1929.

Differences between the Ashby parents strained the marriage, and they divorced in 1935. Ashby's father remarried, but in 1942, when Hal was at the impressionable age of 12, James Ashby shot himself while he was alone in his office. Although Hal always told people in later

4. The Accidental Director

years that his father had committed suicide, Dawson's book suggests that it is not clear if the shooting was suicide or merely an accident that occurred while James was cleaning a gun. Still, Dawson notes that "the circumstantial evidence all seems to point clearly to suicide."[3] Whichever it was, the death of his father had a profound impact on Hal Ashby, who had a troubled adolescence and ended up himself married and a father at age 18. But Hal, unsatisfied with his life in Ogden, quickly left his wife and daughter and headed to Los Angeles to look for other opportunities.

After a divorce and another marriage, Ashby walked into the California State Office of Employment in 1950 at age 21, rather presumptuously seeking a job in the film industry. The woman there told him that she had an entry level job opening at Universal, but that he would have to know how to operate a multilith machine, a type of offset printing press. Ashby hesitated (he had never heard of such a thing) but agreed to take the job, and his career in the film industry began.

Hal Ashby's film career was certainly not a "rags to riches" overnight rise to fame. He bounced around for the first five years, going back to Ogden on several occasions, before he finally decided to make the movie business a full-time commitment. In 1955 he became an apprentice to Robert Swink, a film editor for directors William Wyler and George Stevens, and started an eight-year program that would eventually make him an editor on his own. Ashby viewed the editing suite as his classroom, a place where he learned the art of filmmaking. Intelligent and creative, he had a great mind for the art of film cutting and was able to keep in mind the various clips of film that were needed at a time when movies were cut on upright Moviolas. Furthermore, Ashby was the kind of single-minded and totally dedicated individual that the film industry loves. Once he dedicated himself to his craft, he would edit for hours, smoking cigarette after cigarette in the dank darkness of the edit suite, usually losing track of the time of day (or night). More often than not, in the morning associates found him asleep on a couch after a long night of work. Not surprisingly, this type of attitude and lifestyle took its toll on Ashby's personal life, and two more marriages ended in divorce.

As an assistant editor, Ashby worked on such major films as *The Big Country, The Diary of Anne Frank* and *The Greatest Story Ever Told*. Finally, in 1964, he succeeded in becoming a full-fledged editor on his own and was given his first assignment, editing British director Tony Richardson's black comedy *The Loved One*. Although Richardson ended up taking Ashby's first cut back to England and re-editing it before it was released, this was no doubt Ashby's first big break in films. He was now a certified film editor.

While editing *The Loved One*, Ashby met the man who would become his mentor and eventually lead him out of the editing room and give him an opportunity to direct his first film. Only slightly older than Ashby, Norman Jewison was a Canadian who had broken into the business through television and eventually became a director at Universal. In the fall of 1964, Jewison was getting ready to direct his first independent film, *The Cincinnati Kid*, for producer Marty Ransohoff. In his biography *This Terrible Business Has Been Good to Me*, Jewison says he met Ashby on the MGM lot when he was preparing *The Cincinnati Kid* and Ashby was editing *The Loved One*. "I began stopping by Hal's editing room at the end of the day, watching the changes, smoking a little of Hal's pot and joining him in helpless laughter" at the film.[4] While Ashby regarded Jewison with some deference, the relationship was not all one-sided; Jewison revered director William Wyler and his socially conscious films and was impressed by the fact that Ashby had worked as a longtime assistant to Wyler's editor Robert Swink. Eventually Ashby introduced Jewison to Terry Southern, who would end up co-writing the *Cincinnati Kid* script, and Jewison hired Ashby to edit the film.

The collaboration, a great one for both men, lasted throughout the rest of the decade. After *The Cincinnati Kid* came the Cold War comedy *The Russians Are Coming, The Russians Are Coming*. In 1966, Jewison began production on the film that would win the Academy Award for Best Picture in 1967, the racially charged *In the Heat of the Night*. While its cast and crew were on location in Sparta, Illinois, Ashby was back in Hollywood, running interference with producer Walter Mirisch and United Artists on behalf of the director. According to Mark Harris' book *Pictures at a Revolution*, Ashby was by this time a *de facto* co-producer, handling many more details than an ordinary film editor would.[5]

4. *The Accidental Director*

Hal Ashby receives his Academy Award for best editing on *In the Heat of the Night* (1966) at the 1967 Academy Awards from the legendary British actress Dame Edith Evans. Two years later, in 1970, Ashby will give strong consideration to casting Dame Edith in the part of Maude, before finally deciding on Ruth Gordon. Courtesy Academy of Motion Picture Arts and Sciences.

In the spring of 1968, with the Academy Awards ceremony delayed for two days after the Memphis assassination of Martin Luther King, Hal Ashby won his only Academy Award for editing *In the Heat of the Night*. (The film also won for best picture.) Dressed nattily in a blazer and turtleneck, Ashby accepted the award saying, "I only hope that we can use all of our talents and creativity towards peace ... and love!" It was a great time of professional success for Ashby, who had come light years from his days operating Universal's multilith machine. But for Jewison, a Canadian, the future in America seemed bleak. King and Robert Kennedy had both been assassinated in 1968, and with the streets of Chicago running red with blood from protestors clashing with police at the Democratic Convention that summer, Jewison decided that as soon as possible he and his family would leave America. After the completion of his next picture, *Gaily, Gaily*, the family turned in their green cards and moved to Europe, where Jewison made his next two pictures, *Fiddler on the Roof* and *Jesus Christ, Superstar*.

Unlike Jewison, Ashby seems to have embraced the change and tumult that was in the air in America in the late 1960s. The civil rights movement had resulted in riots and unrest in cities in both the north and the south, but Ashby seemed to sense, even from his remote position as a successful editor in the sheltered world of Hollywood, that the change in the air in America, from the stifling conservatism of the 1950s to the social liberalism of the 1960s, was a good thing. Indeed, the social and cultural upheaval of late 1960s America would come to dominate many of the films that Ashby directed in the decade that followed, so much so that we can now regard Ashby as one of the primary chroniclers of life in this troubled period of unrest and tumult that was America in the late 1960s.

Jewison was now eager to pay Ashby back for his friendship and assistance on the films they had done together, particularly *In the Heat of the Night*. One day while working on *The Thomas Crown Affair*, Jewison turned to Ashby and asked a simple question: "What do you want to do?"

Ashby was stunned. "I want to direct. That's where it's at, isn't it?"

Jewison replied, "Right. So let's find something for you." To reward Hal for the "beyond the call of duty" work he had done on *In the Night of the Night*, Jewison promoted Ashby to associate producer on *The Thomas Crown Affair* and *Gaily, Gaily* and Hal began to "gain some of

4. The Accidental Director

the much-needed experience in the areas of pre-production and production" as well as scouting locations, scripts and casting.[6]

Jewison had a film in the pipeline for production at United Artists, the company that made *In the Heat of the Night*. Titled *The Landlord*, it too had racial themes, although they would be handled a bit more humorously than in *Heat*. Another major difference was that *Heat* was primarily a condemnation by Northerners of the racist actions and attitudes of white Southerners, while *The Landlord* would have a more complex and challenging approach to the subject matter of race relations. As one of the characters in the 2013 film *Lee Daniels' The Butler* says about *In the Heat of the Night*, Sidney Poitier's character is more like a white person's fantasy of what black people should be like than a real flesh-and-blood black person. However, the characters in *The Landlord* are, for white people, more like a nightmare than a fantasy, and this view is expressed frequently by members of the uptight family of the film's protagonist, Elgar Enders.

The Landlord was based on a novel by a young African American writer from Philadelphia, Kristen Hunter, who set the story in her hometown. (Ashby and Jewison changed the setting to New York for the film.) Hunter's novels, which also included *God Bless the Child, The Soul Brothers and Sister Lou, Kinfolks* and *The Lakestown Rebellion*, frequently focused on the trials and tribulations of life as a black person growing up in America. She began writing novels in 1964 and finished *The Landlord*, her second book, two years later. The *Landlord* script was written by African American screenwriter Bill Gunn. Gunn, also an actor and director, would write, direct and star in the 1973 film *Ganja & Hess*, a bizarre horror film about an archaeologist turned into a vampire. It failed so miserably that it effectively ruined Gunn's career.

The Landlord is the story of Elgar Enders, an aristocratic young white Long Islander who buys a tenement building in Brooklyn's Park Slope neighborhood and naively sets out to get rid of the tenants so the building can be improved as part of an overall neighborhood gentrification. Enders gradually comes to appreciate the earthy urban lifestyle of his tenants, which contrasts drastically with Enders' own home life in stuffy Long Island and the interference of his domineering parents. Eventually he moves into the building and becomes romantically involved with several of the female residents, impregnating Fanny, a married woman. When the child is born, Fanny refuses to take it, as does Elgar, and when the baby is adopted, Fanny suggests that the child be adopted as a white baby in order to improve the child's chances of having a good life.

The story of how Jewison turned the directing duties on *The Landlord* over to Ashby, and thus started his friend's directorial career, is filled with contradictions. Ashby frequently said that he simply walked onto the set of *The Landlord* one day and began directing, almost as if he were living out the character of Chance in *Being There*, who stumbles into the job of economic advisor to the president after being a gardener all of his life. The reality, however, is somewhat more complex. As Jewison noted in a 2007 interview, "The reason that I asked [Ashby] to direct it was I was already involved in *Fiddler*. I moved to Europe with my family for the next ten years. I was a little disillusioned at that time."[7] Jewison, a dyed-in-the-wool liberal, was shocked at what happened in America during 1968, and certainly did not want to direct a film as controversial as *The Landlord*. He also saw an opportunity to help his friend and long-time associate move up the film world ladder and become a director. So Jewison negotiated a deal with David Picker of United Artists that would allow Ashby to direct, while Jewison would produce the film, oversee the budget and stand by to step in for his friend if he needed any help. As it turned out, Ashby didn't need any.

The Landlord was an audacious debut film for 40-year-old Hal Ashby, and set forth many of the themes and motifs that would concern him for the next decade or so. Elgar Enders begins the film somewhat innocent and naïve: He shows up at the tenement building wearing a white suit, driving a VW convertible filled with potted flowers. The guys hanging out in front of the building chase Elgar away; the flowers are stolen; and his car tires almost stolen. Despite this discouraging start, Elgar sticks it out and ends up going on a journey of enlightenment about himself, race relations, and the possibility of loving someone from a very different background. All of Ashby's films from this point on feature protagonists who start out innocent in some way, and go on a journey—sometimes an actual trip, sometimes a metaphysical journey, often both—to find a deeper meaning in their lives. In this

4. The Accidental Director

sense, *The Landlord* was the perfect film for Ashby to kick off his career. Ashby later commented, "It really blew my mind when I sat there looking at the dailies and saw so much of me coming out on that screen."[8]

The Landlord opens with a quick shot that appears to make no sense, as it has no connection to what comes next in the film: a group of people at a wedding. It is in fact the wedding of Ashby to actress Joan Marshall, with the director and his new wife front and center. Marshall turns and kisses a man who is not Ashby. According to Nick Dawson, the film of the wedding was made in New York shortly after the movie wrapped, and the recipient of the kiss is Norman Jewison, who had just given away the bride. Marshall's on-screen kiss was Ashby's way of acknowledging Jewison and thanking him for his help in elevating Ashby to the director's chair. This non sequitur beginning has two functions: It asserts a personal level to the filmmaking process, as Ashby has injected a scene from his own life into the beginning of the film (as we will see, Ashby made cameos in almost all of his films, including *Harold and Maude*), and on a second level it suggests that Ashby has been influenced by the avant-garde style of filmmaking that had been going on since the French New Wave asserted itself with Jean-Luc Godard's 1959 film *Breathless*. Peter Bart once suggested to Ashby that if his last name had been Godard instead of Ashby, *The Landlord* would have had an easier time finding an audience and would have been seen as a great film.

Ashby used a cinematic technique in *The Landlord* to visually establish the wide gulf between the world in which Elgar Enders comes from, his privileged Long Island home, and the rundown Brooklyn tenement. Ashby had cinematographer Gordon Willis (who had only recently shot his first movie) photograph the Enders home in soft focus, pastel colors and low contrast. In the tenement scenes, Willis used the style that he utilized when becoming known as "the prince of darkness": The scenes were shot using naturalistic, high-contrast lighting, with many of the images in shadow and darkness, so dark that at times they are almost hard to discern. In this way, Ashby establishes the disparity between the two worlds that Enders inhabits: his parents' Long Island home almost looks like an unreal dream, while the world of his tenants is harshly realistic. Willis would revisit this technique again soon after *The Landlord* when, in Francis Ford Coppola's *The Godfather*, he shot the scenes of Connie's wedding with special lenses in high-contrast lighting. They were then intercut with the scenes in Vito's study that were done with low light, providing the visual contrast that Coppola needed to suggest the Godfather's public life versus his private one.

For his actors, Ashby used a relative newcomer to films, Beau Bridges, as Elgar. Ashby had befriended Bridges, the son of TV star Lloyd Bridges, while working on Jewison's *Gaily, Gaily* in which Bridges played the lead. Ashby also brought back an actress Jewison had used in *In the Heat of the Night*, Lee Grant, as Elgar's mother. (Grant was nominated for a Best Supporting Actress Oscar for *The Landlord*.) The mother-son relationship, which has minimal importance in Ashby's later films, is featured both in this film and even more so in *Harold and Maude*. For *The Landlord*'s Brooklyn scenes, Ashby used a wide variety of African American actors, including Louis Gossett, Jr., who would become a highly successful character actor in the 1970s, as Copee, and Diana Sands as Fanny, as well as the always popular Pearl Bailey as Marge.

The Landlord was budgeted at $2 million and Ashby went $400,000 over budget. The film received a limited release by United Artists, who reasoned that it would play better in urban areas and on the coasts than in rural areas or in the South. The film was a much more ambitious and complex treatment of racial issues than other films of its time, such as the Jim Brown vehicle ... *tick ... tick ... tick...* Critics, the ones that noticed it at least, seemed to mostly like or at least in some way be impressed by the film. Roger Ebert was mostly positive in his October 21, 1970, review, giving it three stars and saying, "Instead of staying on that safe, predictable level, it begins to dig into the awkwardness and hypocrisy of our commonly shared attitudes about race."[9] Nick Dawson notes that *The Landlord*, while not a major box office success, at least managed to turn a small profit.[10] Still, when all was said and done, *The Landlord* went largely unnoticed.

After *The Landlord*, Ashby faced an enormous challenge. Now a director, he couldn't really go back to being an editor, which would have been a step down. His mentor Norman Jewison was gone making *Fiddler on the Roof* in Europe. Ashby was, for better or worse, on his own. For two months in the summer of 1970, he sat around the offices of his friend Charles "Chuck" Mulvehill, a production coordinator for Mirisch Productions, whom Ashby had worked with on *The Landlord*.

4. The Accidental Director

According to Mulvehill, Ashby was "going crazy from the disappointment of the *Landlord* release and from the lack of anything to do."[11] Finally one day, Ashby received a call from Paramount; Robert Evans had a script called *Harold and Maude*, by a novice scriptwriter, and he was interested in having Ashby direct.

5

The Kid Stays in the Picture

In some regards, Ashby would seem like an odd choice to direct *Harold and Maude*. His only directorial effort was an urban-oriented look at troubled race relations, and there was no evidence he could handle a quirky love story between a young man and an old woman. But as it turned out, Ashby was the perfect choice for *Harold and Maude*. His brilliant casting, his sensitive handling of the actors, his decisions regarding location and music, and his uncanny ability to edit a film to perfection, all led to the creation of a movie that would eventually capture the hearts of legions of filmgoers. Additionally, Ashby's own father had died an apparent suicide, and so there was a connection with the fatherless character of Harold Chasen, who repeatedly acts out his resentments at his domineering mother by faking his own suicide.

However, the relationship between Ashby and Paramount during the making of *Harold and Maude* was often rocky. Ashby was individualistic and anti-authoritarian, which is probably one of the reasons that the character of Maude and the entire theme of *Harold and Maude* appealed to him when he first read the script. Although he had come up in the studio system, Ashby tended to think on his own and not be a company man, and when he began to work with Norman Jewison, who was largely functioning as an independent in the Hollywood system, the two men quickly adopted an "us vs. them" mentality when it came to dealing with the suits. This tended to carry over into Ashby's work as a director.

In 1970 Peter Bart was Robert Evans' right hand man and the number two person in charge of Paramount film production. Bart's career began in journalism as the West Coast correspondent for the *New York*

5. The Kid Stays in the Picture

Times, and he had initially met Evans when interviewing him for a feature article for the Arts & Leisure section of the Sunday *Times*. Evans noted that he and the intellectual Bart immediately "hit it off as opposites." Indeed, the bespectacled, highly intelligent Bart and the gregarious, shoot-from-the-hip Evans were an odd couple. But much to the surprise of the Gulf+Western executives, once Evans was put in charge of production at Paramount he immediately brought Bart aboard as his second in command. Evans noted that Bart "doesn't read synopses—he reads the entire text. Where he can read six books over a weekend, I am pressed to finish one in six days."[1]

Bart had been impressed by *The Landlord* and kept Ashby's name in mind. So when Evans decided that Higgins would not helm *Harold and Maude* and was looking around for a director, Bart mentioned Ashby to Evans in glowing terms. Evans was not as enthused, as he regarded the editor-turned-director as an "acid freak." Having initially lied to the studio about the content of the script, Evans was now faced with hiring a director with whom he had virtually nothing in common and whose lifestyle he disdained. Still, there were some hidden benefits about hiring such an oddball. Evans told Bart candidly that if they hired Ashby and things went wrong, they could just pin the whole fiasco on the pot-smoking hippie and be done with it.

Ashby also had some reservations about *Harold and Maude* after initially reading the script. He told Evans:

> I was really concerned that I didn't know if I could make it work because it was fantasy. I just didn't know where I was at the time. I got that thing about everybody says, "We laughed out loud." And I said, "That's what scares me; you're laughing out loud at the page and I'm thinking I'm going to have a hard time making you laugh when you see it on the screen," because sometimes you can be a little more ludicrous on the page than you can on the screen; you can be a little more bizarre.[2]

However, after thinking it over (and considering the lack of alternatives), Ashby finally began to come around and warm up to the project.

Bart remembered later that at one of the initial *Harold and Maude* meetings, Ashby told the Paramount executives that he had had an epiphany that the film could be turned into a "freaky musical"; in addition, Ashby was with another man that Bart took to be Cat Stevens, although this was not possible, since Stevens' involvement in the film was still months away.

The circumstances of Ashby's hiring by Paramount are not terribly clear; for one thing, there appears to be no actual written contract that ever existed for Ashby to direct *Harold and Maude*. In a December 1970 letter to Robert Evans, Ashby noted, "From the inception when my semi-autonomous deal was set verbally or put in a deal memo, Paramount has come back to my agents with enough points to make it quite obvious they were not quite interested in the deal as it was originally discussed." Ashby went on to write that he "could only assume Paramount's attitude was let him go ahead but don't put anything in writing unless, in fact, it was we can't pull it out from under him." He concluded by saying about his deal to direct the film, "In the end, there still isn't a signed piece of paper to be found anywhere."[3]

On the initial budget for *Harold and Maude* dated November 21, 1970, Ashby is referred to as Harold Ashby (his actual first name was William; Hal—not Harold—was his middle name). Ashby complained to Bob Goodfried of Paramount's publicity department when he was referred to as "Harold" in the studio's October press release that announced Ashby's hiring as director. Ashby's salary was to be $3250 per week for up to 18 weeks plus two additional weeks for a total of $65,000, hardly a huge salary for the director of a major studio feature film, even in 1971 dollars.[4]

As it turned out, though the shoot was completed in ten weeks, Ashby would really end up working on the picture for a year and a half.

Ashby was also concerned that he was stepping on Higgins' toes. His initial reaction after reading the script was that Higgins should be the director, so he went to Paramount to implore the studio to "let Colin make his film." But Paramount was dead set against Higgins as director, and told Ashby in no uncer-

Director Hal Ashby lines up a shot. Paramount production chief Robert Evans considered him an "acid freak" but nonetheless hired him to helm *Harold and Maude*. Evans later told Peter Bart that, if the movie failed, they could blame it all on Ashby.

5. The Kid Stays in the Picture

tain terms that he could either accept the job or they would find another director to take the position. Whatever happened, Higgins would not get the job. So, with Colin's consent, Ashby decided to accept, feeling that he could do the best possible job bringing Higgins' vision to the screen. In addition, he would incorporate Higgins into the filmmaking process by making him an associate producer, which would allow Higgins to be on the set while shooting (plus it would be handy to have Higgins, the screenwriter, around for rewrites). Unlike other directors, who might have been jealous of the young screenwriter, Ashby viewed making movies as a largely collaborative experience, and so to his credit he welcomed Higgins along as an important part of the team making *Harold and Maude*.[5]

The September 18, 1970, issue of *Daily Variety* announced that Ashby had been signed on to direct *Harold and Maude*, and on September 24 *The Hollywood Reporter* noted that Howard Jaffe and Higgins would produce the film. With a November 2 start date, Ashby had to work fast. He wanted a producer that he could work with, and his initial meetings with Jaffe, Paramount's designated man for the job, went nowhere. Ashby had mixed feelings about Jaffe, later commenting that he was a "sweet man, but he's a lightweight."[6] Jaffe, meanwhile, was taken aback by Ashby's long hair and hippie appearance and it was clear very quickly that they would not be a good match. Although as late as October 26 Jaffe was still working on the film, by November he had decided to move on to a Columbia project called *The Daughter* instead of continuing with *Harold and Maude*. The decision suited Ashby fine because he wanted to work with Chuck Mulvehill, who could handle many of the day to day operations. Mulvehill became so valuable to Ashby that he would continue working with the director for the rest of Ashby's career.

Shortly after starting work on the film, Ashby persuaded Mulvehill to leave his job with Mirisch Productions and go to work for Lewis-Higgins Productions, Inc. Although Mulvehill had some reluctance about leaving Mirisch, his decision to go with Ashby was a fairly easy one. For one thing, it had been over a year since he had worked on a film, and the inactivity was starting to get to him. Furthermore, Mulvehill seemed excited at the prospects that *Harold and Maude* offered to both himself and Ashby. He wrote to Mirisch executive Patrick Palmer in late September that *Harold and Maude* is "a wonderful piece of black comedy that should be a lot of fun doing."[7]

But problems with Paramount relating to this decision began right from the start, as Paramount executive Jack Ballard was, according to Mulvehill, "doing everything he possibly can to get one of his unit managers on the show" instead of Mulvehill. The situation had gotten so bad that by later September, he and Mulvehill were locked in "a Mexican stand-off" over the issue. Paramount believed that Ashby wanted Mulvehill simply because Chuck would function as the director's mouthpiece, and so would not look out for the interests of the studio. Additionally, Mulvehill was not in the Producers Guild, and thus faced that hurdle in getting hired to work on *Harold and Maude*. Eventually Ashby prevailed, and Mulvehill was eventually credited as co-producer on the film with Higgins. Mulvehill would end up being so critical to the film that he even allowed his car to be used for several of the scenes of Maude driving, and he was also featured in a small part as the man in the junkyard who sells Harold his hearse.

On September 25, 1970, Ashby took out a nine-month lease for Lewis-Higgins Productions at 8803 Appian Way, a Spanish Colonial-style house featuring a turret in the front. It would serve as production offices for the film as well as Ashby's home. Up a winding drive called Lookout Mountain Road, 8803 Appian Way sits high in the Laurel Canyon section of the Hollywood Hills, with a tremendous view of smoggy downtown L.A. on one side and the wide expanse of the San Fernando Valley on the other. At the time, the area was home to some of Southern California's best-known artist and musicians, including Joni Mitchell, Neil Young, David Crosby, Jackson Browne, Michelle Phillips and Carole King (working at that time on what would be her most successful album, *Tapestry*). It was, as music producer Lou Adler said, the period of the "transition from cool to mellow." Given Ashby's penchant for hip music and the beautiful people (and the drugs and sex) that went along with it, his selection of the Appian Way house as a base for his operation should not really be too surprising.

The rent on the Appian Way house was $900 per month. Ashby decorated it with psychedelic paint on the walls and rugs of all kinds, as well as two black cats. Ashby told a writer for *Variety*, "Paramount

5. The Kid Stays in the Picture

asked me where I wanted my offices. I told them I've always wanted a house."[8] The tasks of deciding on locations for the film, hiring crew and casting the actors—a process Ashby called "the most difficult part of making a film"—was about to begin.[9]

The *Harold and Maude* script did not specify a location; we only know that there is a nearby military establishment, some churches, a reservoir and that it is near the ocean (Harold drives his car into the ocean at the end). As Higgins had written the script with the intent that it be his third student film at UCLA, he obviously had no budget or time to shoot it anywhere but where he called home, presumably Los Angeles. Ashby, however, had other ideas. He had learned from Jewison and others that shooting in L.A. meant the studio execs were closer to the filming, and the result would logically mean more interference, something the director was determined to avoid. So, naturally, one of the first things that Ashby did was to begin thinking of alternate locations.

Shortly after being hired in September 1970, Ashby went on scouting trips to Denver, San Diego, San Francisco and, on the East Coast, Boston and New York.[10] In December he wrote to Evans that the East Coast was "still the place that turned me on the most." Ultimately the decision would come down to money. Concerned about the budget, Paramount prepared three comparison budgets to look at the difference in cost between shooting in three various locations: the East Coast, San Francisco and L.A. Although Ashby and Evans had informally discussed making the picture for between seven and eight hundred thousand dollars, when the pencils got sharpened and numbers were put on paper, the figure was a bit higher. Los Angeles was the cheapest location, of course, as the travel and lodging costs were reduced, and the budget came in initially at $863,820. The cost of shooting on the East Coast was estimated at $954,333; the cost of shooting in San Francisco, $957,229.

Eventually these numbers were revised and it appeared that the cost of the filming had risen to $1.3 million, with "the possibility of an additional sixty to eighty thousand dollars being tacked onto the 1.3 if we were to shoot in New England," as Ashby wrote Evans. Ashby went back to Evans and suggested sending Mulvehill east to see if deals could be made that would eliminate the possible overage, and he agreed to drop the East Coast idea if Mulvehill was unsuccessful. When Mulvehill returned, he told Ashby that the risk of a sixty to eighty thousand dollar overage was still there and Ashby ultimately gave up on his hope of shooting in the east and settled on San Francisco. At the last minute Paramount returned to Ashby, demanding that the film be made for 1.1 million; Ashby wrote to Evans, "I looked the budget over carefully and decided the 1.3 figure is an honest one, which I felt I could meet. Now I hear it seems that the big decision lies between shooting in Los Angeles and San Francisco, as it seems Los Angeles is the only way to cut the budget."[11]

In the end, Ashby got his way, with San Francisco slated as the locale for the film and a final budget of estimated costs, both above and below the line, to complete the film at $1,285,000, with shooting scheduled to run from January 4 to February 27, 1971. Ultimately, the film would come in just slightly over budget and principal photography would end on March 13, about two weeks late. But as we will see, the delays were due to bad luck and accidents, not slowness on the part of Ashby and his crew.

San Francisco was the ideal locale to film *Harold and Maude*, and not just because it kept Ashby and company away from the prying eyes of Paramount. Located about 300 miles north of Los Angeles, the San Francisco Bay Area was, in 1971, a teeming metropolis and home to about 4.6 million people.[12] San Francisco, sometimes referred to as "Baghdad by the Bay" and "The Golden City," has long been a popular area for shooting films, known for its fog, rolling hills and beautiful ocean views. Hitchcock had shot several of his films in that area, including *Vertigo* and *The Birds*. The 1968 Steve McQueen thriller *Bullitt* had made ample use of San Francisco's hills in its famous chase sequence. San Francisco also had the water and ocean access that was needed for several of the scenes in the film, including the climactic car crash.

In addition, the Bay Area is home to Stanford University (Higgins' alma mater) as well as U.C. Berkeley, a hotbed of revolutionary political activity in the late 1960s. In 1964, the University of California tried to stop a group of activists who were handing out leaflets on the Berkeley campus and what began as a minor brouhaha quickly mushroomed

5. The Kid Stays in the Picture

into a major protest and the birth of the Free Speech Movement. By the late 1960s, U.C. Berkeley was the main focus of protestors against the war in Vietnam and the campus and surrounding areas were filled with riots and protests on an almost daily basis. The Bay Area's liberal political slant and the tolerance of diverse and artistic lifestyles made it the logical home for someone like Maude, who had clearly been an active revolutionary in her younger days. However, being a cultured and affluent area, it was also not surprising to find a wealthy and upscale family like the Chasens living there as well. In short, the selection of the San Francisco Bay Area as the location to shoot the film worked perfectly.

6

The Most Difficult Part of Making a Film

For a film such as *Harold and Maude*, which was so highly dependent upon characterization, the casting of the parts—especially the two leads—was of critical importance. Ashby was on the record as saying that casting was the most difficult part of making a film. In the case of *Harold and Maude*, decisions had to be made quickly; Ashby was hired in September and initially the start date of the film was to be November 2, although it was later pushed back to mid–December and eventually moved to the beginning of the new year. After recovering from an autumn hernia operation, the director was ready to move forward with cast the film.

For the part of Harold, Colin Higgins favored John Rubinstein, a young actor who had been at UCLA. Rubinstein was five years younger than Higgins and came from an artistic family; his father was renowned Polish-born concert pianist Arthur Rubinstein, and his sister Eva danced and acted on Broadway, and later became an internationally known photographer. Rubinstein began studying theater at UCLA in 1964 and also began acting professionally around the same time, including television appearances and local theater. Eventually Rubinstein had a long and distinguished career on Broadway, as well as many feature film and television credits. He co-starred in the mid–80s TV series *Crazy Like a Fox* with Jack Warden, who played the part of Lester Carpf in Ashby's *Shampoo* in 1975.[1] With his curly, bushy hair and youthful-looking face, Rubinstein seemed to Higgins to be the personification of Harold Chasen as he had imagined him.

Ashby liked Rubinstein, but he had another actor in mind for the part. Ashby was acquainted with director Robert Altman who, like Ashby, had come to directing feature films late in life. Altman began

6. The Most Difficult Part of Making a Film

his career as a director of industrial films and documentaries. In 1970, he had had a breakout hit with the film *MASH*, an irreverent story of Army surgeons working just behind the Korean War front line. An actor named Bud Cort had a minor part in *MASH* as an orderly who makes a small mistake, only to be unfairly blamed by Major Frank Burns (Robert Duvall) when a patient dies. Cort played his one big scene memorably, breaking into tears when Burns castigates him in front of other members of the unit. Altman thought so much of Cort that he featured him in a starring role in his next movie, *Brewster McCloud*. Made by Altman's newly formed production company Lion's Gate, it was a quirky film about a boy who lives in the Houston Astrodome and is building a pair of wings in order to learn to fly. Altman suggested Cort to Ashby, who met with the actor on September 25, shortly after he began work on *Harold and Maude*.

Bud Cort in Robert Altman's *Brewster McCloud* (1970), the film he had just completed before starring in *Harold and Maude*. Ashby instantly felt Cort was right for Harold and cast him over the objections of Colin Higgins, who preferred his UCLA classmate John Rubinstein.

Cort was born Walter Edward Cox in New Rochelle, New York, the son of Joseph P. Cox, an orchestra leader, pianist, and owner of a successful men's clothing store in Rye, New York, and Alma M. Court, a former newspaper reporter and an executive assistant at the MGM offices in New York City. Although he went to religious school and at one point actually considered going into the priesthood, Bud was bitten by the acting bug early on, appearing in local plays as well as trying his hand at painting, for which he also evidenced talent. At the age of 14 he began to study with well-known acting teacher William Hickey at the HB Studios in Greenwich Village. (Hickey would later become best known for playing the part of the patriarch in John Huston's 1985 hit *Prizzi's Honor.*) After high school he applied to the NYU School of the Arts, but the acting department was full; after they saw his art portfolio, he was admitted as a scenic design major in 1967. Bud continued his acting studies, however, along with picking up work in commercials, parts in off-Broadway shows and even soap operas. With his luminous white skin, young face and jet black hair, he was perfect for playing roles that required that particular look. By this time, Bud had changed his name to avoid confusion with the popular TV actor Wally Cox (*Mr. Peepers*). From then on, he would be known as Bud Cort.

Bud formed a comedy team with actress Jeannie Berlin (daughter of comedienne Elaine May) and later with Judy Engles (who would appear in *Harold and Maude* as Harold's computer date Candy Gulf). Bud and Judy won first place during amateur night at the famed Village Gate in Greenwich Village, and then the duo signed a professional management contract. While Bud was appearing in the musical revue *Free Fall* in New York, he was spotted by Altman, who was looking for actors for *MASH*. Bud's youthful, impassive look was perfect for the part of Private Boone, so Bud left the New York theater scene behind and went to Hollywood.[2]

But Ashby had a long list of actors to consider for Harold and, initially, Bud was just one of them. Other actors on his list included Richard Thomas, a year or so before he began his successful run as John-Boy on the TV hit *The Waltons*; Jay North, formerly TV's Dennis the Menace; Colin Higgins' brother Barry; Bob Balaban; Jack Bearden; John Savage; Wendell Burton from *The Sterile Cuckoo*; a pre–*American Graffiti* Richard Dreyfuss; and, surprisingly, rising pop musician Elton John.

Elton John, born Reginald Dwight, was an English piano-playing singer and songwriter who had recently released his debut album in America and had had a top ten hit with the ballad "Your Song." Ashby needed music for the movie, and he thought that John, with his soulful voice and great piano playing, could fill that role and possibly even take the part of Harold himself. John had a baby face at that time, and was largely an unknown quantity in the United States despite his rising

6. The Most Difficult Part of Making a Film

music career. Ashby and Mulvehill visited John after a show at the Troubadour in L.A. in the fall of 1970 and broached the subject of doing the music for *Harold and Maude,* but John had recently finished working on the music for the film *Friends* and wasn't interested in doing any more film work at the time. Plus his career was just beginning to take off, and John reasoned correctly that for the next year he would be too busy to work on music for a Hollywood film. As John decided not to write the film's music, and had no acting experience whatsoever, Ashby ultimately decided it was best to move on to other candidates to play Harold.

With Cort, Rubinstein, Balaban and Barry Higgins leading the contenders, Ashby turned his attention to the even more challenging prospect of casting Maude. There were lots of young actors around,

Ruth Gordon and her husband Garson Kanin in 1949. Kanin, 16 years his wife's junior, was one of Broadway's best known and most successful playwrights. The two collaborated on the scripts for *Adam's Rib* and *Pat and Mike,* films that may have reflected their real-life partnership.

71

but not that many actresses approaching age 80 that might be capable of the role and willing to play an octogenarian sex star. In Higgins' script, Maude appears to have a European background, as she mentions being a young girl in pre-war Vienna. Ashby, therefore, logically began to consider a number of European actresses when he made up his list of choices for Maude.

Ruth Gordon and her husband, writer Garson Kanin, were dining in New York with Broadway producer David Merrick and his wife, and seated at a nearby table was Robert Evans and his actress wife Ali McGraw. McGraw had recently been featured in Paramount's tearjerker *Love Story* as the doomed Jenny, wife to preppy law student Oliver Barrett IV, played by Ryan O'Neal. Released in December 1970, *Love Story* was a major success, bringing in millions for the studio and solidifying Evans' status as the new production genius of Hollywood.

Gordon was one of the grand dames of Broadway, having acted on the Great White Way for over 50 years. But Evans knew her from her work in *Rosemary's Baby*, a Paramount hit made under the Evans regime a couple of years earlier. According to Gordon's 1976 biography *My Side*, Evans stopped by and told her, "I've got a sensational script for you, Ruth." Gordon's first thought was to inquire if there was a part for Ali in the film, because then she would be sure that the film would be made. But to her surprise, Evans (who would later have second thoughts about the casting of Gordon) told her that she would in fact be the star and romantic lead of the film.[3]

After reading the script, Gordon had only one thought: "Nobody could play it but me! It's a terrific part, she's fantastic, big acting scenes, deep and moving, then funny, and I sing a song and dance. Talk about vitality, it leaps off the page, and she's eighty!" Eventually Gordon was informed that the director was to be Hal Ashby, and that Ashby had final say on who would play Maude. And Ashby had a long list of actresses that he was considering, and Ruth Gordon was but one of them.

High on Ashby's list of actresses for Maude was Dame Edith Evans. Evans, born in 1888, was considered by many to be the 20th century's greatest English stage actress. She made her professional stage debut in 1912 and excelled in both classic and modern roles in the West End

6. The Most Difficult Part of Making a Film

of London and on Broadway. She was made a Dame Commander of the Most Excellent Order of the British Empire (the equivalent of a knighthood) in 1946. Evans had largely ignored films until 1949, but acted frequently for the cameras in the 20 years after that: She appeared in Fred Zinnemann's *The Nun's Story* and in Tony Richardson's film version of John Osborne's *Look Back in Anger* (both 1959). Her performance as Miss Western in Richardson's Oscar-winning Best Picture *Tom Jones* (1963) that established her as a major film presence. Coincidentally, it was Richardson who had given Ashby his first break as an editor on his 1965 farce *The Loved One*. More recently, Dame Edith had won a Golden Globe and New York Film Critics Circle Award (as well as an Academy Award nomination) for her performance as the frightened old lady in Bryan Forbes's *The Whisperers* (1967).[4] By further coincidence, when Ashby won his Academy Award for editing *In the Heat of the Night* in 1968, it was Dame Edith who presented Hal with the statuette.

Ruth Gordon in 1969 with her Academy Award for Best Supporting Actress in Roman Polanski's *Rosemary's Baby* (1968). She appeared in her first film in 1915, and her Oscar win signaled a new period of film popularity for the actress at age 72.

Other talented actresses under consideration by Ashby included Eva Le Gallienne, Joanna Roos, Jo Van Fleet, Patience Collier, Elisabeth Bergner, Cathleen Nesbitt (later to be featured in Hitchcock's *Family Plot*), Bessie Love, Dame Gladys Cooper and Isabel Jeans. Other long shots on Ashby's list were the grand dame of the Broadway stage Helen Hayes, Lotte Lenya, Dorothy Comingore (from *Citizen Kane*), Margaret

Lockwood ("too young?" Ashby wondered, in a note to himself), Dame Peggy Ashcroft, silent film stars Pola Negri and Minta Durfee (onetime wife of Roscoe "Fatty" Arbuckle), Simone Signoret, Janet Gaynor, Claudette Colbert and even Dolores Del Rio, although the Mexican superstar of the 1930s would certainly be hard to envision as the feisty Maude.[5]

On October 21, 1970, Ashby took the red eye to New York to audition actresses and make a final decision about who would play Maude. In New York, he met briefly with Ruth Gordon at the Drake Hotel to discuss the part. Gordon finally asked Ashby bluntly, "Well, do you want me?"

"Well, of course, I want you," the director replied. "Everybody wants Ruth Gordon." But ultimately Ashby was noncommittal, later admitting that the meeting he had with Gordon was too brief to let him know if she was right for the part. In the end, he told the actress he was flying to Europe to meet with other candidates for Maude. "The hell with him," Ruth Gordon thought.[6] Later than night, Ashby flew to London, arriving on Friday the 23rd. After checking into the Grosvenor House and taking a brief respite, he began a series of meetings at the Dorchester Hotel. At one p.m. he met with Patience Collier, who was appearing in Jewison's *Fiddler on the Roof*, but at 60 she wasn't the right age for either Maude or Mrs. Chasen. At 3:00 he met with Evans, at 4:00 with Cathleen Nesbitt and at 6:00 with Vivian Pickles, whom Ashby was considering for the role of Harold's mother.

On Saturday the 24th he met with Richard Portnoy, Silvia Coleridge, Bessie Love and Isabel Jeans. Dame Sybil Thorndike, Ashby noted, was "just out of the hospital, very frail" and at nearly 90 was too old for the part. Lila Kedrova, the countess in Hitchcock's *Torn Curtain*, was on Ashby's list for a meeting, but at 52 years old was far too young for Maude, and a little too old and too European for Mrs. Chasen. Ashby later visited Dame Gladys Cooper at her home on the Thames to discuss the part with her. Still in London on the 26th, he called Norman Jewison, who was hard at work on *Fiddler*, for some advice and to catch up, and later tried to contact director Stanley Kubrick through his representative.[7]

After returning to Hollywood, Ashby had a lot to consider. Edith Evans or one of the other actresses he'd met in England would give the part of Maude great stature, but in the end, as he commented later, he

6. The Most Difficult Part of Making a Film

"kept drawing myself back to the feeling the role should be played by an American." Ashby had a second meeting with Gordon in her Hollywood home and the actress thought the part was now hers for sure, but Ashby continued to be noncommittal. "To hell with him in spades!" Gordon thought. Eventually Ashby came to the conclusion that "Ruth Gordon would be the best Maude. The character was there in her optimism, her energy." She could also bring a comic flair to the part that some of the others were lacking. Despite Higgins' reservations, by early November Ashby had made up his mind, and the part was finally offered to Ruth Gordon.[8]

Ruth Gordon Jones, better known as Ruth Gordon, was born on October 30, 1896, in Quincy, Massachusetts. The daughter of a former ship captain, she decided on her life's work after seeing a performance by stage actress Hazel Dawn, who became her acting idol. Over the objections of her father, Gordon embarked upon a theater career, studying at the American Academy of Dramatic Arts and getting her first positive newspaper notice for her Broadway debut in a 1915 production of *Peter Pan*. Influential critic Alexander Woollcott described her performance as one of the lost boys as "ever so gay" and Woollcott became a valued and powerful friend to Gordon, encouraging her and promoting her career.

Gordon was one of Broadway's biggest stars of the 1920s and '30s, but her private life was marred by the premature death of her first husband, actor Gregory Kelly, who died at the age of 36 from heart disease. The diminutive (five foot), high-energy Gordon would bear only one child, a son named Jones Harris, born in 1929 as the product of an out-of-wedlock relationship with the much hated Broadway producer Jed Harris. In 1936, Gordon appeared for the first time in England at London's Old Vic Theatre in William Wycherley's play *The Country Wife*. It co-starred her future rival for the part of Maude, Edith Evans.

In 1942, Gordon married the brilliant playwright Garson Kanin, 16 years her junior. The marriage lasted more than four decades, throughout the rest of Gordon's life. While combining Broadway stage work with appearances in such films as *Abe Lincoln in Illinois* (1940) and *Two Faced Woman* (1941), Gordon began to collaborate with Kanin on writing projects. Kanin directed Spencer Tracy on Broadway in 1945 and he and Gordon became friends with Tracy and Katharine Hepburn; Kanin and Gordon wrote the screenplays for two of the couple's best known comedies, *Adam's Rib* (1949) and *Pat and Mike* (1952), which may have reflected the real-life partnership between not only Tracy and Hepburn, but Gordon and Kanin as well. Gordon and Kanin also wrote the screenplay for the Judy Holliday feature *The Marrying Kind* (1952) and Kanin wrote *Born Yesterday*, a huge Broadway hit that was made into a 1950 film starring Holliday, William Holden and Broderick Crawford.

Emblematic of the generosity and encouragement of others by Kanin and Gordon is a story related in *Mad as Hell,* Dave Itzkoff's book about the making of the film *Network*. In New York in 1946, Kanin ran into writer Paddy Chayefsky, with whom he'd become acquainted during the war. The down-on-his-luck writer was working in his uncle's print shop, trying to get his career going. Kanin and Gordon arranged for a $500 advance (then a fairly large sum) for Chayefsky to write his own play, "a gift, essentially, to get him out of his print shop job," as Itzkoff notes.[9] With their help, Chayefsky was soon a full-time writer. He went on to pen the screenplay for *Marty*, 1955's Best Picture Oscar winner.

In the 1960s, after being long absent from movies, Gordon returned to the big screen. She was featured as Natalie Wood's eccentric mother in *Inside Daisy Clover* in 1965, before taking on the role which—save for *Harold and Maude*—she would probably be best remembered for: Mia Farrow's demonic neighbor in Roman Polanski's *Rosemary's Baby* (1968). Gordon was nominated for an Academy Award for *Inside Daisy Clover* and she won the statuette for her over-the-top performance as Minnie Castevet in Polanski's film. After walking to the podium and accepting the award from Tony Curtis, Gordon joked, "I can't tell you how encouraging a thing like this is!" After the audience laughter died down, she went on to note that the first film that she was ever in was in 1915, an era that was dominated by names like D.W. Griffith, Charlie Chaplin and Mary Pickford.

At the age of 72, Ruth Gordon was back and was becoming known to an entire new generation of filmgoers who had missed her movies from the 1940s, and whose parents had been too young to see Gordon as a Broadway star in the teens and 1920s.[10]

6. The Most Difficult Part of Making a Film

After her Academy Award win, Gordon begin to act in films and television much more frequently than she had in the past. Her first film after *Rosemary's Baby* was another horror film, the 1969 shocker *What Ever Happened to Aunt Alice?* Something of a follow-up to the 1962 hit *What Ever Happened to Baby Jane?* (the film that briefly resurrected the careers of Joan Crawford and Bette Davis), *Aunt Alice* featured Gordon as a woman who applies for a housekeeper's job in the Tucson, Arizona, home of widow Clara Marrable (Geraldine Page). Her true intention is to find out what has happened to her friend Miss Tinsley (Mildred Dunnock), who previously held the housekeeper's job, and the results are quite shocking. Next, Gordon took on the role of Mrs.

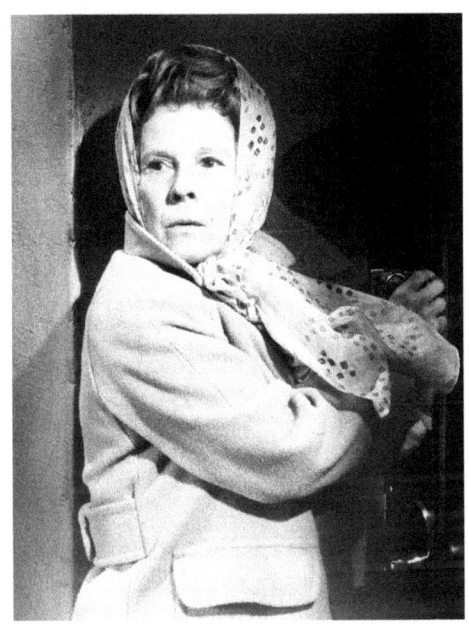

Gordon in *Whatever Happened to Aunt Alice?* (1969). She again wore the scarf seen in this picture in *Harold and Maude,* partly to obscure her face during the fast driving sequences when her young stunt double, Pamela Bebermeyer, was at the wheel.

Hocheiser in Carl Reiner's 1970 farce *Where's Poppa?* Here Gordon played the senile mother of New York attorney Gordon Hocheiser (George Segal), who meets the woman of his dreams, Louis Callan (Trish Van Devere). Unfortunately, Hocheiser now begins to worry that his mother's eccentric behavior will scare off his new girlfriend, and he begins to plot to send her to a rest home despite a promise to his father to always take care of his mom.

Why did Ashby pick Gordon, an American, over such esteemed English and European actresses? For one thing, at 74 the feisty Gordon was exactly the right age to portray Maude. During the course of the film, Maude has to ride a motorcycle and perform other physical activities that a frail old woman might not be able to do; Gordon, fairly spry for her age, was able to do these activities with no problem (the one exception being some of Maude's driving scenes, for which Ashby employed a stunt double). Gordon did take a one-and-a-half week "rest break" during the filming and returned to New York from late January until mid–February (she wasn't needed during that time, as the scenes at the Chasen home and with the psychiatrist were being shot).

In the end, her success playing Maude was due to a pixie-ish quality that made Gordon seem youthful for her age. (Perhaps being married to a man 16 years her junior had something to do with this.) This quality—as well as Gordon's in-bred Yankee charm—made the character of Maude resonate with moviegoers. Bud Cort told *New York Times* writer Leticia Kent that Gordon was "like a 15-year-old teenybopper. She jukes around. And she's got more energy than anybody I know—including me."[11] Seasoned by years of work on the New York stage, Gordon was a true professional in every way, and her acting chops helped her pull off lines of dialogue that might have been a stretch for a lesser actress. Ultimately, Ruth Gordon had what she needed to successfully play a part that, in the hands of many others, might have been unbelievable, perhaps even laughable.

On November 12, Edith Evans sent a handwritten note to Ashby, replying to his decision to cast Gordon as Maude. "To cast Ruth Gordon is a stroke of genius," the British actress wrote, and indeed it was.[12] On December 4, Ashby wrote formal letters to all the actresses that had met with him, thanking them for their time and informing them that after "many weeks of anxiety, frustration and self doubt, I have at long last made the decision to cast Ruth Gordon in the title role of *Harold and Maude*." He signed it, as usual, "Much peace and love, Hal Ashby."[13] The contract hiring Gordon was signed on December 4 between Lewis-Higgins Productions and TFT Corp. of New York; it provided Gordon's services as an actress for ten weeks, with two additional free weeks. The total compensation was $25,000, plus additional payments of up to $50,000 from the film's net profits, if there were any. (There would be, but not until years later.)

The two biggest supporting parts were Mrs. Chasen and Uncle Victor. For Mrs. Chasen, Ashby met in New York with Barbara Bel Geddes, but ultimately decided against using the co-star of *Vertigo*.

Other names on his list were Diana Douglas, Barbara Harris (whom Ashby would later cast in the unfortunate *Second Hand Hearts*, released in 1981), Celeste Holm, Sheree North (Ashby noted to himself that the former singer and rival to Marilyn Monroe was "not right") and Cloris Leachman. Leachman had many of the qualities that seemed right for Mrs. Chasen, but she was just beginning a run on TV's *The Mary Tyler Moore Show* in the fall of 1970. In 1971 she would win the Best Supporting Actress Oscar for her performance in Peter Bogdanovich's *The Last Picture Show*.

In the end, Ashby returned to Vivian Pickles, whom he'd first met in London in October. (She had been in the John Schlesinger film *Sunday Bloody Sunday*, and Schlesinger recommended her to Ashby.) Pickles remembered, "Hal was interviewing all the famous dames in a penthouse suite at the top of London's Dorchester Hotel. The dames were all very much up for Maude. It's a wonderful part, and they were all so keen for it. After the interview, Hal decided to play Maude as American and Mrs. Chasen as English-American."[14]

By this casting, Ashby had tinkered with Higgins' concepts in the script, in which Maude is European and Mrs. Chasen is American. Born on October 21, 1931, Pickles was not quite 40 when filming on *Harold and Maude* began, making her just barely old enough to play Harold's mother. A child actress who starred at age 14 as Alice in a BBC production of *Alice in Wonderland*, Pickles was educated in Paris, then returned to the London stage, appearing with Roger Moore in *I Capture the Castle* at the Aldwych Theatre. In addition to theatrical work, she appeared in several British television series in the early 1960s, then was cast by Ken Russell in the lead role in *Isadora Duncan, the Biggest Dancer in the World*. This was actually the first film that Ashby saw her in; he was later quoted as saying "Vivian Pickles is one of the finest actresses in the world."[15]

Casting Pickles did bring about some problems. Mulvehill remembered that they had problems with immigration getting Pickles a work permit, as there were objections from the U.S. government about an English actress hired for the part of an American. Pickles' accent was not a problem, as her refined background merely gave her the tone of a woman who was elegant-sounding, highly educated and well-traveled. In 2012, Pickles commented, "*Harold and Maude* is the only job I've done where I haven't wanted to change something after I've seen it.

Hal was so inspiring, with a most wonderful, genuine, appreciative smile of warm approval that spurred you on." Pickles also mentioned that Ashby "really loved my ideas" for her character in various scenes, and there is no doubt that her memorable performance added much to the film's black comic tone.[16] Pickles was scheduled for two weeks work and paid $10,000.

For Uncle Victor, identified in Higgins' script as "General Bradley's right hand man," Ashby also had a long list of possibilities. These included Barnard Hughes, Hume Cronyn, Murray Hamilton, William Daniels, Gene Hackman and Carroll O'Connor. Hughes was likely unavailable, as he played a critical supporting part in Arthur Hiller's *The Hospital*, a film that, like *Harold and Maude*, was released in December 1971. Hamilton and Daniels had both appeared in Mike Nichols' 1967 film *The Graduate* (Hamilton as Mr. Robinson and Daniels as Benjamin Braddock's father) and Ashby must have realized that, since *Harold and Maude* would attract a very similar audience to *The Graduate*, these two actors would carry too much baggage from the previous film. Nineteen seventy-one was the year Hackman broke through to star status in William Friedkin's *The French Connection*, and O'Connor was just beginning his long-running role on TV as Archie Bunker in *All in the Family*, so these two were likely both unavailable or too expensive for the part of Uncle Victor.

Ashby finally settled on an actor who was less familiar to moviegoers of the time than these other actors; his name was Charles Tyner.

Born in Virginia in 1925, Tyner was a World War II veteran who studied acting with the famous Stella Adler. He appeared on Broadway in two Tennessee Williams plays, *Orpheus Descending* in 1957 and *Sweet Bird of Youth* in 1959. He was reunited with his *Sweet Bird of Youth* co-star Paul Newman in the 1967 film *Cool Hand Luke*, in which Tyner played a sadistic prison guard. Ashby knew Tyner because he played Dr. Lazarus in Jewison's 1969 flop *Gaily, Gaily*, which Ashby associate produced. For his part as Uncle Victor, Tyner was paid $3,000 for one week's work.[17]

Other parts in the film were cast by Ashby and well-known Hollywood casting director Lynn Stalmaster. George Wood (credited as G. Wood) would play the deadpan part of the psychiatrist who deals with Harold and his hang-ups. Eric Christmas, a character actor who came to acting rather late in life, would stealing most of his scenes as

6. The Most Difficult Part of Making a Film

the frustrated priest harassed and harried by Maude; the $1000 he was paid for his part was undoubtedly the best investment that the film made. Maude's friend Madame Arouet was played by Marjorie Eaton, a San Francisco-born actress who had played a nun in the 1966 film *The Trouble with Angels*. All of Madame Arouet's scenes were eventually cut, so Eaton did not appear on screen in *Harold and Maude* and was not credited. The character of Glaucus was played by well-respected Irish actor Cyril Cusack, who also saw many of his scenes cut. (He appears in just one scene, doing a nude sculpture of Maude, though his character is mentioned several other times.) An indication of the respect Cusack received was his high billing in the film, behind Gordon, Cort and Pickles, and the fact that he earned $3500 for his part, making him the highest-paid supporting actors after Vivian Pickles.

Other parts were cast in short order. Ellen Geer, daughter of respected actor Will Geer (grandpa on *The Waltons*) went up to Ashby's Appian Way home to meet the director and the two immediately hit it off. She was cast in the important part of Harold's final computer date Sunshine Dore. Cort's comedy partner Judy Engels was cast as Candy Gulf, Harold's short-lived first date. For Edith Phern, Harold's second date, an actress resembling a "female Don Knotts" was supposed to be cast; Shari Summers, who after the film married Charles Mulvehill, took the role.[18] William Lucking was cast as the motorcycle cop who tries to chase down Harold and Maude when they go to replant the little tree. Lucking is only in one shot of the finished film.

Harold and Maude was largely ready to go, except that trouble was brewing between Hal Ashby and Paramount, and before cameras rolled, things finally came to a head.

7

I Feel I Could Make This Film About as Funny as the Vietnam War

On Monday, November 23, Ashby arrived at Paramount for a meeting with Robert Evans and other Paramount executives to discuss progress on *Harold and Maude*. Having decided on Ruth Gordon as Maude, Ashby was excited about the meeting. A few weeks earlier, he had given Evans a script for a film called *Owen Butler* that he hoped Evans would read and consider as Ashby's next project. He had ideas for *Harold and Maude* that included what music would be used, advertising and publicity for its eventual release, and his desire to have Mulvehill as co-producer. Ashby also hoped that these discussions would also lead to further talks about his eventual career making films at Paramount.

Ashby was taken aback from the first moment the meeting began. He was told that the budget, which had been previously agreed upon as $1.3 million, was being cut to $1.1 million. This would mean that the film could not be shot on location in the San Francisco Bay Area, but would have to be shot in Los Angeles, which was the only viable place to meet that budget number. He was told that the start date was being pushed back beyond December 14. And he was told that Paramount insisted upon having a location manager on the film who was essentially an auditor and would control the spending to make sure the film did not go over budget. No future projects or scripts with Ashby were discussed.

Hal returned to his offices crushed. After a number of sleepless nights, he finally wrote Evans a letter to address the situation. In the December 1 letter, Ashby essentially quit as the director of *Harold and Maude*. This was either an enormous crisis of confidence on his part,

7. About as Funny as the Vietnam War

or a canny power play intended to get Paramount to do things Ashby's way. Or it was a little of both? Whatever it was, it ended up working.

For several months, Ashby had been trying to procure the services of Gordon Willis, his director of photography on *The Landlord*, for *Harold and Maude*. A brilliant cameraman, Willis had learned his craft serving in the Air Force during the Korean War, and had come up in the industry working in New York on documentaries and in advertising. Willis was in the cameraman's union, but only for work on the East Coast; as *The Landlord* was shot in New York, this was no problem, but when it appeared that *Harold and Maude* would be shot in California, trouble arose. Ashby desperately wanted Willis for his second film; as he wrote to Evans, this would "eliminate one great problem of communication with the cameraman." On October 15 Ashby had written Willis a letter offering him the job. But Paramount told Ashby that if he hired Willis without Willis joining the West Coast union, the director risked of shutting down all the films in production on the West Coast. After a series of delays, Ashby faced a time conflict with Willis' commitment to work on Francis Ford Coppola's *The Godfather* (also a Paramount film) being shot primarily in New York. As Ashby wrote to Evans,

> Then Paramount arbitrarily decides I can't start the picture on December 14th, and that's the way it stands until a week is killed and I have to jump up and say this means Paramount is canceling the project. Then I'm told the union says no to Gordie's coming out here at all. Now I say Paramount didn't try very hard; in fact, I say Paramount said that I couldn't start the film December 14th, and to insure their position, they killed it with the union.[1]

Ashby's December 1 letter to Evans included a litany of other complaints. He beefed about interference from Paramount executive Jack Ballard, who was requesting that all hiring be cleared with him first. It was Ballard who demanded that a Paramount auditor be on the location during the shooting. Furthermore, when Ashby had suggested that Ken Ryan be hired as auditor, Ballard denied the request and Ryan was lost to work on a Warner Bros. film. Furthermore, Ashby wrote to Evans that "you were going to speak with those in authority at Paramount to see why our unit couldn't be set up on a similar basis to those functioning autonomously out of Universal and Twentieth [but] to this day, I've never heard another word about it."

Ashby was perhaps most upset about Paramount's eleventh-hour decision to revise the budget to a figure that would rule out Northern California as a location. "Now," Ashby wrote, "I hear it seems that the big decision lies between shooting in Los Angeles and San Francisco, as it seems Los Angeles is the only way to cut the budget. As you know, my thoughts in this area have never changed."[2]

Ashby went on to tell Evans how disappointed he was during the November 23 meeting, as he came in ready to discuss all the matters related to *Harold and Maude* as well as getting "into an area of discussing how Paramount feels about films and filmmaking and the direction that we're going to take to achieve those aims." Ashby was upset that, as far as he knew, after five weeks his *Owen Butler* still hadn't been read. Ashby felt "floored" when, during the meeting, he was hit with the possible budget reduction and the "arbitrary decision as to when I can start and not start and a failure to get my cameraman who I'd been told many, many times that I could have under certain conditions but, in the end, I could not have even when those conditions were met."

Ashby concluded the letter by stating that "the energies and creative juices have indeed finally been tapped and it would, I'm afraid, have to take its toll on the film, and *Harold and Maude* deserves better than that." He added the following grim P.S.: "I feel I could make this film about as funny as the Vietnam War."[3]

Did Ashby really intend to quit *Harold and Maude* just as the film was about to go into production, or was this just a bluff to get his way with Evans and the studio? It's hard to say, but the tone of the letter makes it hard to believe that it was purely a bluff. Ashby had been around the studio system for years (even as it was unraveling) and knew how to play political games, but it appears that he was genuinely stung and hurt at having a series of indignities heaped upon him just as the film was ready to begin shooting. In the first paragraph of the letter, he speaks of "another sleepless night" that he has suffered through, apparently in order to make Evans understand how upset and overwrought he was with the situation. He added, "I do believe it would be a great mistake, on both our parts, for me to continue to work on this film."[4]

7. About as Funny as the Vietnam War

It appears that Ashby was playing his final card in order to proceed with the film the way that he hoped. He knew that *Harold and Maude* was a quirky and idiosyncratic project (Evans had called it "impossible to cast"), that Evans would not let Higgins direct, and that finding another director at this point would severely hinder and possibly even scuttle the film. In threatening to quit, Ashby was trying to get Paramount to agree to let him make the film on the budget of $1.3 million that he felt was "an honest one, which I felt I could meet."[5] He was trying to get Paramount to agree to let him shoot in the Bay Area, away from their prying eyes, and without an auditor watching his every move.

His gambit appears to have worked. On Tuesday, December 2, the day after the letter was written, Ashby had a meeting with Evans, Stanley Jaffe and some of the other Paramount executives to discuss the situation. A budget of $1.25 million was approved, giving Ashby the ability to shoot in San Francisco. Although the meeting ended before Hal could air all the issues he had in mind, a series of later meetings with Bart and some others satisfied the director that, despite not getting all the autonomy he sought, he could move forward.

But black clouds continued to hover over Ashby and the production, ultimately foreshadowing the uphill climb that *Harold and Maude* would face on its release about a year later. Ashby was still concerned that he had been fulfilling most of the responsibilities of the producer and that Paramount still had not settled on anyone to replace the departed Howard Jaffe. The studio was leaning towards hiring independent producer Leon Roth, but Ashby suggesting saving the $20,000 that hiring Roth would cost by giving the job to Mulvehill, who would have been willing to do it for his present salary and screen credit. "I have Chuck with me because I trust him," Ashby wrote to Evans.

> I know what he is saying [about costs] is honest. One of my primary concerns, at this stage, is to allow myself the freedom to get on with more creative aspects of making this film, and not be bothered with such items as taking a whole night to write this letter. Believe me, when Chuck takes over as producer, a great load will be gone from my shoulders.[6]

In the end, Roth was not hired for *Harold and Maude* and some of the money was used to hire Wes McAfee as unit production manager. A veteran of several television series, McAfee had recently worked on the film *Billy Jack*. According to Jeff Wexler, McAfee served as an uncredited producer on *Harold and Maude*, and he did most of the work finding the locations for the film and signing off on all the film's location agreements.

Harold and Maude's final production budget, prepared in early 1971, noted above-the-line costs (producer, director, writer and cast) at $303,600. The cast was budgeted at $92,800, a sum fairly common in 1971 for a non-star vehicle such as *Harold and Maude*. Below-the-line costs (pretty much everything else) came in at $892,900, which included $245,100 in location costs, $81,800 for editing and $40,500 for production staff. The total cost to complete the film, not including prints and distribution, was anticipated to be $1,285,000.

For good reason, Ashby was also worried about the fact that the project still did not have a cameraman on board. He mentioned in a December 7 letter to Evans that he was considering Conrad Hall and David Walsh for the position, but neither worked out. Ashby turned to veteran Haskell Wexler, director of photography on *In the Heat of the Night*, and he too was unavailable. But Wexler recommended John Alonzo to Ashby. Alonzo had seen *The Landlord* and was very impressed by it; after he met with Ashby and read the script, he agreed to work on the film.

Alonzo had met Wexler in Europe while working on a documentary on the conductor Zubin Mehta. He had recently done a number of TV shows and documentaries, but had just begun to work on feature films, including the Roger Corman low-budgeter *Bloody Mama* and the car chase film *Vanishing Point*. Despite Alonzo's relative lack of experience in features, Hal had a good feeling about the dark-haired Alonzo after meeting with him. When Alonzo read the script, he "was very impressed with the philosophy" of the film.[7] Like many of the people involved in *Harold and Maude*, Alonzo was fairly young, 36, and relatively inexperienced. Ashby took a gamble: On December 22, he decided to hire him.

With most of the rest of the crew falling into place, Ashby still faced a final decision on the actor to play Harold.

Since September, Ashby had been leaning towards Bud Cort; in their first meeting, Cort confidently told Ashby, "I'm playing this part,"

7. About as Funny as the Vietnam War

to which Ashby replied, "Well, I guess you are!"[8] But the director also knew that Higgins was holding out hope that his UCLA classmate and first choice, John Rubinstein, would be selected. He had ruled out Elton John and several others, but there were a few additional contenders that Ashby wanted to consider before a final decision would be made. Bob Balaban was still in the running; the 25-year-old had played small parts in *Midnight Cowboy* and *Catch-22*, but at the time he was virtually unknown to audiences. (With his round glasses and receding hairline he has since become well-known as a film-TV character actor.) Balaban came from a show business background, as his family owned the Balaban and Katz movie theater chain that dominated the Midwest and his uncle Barney had been head of Paramount for many years. With his thick glasses and slight build, Balaban fit the part of a nerdy Harold.[9]

Other contenders included Danny Fortas, Todd Susman and John Neilson, young actors with little to no experience. On December 8, Ashby fashioned a memo indicating how much these Harold contenders would cost if selected for the part. The most experienced actors, Cort and Rubinstein, would receive the highest pay, $27,500, for the ten-week shoot. Balaban would be paid $20,000 if hired, and the other three would receive salaries ranging from $1250 to $900 per week, with a ten-week guarantee. Ashby decided that it would be best to invite these six actors to the Appian Way house for an informal screen test, shot on video tape; he got Haskell Wexler to shoot them, and copies of the videos were sent to Evans for his review.[10]

The tests took place on Monday, December 14 and Tuesday the 15th. Ruth Gordon was on hand to do the tests with the various candidates, partly so that Ashby could get an idea of the chemistry between them. Bob Balaban was scheduled first, at 8:00 AM on Monday, followed by Susman and, after lunch, Neilson. Gordon noted that Neilson was "not right at all."[11] Cort was the first to be seen on Tuesday, followed by Fortas and Rubinstein in the afternoon. The actors performed two scenes, the first one walking outside on the street and the second, longer scene inside, set in Maude's home. This was the scene in which Harold is given his most dramatic lines, as he tells Maude the story of his first "death" at prep school and the reason he continues to re-live it through his fake suicides.

In the end, Bud Cort, Ashby's first choice all along, was given the part of Harold. Higgins was disappointed that Rubinstein was not chosen; the young writer was initially irritated by Cort's penchant to improvise instead of reading the words as written. But in 1979 he commented, "I think Hal made the right choice. I think Bud goes beyond playing the part and becomes the part."[12] Haskell Wexler's son Jeff, who helped his father shoot the tests, later said, "It was obvious to all of us that Bud was the absolute best choice."[13]

By casting Cort, Ashby tapped into the ghoulish nature of Harold Chasen. Obsessed with death, Harold repeats ritualized fake suicides for his mother's benefit; these are not the actions of a normal human being. Ashby realized that he needed an actor who would express the deep psychological issues faced by Harold, and he felt correctly that Rubinstein would not bring the necessary gravitas to the part. Cort, with his jet black hair and chalky white face, looked like someone who might have emerged from the Addams Family, a distant cousin to Morticia perhaps; or even a relative of the morbid late-night TV host Vampira. Moreover, Cort's blank and impassive face perfectly reflected Harold's damaged and complicated psychological condition.

With the main parts cast and Alonzo finally on board as photographer, the additional members of the *Harold and Maude* crew came together quickly. Michael Haller, an art designer who had recently worked on George Lucas' first feature *THX 1138*, came aboard as production designer. His contributions were many, from the idea to have Maude's apartment be an old railroad car to the marching band that passes in front of the church after the funeral. According to producer Mulvehill, Haller was the "unsung hero" of the film.[14] Steve "Sy" Silver, credited as a production associate on the film, served as an assistant art director and set decorator. In 1974 Silver created the San Francisco theatrical parody show *Beach Blanket Babylon*, which is now past its 40th year and considered the longest running musical revue in theater history. Michael Dmytryk, son of director Edward Dmytryk, served as Ashby's first assistant director. Edward Dmytryk had been a member of the "Hollywood Ten," along with Dalton Trumbo, the writer that Edward Lewis had helped get off the blacklist by giving him a screen credit on *Spartacus*. Jeff Wexler, living in San Francisco at the time, became a production assistant, in charge of all props. Robert Enrietto, another relative novice, was hired as second assistant director. William Theiss signed on as costume designer and he, along with hair and makeup artists Kathryn Blondell and Bob Stein, would give Mrs. Chasen her memorable look.

7. About as Funny as the Vietnam War

As Ashby read a handful of telegrams he received in late December, congratulating him on the start of filming of *Harold and Maude* (including one from Bob Evans, saying that *Harold and Maude* would be the "big success of 1971"), he could only look forward to the future with hope. While it would not all be smooth sailing, the filming of *Harold and Maude* was about to get underway, and nothing could stop it now.

8

Bay Area Bound

With the first day of shooting (January 4, 1971) approaching, Ashby and Mulvehill worked furiously over the holidays, getting the film ready to go in front of the camera. An "atmosphere list" and script continuity was created for the film, listing all the locations where shooting would occur, and designating the number of small parts and extras that would be needed. The Ann Brebner Agency, a local casting agency that had worked on a number of San Francisco films such as *Bullitt* (and would work later on *Family Plot, The Right Stuff* and others), was engaged to hire actors for the smaller parts, such as extras and the mourners at the funeral and cemetery scenes. The schedule for the film was tight, with less than two months planned for the shoot; cast and crew would work six days a week for the most part, with only Sundays off.

The city of San Francisco, where only one extended scene would actually be shot, sits atop a finger-like peninsula that runs up from the south bay and San Jose area through an area that we now call Silicon Valley. Most of the film would be shot in this lower peninsula area that makes up the Silicon Valley, including Hillsborough, Redwood City and Palo Alto. A big advantage to filming in the Bay Area was that there was clearer and cleaner air than Los Angeles in the early 1970s. The bay fog, which comes almost every morning, clears by afternoon, lifting and removing many pollutants from the air. The background of the film would be filled by the area's green rolling hills and blue skies, giving it a fresh look it would have lacked if it was filmed in the smoggy valleys of Los Angeles.[1]

When crew and actors arrived in the Bay Area in early January, they checked into the Los Prados Hotel on South Norfolk Street in San Mateo, about 19 miles south of downtown San Francisco, near the San Francisco Airport. The Los Prados was a modest hotel; it's now a Best

Western Motel located behind a strip mall, just off of Highway 101. The hotel's location was strategic, situating the crew near where the majority of the shooting would be done, on the peninsula south of San Francisco. The house seen as the Chasen family home was the Rosecourt mansion, located in Hillsborough, about seven miles from the hotel. Colin Higgins occupied room #117 in the hotel's rear, facing towards the 101 Freeway.

Not everyone stayed at the Los Prados. On most films, a certain amount of status has to apply amongst crew and actors, and that often translates down to things such as accommodations. Befitting her status as the star, Ruth Gordon stayed at the more opulent Huntington Hotel, a prestigious 1920s hotel on San Francisco's Nob Hill. For a shorter shoot, Gordon would likely have stayed at one of the better known hotels such as the St. Francis or Fairmount, but since this stay would go on for 13 weeks, Gordon chose the Huntington as it offered a small kitchenette for preparing some of their meals. She was also provided with a Winnebago. Gordon had to get up at 5:00 a.m. to make the one-hour drive down the peninsula for most of her scenes.

In her 1976 biography *My Side*, she wrote, "It began when Garson and Carl Klavik and I flew to San Francisco to help me be Maude. What a start to the new year! A movie I loved, my husband I love moves his work to Nob Hill to live at the Huntington Hotel, where everyone makes life easier, and with us Carl Klavik, who knows how to do everything."[2] Klavik, a six-footer who towered over the actress and her husband, was an all-around assistant whom Kanin described in a 1977 newspaper article as "the man who handles our affairs in California."[3]

Ashby and Mulvehill stayed in a rented home at 1835 Elmwood Road in Hillsborough. Bud Cort stayed at another short term rental in town.

If possible, films are shot in sequence, allowing the actors to develop their parts naturally as time goes on. However, for many films, this approach is not practical, and *Harold and Maude*, with its extensive location shooting, was one of those films. As the locations were only available at certain times, the crew had to jump around filming scenes out of sequence; this presented a particular challenge for Cort and Gordon: Their characters' relationship develops slowly over the course of the film. Early in the shoot they had to shoot scenes in which their romantic relationship is fairly well advanced.

For Cort, a Method actor, this was particularly problematic. Cort brought daisies for Gordon on the first day of shooting, in the hopes that it would help them develop a personal relationship that would translate into on-screen chemistry. Cort later said that Gordon was initially "all business. The first day of shooting, Ruth came up to me and said, 'You know what Spencer Tracy says is the secret of great acting?' 'No, Miss Gordon?' 'Hit your mark, and learn your fucking lines!' And she walks away."[4] Gordon continued to keep a detached, professional attitude towards Cort during the course of the filming, which made the on-screen chemistry difficult. However, after Cort sent Gordon flowers while she was on her break in New York with a note signed "Dear Maude, I miss you. Love, Harold," the relationship warmed up considerably. Jeff Wexler later observed, "Ruth seemed to treat Bud more like the troubled son she never had, kind, understanding and nurturing while being amazed at what a mess he was."[5]

The *Harold and Maude* set was an unusually egalitarian affair. Everyone had their part to do, but everyone pitched in to help and, as was Ashby's style, everyone's input was considered important. Ann Nolan, who had a small part in the film, later wrote that she was surprised when she came on the set because initially it was impossible for her to tell who was the film's director.[6] Ashby also allowed actors the freedom to improvise and add to their parts with bits of business that were sometimes made up on the spot. According to actor Edward Vasgerdsian, who played a small part as a soldier in the scene at the V.A. Hospital, Ashby was "the kind of guy as an actor you really want to work with."[7] John Alonzo was amazed that Ashby never gave him any camera directions, or even told him where to put the camera. He would just show Alonzo how the scene was blocked out, and let him take it from there.

The first day of filming on *Harold and Maude*, January 5, dawned sunny and bright. Ruth Gordon wrote later that Ashby was a "soother" and had "blond long hair, long blond beard, spiffy brown leather jacket, combat boots" as well as first day jitters.[8] The cast and crew were in Redwood City, a small bedroom community and the county seat of San Mateo, to shoot scene #70, in which Maude discovers the little tree

8. Bay Area Bound

that needs to be transplanted to the forest. The scene involved Maude's confrontation with three police officers who are trying to figure out why a car was driven up onto the sidewalk. Maude's carefree and irreverent attitude towards authority figures is first established in this scene.

For a location, Ashby utilized the San Mateo Hall of Justice, located at the corner of Marshall and Hamilton Streets in downtown Redwood City, and also imposed upon Mulvehill for the use of his Plymouth sedan, which would be towed behind a flatbed camera truck for the dialogue scenes. For her driving scenes, Gordon wore an old pink silk India scarf that she had worn in the 1969 film *What Ever Happened to Aunt Alice?* The scarf would serve a dual purpose: first, as a reference to the earlier film, but on another level it served to obscure the driver's face. Gordon, a lifelong New Yorker, had never done much driving, so it had been determined that much of Maude's wild, out-of-control driving would have to be done by someone else. But who would that be?

Gordon remembered her stunt driver as "Suzy," namely Susan Madigan, Gordon's stand-in on the film. In her biography, Gordon noted that Suzy was "nineteen, adorable round face, snub nose, long light brown straight hair" and that she "looked exactly the way I'd like to have looked."[9] Madigan would go on to a short career in films, most notably as a newlywed in the film *Airport 1975*. But Madigan, who was credited on the film as "Girlfriend" (she is the girl sitting in the yellow car with Tom Skerritt's motorcycle cop in one of the Dumbarton Bridge scenes), was born in 1956 and thus was only 14 when *Harold and Maude* was filmed, so she could not have been the driver. Gordon's replacement driver was actually her stunt double, 20-year-old Pamela Bebermeyer. In addition to the scarf, Bebermeyer wore a rubber mask (specially created from a mold of Gordon's face) which would create the illusion that it was Maude, not a 20-year-old, behind the wheel.

Visiting the bustling downtown Redwood City area today to see the location, the San Mateo County building still looks very similar to the way it did in 1971, except that the sidewalk has been redone and the trees removed. There is a small plaque on the sidewalk where the filming took place, presumably in honor of *Harold and Maude*, noting, "Redwood City Historical Site No. 19."

All did not go smoothly on the first day of shooting. As it was a weekday, people were going in and out of the Hall of Justice for court dates, meetings with the San Mateo County Board of Supervisors and other business. With the filming taking place on the sidewalk in front of the building, many people were upset that they were delayed entering the Hall of Justice. ("Redwood City Snafu," an article in the January 14, 1971, *Palo Alto Times*, quoted the sheriff as saying that the confusion occurred because he believed that filming was going to take place at the City Hall, not the Hall of Justice.) Ashby agreed to shut down the shoot early to allow the public access to the building; they would return on Saturday the 9th, when the Hall was closed, to get one final shot that was needed.

Day two, Wednesday, January 6, was a long day of filming, beginning in the morning with the scene in which Harold buys a used hearse that later infuriates his mother so much that she gets rid of it and replaces it with a sports car. The scene was shot at the Mayco Salvage Company at 114 Harbor Way in South San Francisco. The hearse, a 1959 Cadillac, was purchased by Lewis-Higgins Productions for use in the film and was auctioned off when filming was complete. After having several different owners, the car was purchased in 1975 by a fan of the film who—by his own admission—had seen *Harold and Maude* "somewhere between 150 and 200 times." For several years the owner, who prefers to remain anonymous, frequently drove the hearse around the Bay Area, but eventually stopped driving it and, in 1979, put it in storage to preserve it due to its historical importance. Pictures of the hearse as it looks today can be seen on the website "Grim Rides," run by a group of hearse enthusiasts located in California's Central Valley.

Next the scene in which Harold and Maude picnic at the construction demolition site was filmed at nearby Herauf Concrete Accessories. After lunch, the crew headed over to the east side of the Bay Area for shots of Harold and Maude sitting in the Emeryville mud flats, looking out across the water, holding hands as they clearly grow closer to each other emotionally. This is the scene in which Maude makes the moving speech about Dreyfus and the birds, and Harold looks down and notices the concentration camp numbers tattooed on her arm. Noise from the nearby freeway created difficulty for the sound man.

Ashby was never really happy with the shot of the tattoo but it ended up being one of the most memorable scenes in the film. On February 20, the crew would return to this site for reshoots.

Emeryville at the time was a largely industrial area like South San Francisco. A small city that now has about 10,000 residents, it is tucked

8. Bay Area Bound

on the east side of the Bay Bridge between the much larger cities of Oakland and Berkeley. Berkeley, home to the "free speech" movement in 1964, had been a hotbed of anti-war activity in the late 1960s, and many of the artists and political activists associated with the city also came to live in Emeryville. In the years since 1971, Emeryville has largely shed its status as a smokestack city and become a trendy place to live and work, inhabited by upscale retail, hi-tech and biotechnology. Emeryville is also the home to Pixar Animation, Disney's computer animation company.

The Emeryville locale was undoubtedly chosen because of its beautiful view of San Francisco, which could be nicely photographed as the sun set romantically in the west. The scene takes place in what is called the Emeryville mud flats (or sometimes the salt flats), an area towards the bay waters that is surrounded by landfill. At the time, the Emeryville mud flats contained wood sculptures and other artwork placed there by the burgeoning artist community that was moving into the city of Emeryville and beginning to inhabit the lofts and empty warehouses that were being abandoned by departing industry. A few

The Emeryville Mud Flats was the site of one of *Harold and Maude*'s most memorable scenes. The area is now part of the McLaughlin Eastshore State Park.

of the wood sculptures can be seen in the film. Today, the wood sculptures have been totally cleaned up and the Bayfront area (named McLaughlin Eastshore State Park) is meticulously maintained, as it is now part of the East Bay Regional Park District.

In the hopes of adding an anti-war message to the film, a wood sculpture was built on the set with the words "Fuck War"; shortly thereafter, the police arrived and removed the first word, leaving only "War." Eventually all those shots had to be cut to avoid saddling the film with an unwanted "R" rating for language (use of the word "Fuck" was not allowed). One shot of the "Fuck War" sculpture did make it into a trailer created by Pablo Ferro (this trailer was ultimately never released). The reverse angle shots of Harold and Maude did reveal the Highway 80 freeway that runs along the East Bay shoreline and a freeway sign indicating the off-ramp for "Ashby Ave." in Berkeley. While this was not planned, it did serve as a happy accidental homage to the director. (A major street, Ashby Avenue runs through Berkeley.)

On January 7, the crew headed to the west of San Mateo, to the coastal area of Half Moon Bay, in their Cinemobile (a compact production unit on wheels, designed to carry crew and equipment to various locations) to film the daisy fields sequence and the shots of planting the little tree in the forest. Half Moon Bay is a small community along Highway 1, about 25 miles south of San Francisco and ten miles west of San Mateo. Despite some confusion about the actual locations of the shoots, eventually all cast and crew arrived in the right place and 11 setups were taken on January 7, shooting the scene in the daisy fields. On the 8th, the scene in which the little tree is planted in the forest was filmed, but it was not completed; the crew returned January 21 to complete this scene. On Saturday, January 9, the first week of filming ended with shots of the vegetable field and the greenhouse at the Nurserymen's Exchange in Half Moon Bay; then back to the San Mateo Hall of Justice in Redwood City to finish the filming that was interrupted on Tuesday.

The week of January 11 commenced with scenes in which Maude begins to drive Harold home in his hearse after the outdoor funeral at Holy Cross Cemetery. The cemetery is located at 1500 Mission Road

8. Bay Area Bound

in Colma, a small city just south of San Francisco. Around 1937, San Francisco residents voted to no longer build cemeteries within the city proper and, as a result, there are only three cemeteries within San Francisco city limits. (One of them, the historic graveyard next to Mission Dolores, is prominently featured in Hitchcock's *Vertigo*.) As a result, Colma, located just to the south of San Francisco, is known as the "city of souls." Colma is home to only 1,400 (living) residents, but it has 16 cemeteries, of which Holy Cross is the oldest and largest. Holy Cross Cemetery is the burial site of such luminaries as former California Governor Pat Brown, as well as Yankee superstar "Joltin' Joe" DiMaggio.[10]

At this time, scenes were also photographed at the Golden Gate Cemetery on Sneath Lane in San Bruno, a massive veterans' cemetery with well over 100,000 internments. An impressive shot of Harold and Maude sitting amongst hundreds of tombstones was filmed with a long

Holy Cross Cemetery today looks very much as it did during the filming of *Harold and Maude* almost 45 years ago (photograph by the author).

zoom lens; in the finished film, this shot was incorporated into the daisy field sequence to subtly suggest the horrific consequences of war.

From January 12 to 15 the crew was in Palo Alto, filming the extended funeral sequence in which Harold first meets Maude. The location was the St. Thomas Aquinas Church, located at 745 Waverly Street at the corner of Waverly and Homer, near Stanford University and in the north edge of the residential district known as "Professorville."

A registered historic landmark, built in 1902, St. Thomas Aquinas Church, Palo Alto's oldest church, has a beautiful round stained glass window (the first shot of the sequence begins on this window and zooms out to reveal the funeral) and wooden arches in the distinctive carpenter gothic style.[11] While shooting the funeral scene, Ashby became fixated on the irony of the Permaseal icon on the side of the coffin, so the sequence includes a closeup shot of it as the pallbearers carry the coffin out of the church. An additional scene was shot at the church in which Maude borrows Harold's pen and adds smiles to the

The *Harold and Maude* crew got one of the film's most impressive shots at the massive Golden Gate Cemetery in San Bruno.

8. Bay Area Bound

Where Harold met Maude: the front steps of the St. Thomas Aquinas Church.

statues of the saints. This scene was eventually cut from the film, although the priest refers to it later when he confronts Maude after the outdoor funeral.

Adding to the black comic atmosphere of the funeral, production designer Haller remembered a situation that had recently occurred at his father's funeral, when a marching band passed just as the funeral procession was coming out of the church.[12] Ashby loved the idea, and the high school band from nearby Sunnyvale was recruited to march past as the pallbearers exit the church with the coffin. This scene was shot on Friday the 15th, as was the sequence in which Maude formally introduces herself to Harold on the stone front steps of the church. At this point she proceeds to produce a ring of keys and steal a Volkswagen parked in front of the church; Gordon's stunt double drove off in the Volkswagen wildly as the priest (Eric Christmas) emerges from the church, sputtering, "That lady stole my car!"

The crew returned on Saturday the 16th to Holy Cross Cemetery to shoot additional funeral scenes as well as the scenes of Harold driving Maude home. That night, Ashby, hoping to allow his cast and crew to get to know each other better, threw a party at the home he was renting in Hillsborough. After the party began, Jeff Wexler suddenly realized that Ashby wasn't there and went looking for him. He found the sometimes reclusive Hal sitting alone in one of the rear bedrooms. Hal asked, "Is there anybody out there?" When Jeff replied that there were, and that people were hoping to see him, Hal confessed that he wanted to have a party, but didn't know if he actually wanted to go to the party. According to Wexler, Ashby wanted the group to get along well, but was reluctant to socialize with the cast and crew. However, after the two of them smoked a joint together, Hal seemed to relax and came out to join the crowd and ended up having a great time.[13]

Further driving scenes were photographed on the 18th of January, but inclement weather made filming difficult, and the initial shoot with the motorcycle cop at the Dumbarton Bridge was postponed and rescheduled for February.

The cast party held at Ashby's rented house and the final wrap party at Steve Silver's would be the only two formal events held for the *Harold and Maude* cast and crew. There were other opportunities to socialize, however, and one of them came during the viewing of the dailies that were watched each evening after that day's filming was completed. Unlike other directors, Ashby (in his communal and collaborative style) allowed all the actors who were present to watch the dailies, whether or not they had been part of that day's filming. What evolved from this, somewhat naturally, were three distinct sections in the screening room. Up front, sitting on the floor on comfortable pads, were the pot smokers (including Hal). In the middle section sat the people whom Ellen Geer described as "the squares" (including herself) who were content to drink soft drinks. In the back, sitting on stools, were those who preferred adult beverages such as director of photography Alonzo. In the end, a "great community" was formed by these people who were not all exactly alike, but who had come together to make a unique movie and now found themselves forming a deep bond with one another.[14]

8. Bay Area Bound

January 20 was the first day of filming for Charles Tyner as Victor Ball, Harold's uncle. The Redwood City Chamber of Commerce offered to let the crew use their offices at 1006 Middlefield Road for a scene in Uncle Victor's office, and filming took place there from January 20 to 22. In the script, Uncle Victor is described as a "one-star general with an amputated right hand" (which Higgins obviously intended as a sick joke, since Mrs. Chasen describes her brother as "General Bradley's right hand man"). On the set, Michael Haller and the crew decided to take the joke one step farther by making a mechanical device that Uncle Victor could pull on to move his empty sleeve into the form of a salute as he looks at the picture in his office of patriot Nathan Hale. Tyner later humorously told a reporter that he could play the part of Uncle Victor with "one hand tied behind my back," which was exactly what he did.

Uncle Victor's persona is further embellished when the script was changed to refer to him as General MacArthur's (rather than General Bradley's) right hand man. In the 1970 film *Patton*, released shortly before *Harold and Maude* started shooting, Bradley is played by sympathetic character actor Karl Malden and depicted as a softer alternative to the militaristic Patton; as a result, Victor's allegiance was changed from Bradley to MacArthur, who would have seemed like a figure of greater military authority to movie audiences of 1971.

Prominent on the wall behind Uncle Victor's desk is a picture of President Richard Nixon, an obvious authority figure. (The priest and the psychiatrist also have pictures of their "bosses" behind their desks— the Pope and Sigmund Freud, respectively—which we see during the later sequence in which the three men admonish Harold about the problems he faces in marrying Maude.) Nixon was a recurring subject of ridicule for Ashby in his films; as Nick Dawson points out, there are also references to Nixon in *The Landlord*, *The Last Detail* and *Shampoo*. Towards the end of *Shampoo*, which is set on Election Day in 1968, there is even a clip of Nixon speaking ironically on TV the morning after his narrow victory over Hubert Humphrey.

Next after the Uncle Victor's office scenes was the lengthy sequence in which Harold and Maude deceive Uncle Victor into believing that Harold is mentally unfit for the military. Originally this scene was set at a reservoir, with Harold tossing Maude into the rushing waters of a dam. For the film, however, it was decided to shoot this sequence at the ruins of the Sutro Baths in San Francisco, so that Maude could drop down through a hole apparently into the ocean. The scene that directly precedes it, where Harold rides in a car and walks with Uncle Victor through what appears to be a military hospital, was shot at Sutro Heights Park, just above the ruins of the baths.

Self-made millionaire Adolph Sutro developed the Sutro Baths in 1894, along the Pacific Ocean in San Francisco just north of the Cliff House restaurant. Sutro's oceanfront complex included an aquarium and a massive public bathhouse that covered three acres and boasted impressive engineering and artistic details. Sutro, who died in 1898, sought to provide a healthy, recreational and inexpensive swimming facility with seven swimming pools kept at various temperatures. The Pacific Ocean during high tide could provide the 1.7 million gallons of water required for all the pools in just one hour. But for all their glamour and excitement, the Sutro Baths were not commercially successful over the long term. During the Depression, the owners converted the baths into an ice-skating rink but the Sutro Baths never regained its popularity and the ice-skating revenue was not enough to maintain the enormous building. A 1966 fire destroyed what was left of the baths, and plans for high rise apartments on the site were scuttled. The concrete ruins just north of the Cliff House are the remains of the grand Sutro Baths and have been part of the Golden Gate National Recreation Area since 1973.[15]

On January 23, the preliminary sequence was shot at Sutro Heights Park, a small park located on a bluff above the actual ruins, as Harold and Uncle Victor ride in a chauffeur-driven car through what appears to be a veteran's hospital, discussing Harold's future in the military. In the background, Edward Vasgerdsian, a local actor who still lives in the Bay Area, played one of the disabled soldiers (wearing his own military uniform) as Harold and Uncle Victor walk ahead of the car. While waiting for the action to begin, Vasgerdsian decided that if his character—who was using crutches—tried to salute Uncle Victor, he would probably fall to the ground. When the cameras rolled, Vasgerdsian improvised this action, with his character sprawling out and rolling on the ground comically. The action worked perfectly, highlighting the absurdity of the conversation between Harold and Uncle Victor, so Ashby kept the shot in the film, although he did not end up using the take in which Vasgerdsian tried to salute.[16]

8. Bay Area Bound

The Sutro Baths sequence was shot in the plaza of the ruins from January 25 to 27. As Harold and Uncle Victor talk over his past military triumphs, Harold become increasingly enthused about the idea of hand-to-hand combat, eventually even frothing at the mouth at the thought of taking "souvenirs" of his kill, including hair, teeth ... even private parts! Harold enthusiastically pulls out a shrunken head (which Mulvehill notes had to be fashioned impromptu by the crew out of gaffer's tape when the prop man forgot the actual shrunken head) and waves it around until Maude, protesting for peace, interrupts him.[17] The scene, one of the few in the movie that came close to making an actual political point, is played for great comic effect by Cort and Gordon, with Tyner playing straight man brilliantly.

Eventually Maude falls through a pre-existing hole—presumably to her demise—and disappears into the dark waters below. Ashby got a great shot of the reflection of Uncle Victor looking down into the water anxiously, his empty right arm extended impotently after the

The ruins of the Sutro Baths along the Pacific coast, where the scene was filmed. In the movie, the locale was established with a shot from exactly this vantage point, near San Francisco's famous Cliff House restaurant.

Taking a break from shooting the "protesting for peace" scene at the Sutro Baths ruins. Left to right: actor Charles Tyner, Hal Ashby, Bud Cort, Ruth Gordon and director of photography John Alonzo.

struggle between himself, the old woman and his nephew. Gordon's stunt double Pamela Bebermeyer recalled that the shot was accomplished when two men in the crew held her up on brooms, and she dropped down through the hole into the cold, shallow waters of the Pacific Ocean below. Although Ashby was apparently never really satisfied with it, the sequence became one of the most memorable in the film.

With Tyner's sequences complete, Gordon was able to take a break and return to New York, as filming with Vivian Pickles at the Chasen home was about to commence and Ruth would not be needed. Beginning January 28 and lasting through February 11, the *Harold and Maude* crew would film at a unique location called the Rosecourt Mansion in Hillsborough, one of the Bay Area's most affluent suburbs.

9

The Rosecourt

Helen M. de Young Cameron was a San Francisco aristocrat. She was born in 1883 to Michael H. de Young, the founder (with his brother) of the *San Francisco Chronicle*. He would also establish the well-known de Young Museum in Golden Gate Park. Helen grew up amidst wealth and affluence: Educated in Europe, she became an accomplished musician and harpist, eventually being presented at the Court of St. James in London and making her debut at the family home in San Francisco in 1905. A socialite known for her good works, Helen married George Toland Cameron in 1909. He was a socially prominent San Francisco businessman ten years her senior; his family made its money in the concrete business during the growth years of the late 19th century.[1]

When Michael de Young died in 1925, George Cameron took over as publisher of the *Chronicle*. Although it would eventually become the dominant newspaper in San Francisco, at the time the *Chronicle* was the second place newspaper, behind William Randolph Hearst's *Examiner*. Cameron was well known around the offices of the *Chronicle* for his bow ties and patrician attitude, seemingly believing that everyone came from the same high social strata as he. The story goes that Cameron once got on an elevator with a copy boy and, looking over at the obviously poor man, asked, "May I give you a ride to your club?"[2]

Helen and George lived in one of the unique homes of the San Francisco peninsula, the Rosecourt Mansion. Built for the Camerons in 1913 by famed architect Lewis Parsons Hobart, the Rosecourt was located in one of the most exclusive areas of lower Hillsborough. Hillsborough was then—and still is now—one of the most exclusive suburbs in the country. Located 17 miles south of San Francisco, Hillsborough has the highest income of places in the United States with populations of at least 10,000 people. An incorporated town that has no commercial zoning, Hillsborough has within its borders only large, exclusive homes and no businesses except for the Burlingame Country Club and golf course.

Named "Rosecourt" for the pink color of its brick, the cobblestones in front of the home were imported from Michael de Young's San Francisco home, which was destroyed in the 1906 earthquake. With 17 rooms, six bedrooms and 7.5 bathrooms, the 12,220-square foot mansion was located in 1971 on a roomy 7.5 acre parcel (some of which can be glimpsed in the sequence in which Harold arrives home driving the hearse). In subsequent years, the parcel was subdivided and the home—which still looks much the way it did when the movie was shot—now sits on a much smaller lot (less than one acre), facing from the rear onto the Burlingame Country Club golf course.[3]

Despite their opulence and beautiful home, the Camerons were never blessed with children. Helen furnished the Rosecourt with expensive artwork and added a music room which included an antique Estey

The Rosecourt mansion today, looking very much as it did in 1971 when it was used in *Harold and Maude*. The surrounding area, however, has changed considerably.

9. The Rosecourt

pipe organ. On October 3, 1955, George Cameron died of a heart attack, leaving Helen a widow with a fortune of $9 million. Fourteen years later, on July 22, 1969, Helen died at age 86 at her home, also of a heart attack. As there were no direct beneficiaries to take over the house, the Rosecourt was put up for sale. In August 1970, a new listing was announced of a "handsome 17-room house on 7 1/2 acres in Hillsborough," the Rosecourt, "distinguished estate of the late Mrs. George T. Cameron." It announced that inspection was available by "appointment with custodian, Mr. Henry Dieckoff." The home was offered at $550,000 as a whole, or in part at a negotiated price. Dieckoff, who had been the Camerons' butler, would play a part in the filming of *Harold and Maude*.[4]

For the *Harold and Maude* filmmakers, the timing couldn't have been more perfect. The Rosecourt was available for their short-term rental while it was on the market, fully furnished with antiques, artwork and other accessories. By early November, Ashby had settled on the Rosecourt as the location for the Chasen home; it would be a coup, because the filmmakers could not only utilize the estate, but the home furnishings and artwork as well. The furnishings were dominated by French styles that were classical and elegant and perfectly suited to a home owned by a woman such as Mrs. Chasen. Since everything would be in place, there would be no need to spend time and money designing and dressing sets; they could simply use what was there. However, two problems emerged in the early going. One was the issue of insurance in order to protect the valuable artwork and artifacts in the home, which included an original Rembrandt. A nervous Ashby remembered later, "You can imagine working in those kind of surroundings. Rare antiques, two hangings worth a million each. I didn't even dare smoke a cigarette for fear I'd burn something."[5]

Cooper, White and Cooper, a well-established San Francisco firm located in the downtown financial district, handled the rental of the estate. On November 5, David DeMarco, Paramount's Director of Corporate Insurance, met with attorney Alan Fox in his San Francisco office to discuss the lease. The Cameron estate was seeking a $7.5 million insurance policy to cover the estate and its belongings, but

DeMarco argued that Paramount's insurance company would never insure for a figure so high. After considerable negotiation, DeMarco proposed insurance of $750,000 to cover the artwork and $550,000 for the home, for total insurance coverage of $1.3 million. Once filming commenced at the Rosecourt, DeMarco visited the site to make sure that due care was being taken. On February 1, DeMarco wrote to Scott Milne of Albert G. Ruben & Co. in Beverly Hills, stating that he had just returned from the *Harold and Maude* location and that the crew was taking "extraordinary precautions to protect the physical properties which are at risk." He noted to Milne the difficulties in coming up with the right amount of insurance for the property due to its large values.[6] In the end, nothing was damaged and no insurance claim was made.

The second problem that arose was resentment from the community about the presence of a film crew. As Ashby recalled in a 1972 interview with Marilyn Beck, "The last time a film company was there was for an Otto Preminger project and I understand he went through the community like a storm trooper, leaving residents with strong feelings that they'd just as soon film companies didn't invade their borders again."[7] But on December 16, after much debate, the Hillsborough Town Council voted to allow the filming *if* it all took place on the Rosecourt grounds and not on any public thoroughfare or street; and that that the main gate at Rosecourt "will be kept closed during the entire time you are on the grounds, specifically including the time you are filming." On December 23, a nervous Alan Fox wrote to Mulvehill informing him of the town council's decision to give its approval, but emphasizing that the filmmakers had to abide by the rules of the town and that they had made an "agreement to locate and maintain all your photographic, sound and other equipment on the Rosecourt premises and not on any Town property or thoroughfares."[8] He noted that they may have one or more persons on the premises to enforce these requirements (presumably Henry Dieckoff) but that they must "rely primarily on you to enforce the requirements." Filming eventually proceeded with no difficulty and, according to Ashby, "we weren't given one bit of trouble. Everything went fine."

On November 23, Alan Fox sent Mulvehill a proposed agreement for renting Rosecourt for use in the film. The agreement was agreed to between Lewis-Higgins Productions and Sheldon G. Cooper, the

9. The Rosecourt

senior partner of the firm and the surviving trustee of trust funds under the last will of George Cameron and executor of Helen's will. The agreement designated the term of rental as 32 days, commencing December 31, 1970, and ending January 31, 1971, with an option to extend this period by 14 days. The cost of the rental was $1500 per day for a minimum of eight days. A payment of $12,000, covering the eight-day minimum, was due and payable in advance at the signing of the agreement.

With the insurance taken care of and the Town Council having given its approval, all looked well, but filming still could not proceed: Vivian Pickles, who was to play Mrs. Chasen, was needed for most of the scenes in the home, and she was in Europe working on *Nicholas and Alexandria*. Delays in the production of that big-budget costume film kept Pickles there longer than expected, so the house rental agreement was modified: a January 15 start date with a February 14 end. Further complications ensued involving Pickles' immigration work status, as the authorities had to be given a good reason why an English actress had been chosen for a role that could have been filled by an American. Understandably, Ashby became very anxious at the thought of having to start filming at the estate without his Mrs. Chasen. In a 2011 interview, San Francisco casting director Ann Brebner, a local legend in the Marin County acting community, remembered that the worried Ashby turned to her in a production meeting and suggested that she (Ann) might have to play the part if Pickles did not arrive in time. Forty-eight years old in 1971, Brebner was the right age to portray Harold's mother, but was not a member of the Screen Actors Guild, so there would have been union troubles if she had taken over the part. When Pickles arrived in the nick of time, Brebner lost her chance to enjoy the limelight.[9]

On January 28, the first day of filming at Rosecourt, the long shot that Higgins had originally designed to open the film was completed in the Rosecourt's ornately filled music room in the north wing of the house. As mentioned above, the music room was a 1925 addition to the home. The camera follows Harold's shoes as he crosses the room, writes himself a name tag ("Harold Parker Chasen"), puts on a record, lights some candles and then appears to hang himself. In an overhead shot we see Harold swinging gently. A specially constructed noose was designed to attach to Cort's clothes so that he would not actually strangle to death. In a reverse angle behind Cort's hanging body, we see Vivian Pickles enter the room.

Shooting this scene was not without its risks. Cort wanted to make the fake hanging look realistic, so he pushed it as far as he could. He later told a reporter, "[W]hen we did the hanging sequence, I said, 'Hal, when we do these suicides, I want them to be so real that the crew thinks I'm actually killing myself. If I'm really in trouble, I'm going to give you a signal by raising my little finger, which means I'm in trouble and you have to stop it.' If you look at that sequence now, you actually see my little finger start to come up at one point."[10] Higgins had originally conceived this as one lengthy shot, but too much complex camera movement and focus-pulling would have been required, and the shot was divided with edits into several different angles. Still, the desired effect of shock and black humor was achieved in this *tour de force* opening sequence.

January 29 included filming of the dinner scene with Harold, Mrs. Chasen and her guests, as well as the shot in the front of the mansion when Harold arrives home driving the hearse. On the 30th, the scene when Mrs. Chasen first informs Harold about the computer dates was shot, as well as the scene in the pool where Harold commits a mock drowning. Although the weather in the Bay Area is relatively mild during the winter, with high temperatures in the mid– to upper 50s, it was still too cold to shoot the scene without heating up the pool so that the actors would not freeze. Several days were spent getting the pool to the right temperature.[11] Fortunately, the sun cooperated on this day, allowing the scene to be shot with the appearance of bright sunlight. The script called for the scene to be shot with Mrs. Chasen looking through a window in the pool house at Harold floating underwater, but the pool at the Rosecourt was not equipped with this type of window, so a modification had to be made and Pickles was filmed swimming past an apparently drowned Harold, ignoring him. A full-size dummy of Bud Cort (created for a scene that would be shot later) floating in the pool was also used to help the actor avoid spending time in the frigid cold water, and to complete the lengthy shot that was needed as Mrs. Chasen swims past Harold. Jeff Wexler noted that Cort was "actually quite nervous about the water stuff" but it all came off without a hitch. An under-

9. The Rosecourt

water camera rig was used to complete this sequence.[12] Further retakes of this scene were filmed on February 3 and 5.

Pickles' favorite scene was shot on February 1, as Harold sits in a chair stone-faced while his mother fills out his computer dating form, answering the questions for him. Eventually, Mrs. Chasen—the ulti-

English actress Vivian Pickles during the filming of one of the scenes at the Rosecourt. Pickles impressed everyone with her ability to ignore the camera while acting. She did not always get along well with Bud Cort but nevertheless later remembered her *Harold and Maude* experience fondly.

mate egotist—begins answering the questions as if she, herself, was the one entering the world of computer dating. Ashby had makeup artist Bob Stein make Cort's skin up to look particularly white and chalky in these early scenes of the film, so that after he meets Maude the audience can literally see a transformation occur as Harold becomes more "alive." By the later scenes of the film, his white skin was made to look a more normal color, showing that, through his relationship with Maude, he had left his hermetically sealed indoor world and become part of the living.[13]

Cort's old comedy partner Judy Engles was on the set for her scenes as Candy Gulf, which were shot on February 2 and 3. Cort improvised a few times on the film, including the scene in which he and his mother look after the departed Candy, by turning and giving a sly look to the camera while Pickles looks at him, annoyed. Ashby held on the shot with expert timing, and it turns out to be one of the funniest scenes in the finished film. Also on February 3, outdoor scenes at the estate were shot, including the sequence in which Mrs. Chasen gives Harold his sports car. The script called for the car to be an MG, a British sports car, but production designer Haller persuaded Ashby to use a Jaguar, which Harold then transforms into a "mini hearse" using a welding torch. Higgins favored the MG, but Ashby and Haller reasoned that the Jaguar was better known to American audiences and would have more impact in the final scene, when the car roars over the cliff.[14] Cort also improvised later in the scene when Mrs. Chasen is shocked at seeing the transformed Jaguar, by giving her "the finger" behind her back; Ashby left the shot in the film.

Harold's final computer date, Sunshine Dore, a "stringy, long-harried actress" according to the script, was portrayed by Ellen Geer, and her scenes were filmed from February 4 through 6. Geer, who came from an acting and theatrical background, had only recently begun her film career with a small part as a nun in Richard Lester's *Petulia* (1968). Most of her subsequent experience was in television.

The main scene between Harold and Sunshine was shot in the music room, where the initial "hanging" scene had been filmed. With different lighting and rearranged furniture, it is difficult to recognize it as the same room. While shooting the scene where Harold and Sunshine walk across the room, something interesting happens that illustrates the free-form nature of the filming of *Harold and Maude*. In

9. The Rosecourt

character as Sunshine, Geer (wearing high-heeled boots) slipped on the slick floor during a take. With her theatrical background, she didn't break character and kept going, despite hearing a snicker coming from behind the camera. Although Ashby later shot additional coverage of the scene, he decided to leave the unplanned slip in the shot, as it gave a feeling of realism and awkwardness to the character of Sunshine.

Of Harold's three dates, Sunshine—being an actress herself—is the only one who sees through Harold's ruse as he performs the ritual of Hari Kari and picks up on it herself, jumping in and performing Juliet's part in the death scene in *Romeo and Juliet*. Geer relied on her knowledge of Shakespeare to perfect her character; as a result, the sequence became one of the most memorable in the film. In the script, Mrs. Chasen enters the room carrying a tray of drinks and, seeing Sunshine apparently dead, drops it. For the film, Ashby had decided to employ Henry Dieckoff, the butler who actually worked at the estate, to play the Chasens' butler and carry the tray into the room with Mrs. Chasen. When Ashby ordered Dieckoff to drop the tray, he demurred, saying that a real butler would never do something that unforgiveable. Ashby, always one to listen to the views of others in a collaborative way, decided that Dieckoff was right, and instead had Pickles absentmindedly drop the drink that she was holding as she tried to place it back on the tray. This achieved the same slapstick effect and punctuated the scene perfectly.

Ellen Geer recalled her week on the *Harold and Maude* set as a wonderful experience. She enjoyed working with Pickles, whom she called a "warm and kind human being"; their shared experiences in the theater allowed them to form a bond. She also became friends with Cort and, as someone who knew how to play the banjo, she ended up sharing with him some rudimentary knowledge of the instrument that allowed him to pluck out some notes when it was needed in later scenes. The two later took a musical comedy singing class together, although she admitted that both were "scared to death" and ended up sitting in the back row to avoid embarrassment. She also had effusive praise for Ashby who, she said, created "an actor's dream of security within the space" that he set up.[15]

On Monday, February 8, Harold's computer date with Edith Phern was shot. Playing Edith was young Shari Summers, a Bay Area native who had only had some minor experience in television roles before this film. Her casting ended up being a fortunate one for both her and producer Chuck Mulvehill; a romance blossomed on the set and, after the film, the two were married at Ashby's home, and remain married to this day. This scene was notable for getting the biggest laugh during previews: Harold pulls out a cleaver and proceeds to chop off his hand as Edith looks on in shock.[16] *Daily Cal Arts Magazine* reporter Bill Royce, who was on hand while this sequence was filmed, wrote, "[Vivian] Pickles has the additional virtue of being an uncommonly excellent actress."[17]

A major earthquake, registering 6.6 on the Richter scale, rolled through California on February 9 at 6:00 in the morning. This temblor was felt 300 miles to the south, in the northern San Fernando Valley area of Los Angeles. There was a sense of alarm amongst some members of the cast and crew, as most of them lived in the greater Los Angeles area and were understandably concerned about the safety of loved ones and the potential of damage to homes and property. The earthquake was a substantial one, causing hundreds of millions of dollars of damage, freeway collapses, power outages and the disruption of the lives of hundreds of thousands of people. The earthquake anticipated the 1994 Northridge earthquake, as it was in the same general part of Los Angeles. Ruth Gordon and Garson Kanin had returned from their trip to New York to their home in Los Angeles in time to experience the earthquake.

The earthquake did not cause any delays in the filming of the movie. Once it was verified that family and friends in the area were all right, production proceeded on schedule. The only really noticeable effect that the earthquake had on the film was a disruption in the delivery of dailies processed by a lab in Los Angeles.

On the day of the earthquake and the next day, February 10, the special effects crew was busy with plenty of fake blood, as Harold's mock suicide in Mrs. Chasen's bathtub was filmed. The mirrored walls in the bathroom gave the crew fits (they had to make sure they weren't seen in the reflection), but after a day and a half the needed shots were in the can.

Also on the 10th, the sequence of Harold in his room with the var-

9. The Rosecourt

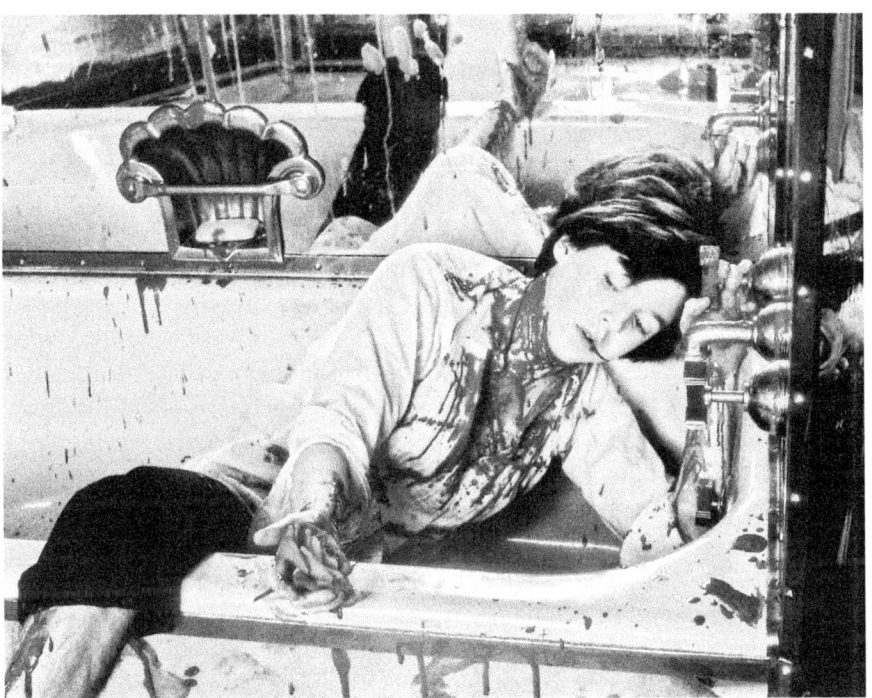

For his mother's benefit, Harold (Bud Cort) pretends to have slashed himself to death.

ious implements of his suicides was filmed, including the dummy head and body used during the pool scene. In 1972, Colin Higgins described this scene (which did not appear in the finished film) to author Michael Shedlin in *Film Quarterly*:

> It opened up with a shot of a large, silver-plated serving dish. A hand comes in and removes the cover and there, on a little bed of parsley, is Harold's head. Two hands come into the frame and pick up the head, and we move back and there's Harold holding his head and looking at it. He sort of peels off the latex blood and walks over to his bedroom chair where a headless dummy sits. He puts the head on the dummy, but the head really isn't sitting right, and he goes into the closet to find something.
>
> Swing around to the door and his mother enters in an evening gown. She says, "Now listen up, Harold. Your computer date will be arriving and it would be nice if..." and so forth. Cut to the closet and Harold is just sitting there listening to her talk to this dummy in the chair. And

then she says, "Well, I've got to go to this ballet with the Fergusons..." and she turns a little. "You're looking a little pale, Harold. You try to get a good night's rest..." and she leaves.[18]

Although this scene fit the black humor of the rest of the movie, Ashby ultimately decided that it was superfluous and didn't use it in the movie.

On February 11, filming finally wrapped up at the estate with the scene (set in Mrs. Chasen's bedroom) where Harold tells her that he is marrying Maude. For this scene, Cort had normal color in his face, to indicate that his relationship with Maude had literally brought him back to life.

Cort's Method acting techniques occasionally caused problems when sharing a scene with a classically trained actress such as Pickles, with whom he had never worked before. Cort recalled that, during the scene in which Pickles tells him he's going to have to join the army, he slowly raised his middle finger, sucked on it, then held it up at her throughout her speech. "She finished and ran off the set," he remembered. "Then Hal said, 'Oh my god, Bud, you can't do that! It was great, but she's pretty down, you have to apologize to her!'"[19] Perhaps in order to make up for such behavior, Cort gave Pickles a posy at the conclusion of the filming of their scenes. But the flowers would only go so far, and in 1997 Cort recalled, "I tormented her so much that when I finally went to London after the shoot, I tried to look her up, and she wouldn't even see me. I had to beg her to finally let me see her, and when I finally did, we became good friends." As a classically trained actress, it was inevitable that Pickles would come into conflict with Cort's improvisational Method style, but part of the problem also stemmed from the fact that, with the actress' late arrival on the film, the two had virtually no time to prepare before they started shooting.[20]

Cort did get along well with d.p. Alonzo, who took special care in shooting the actor's translucent skin. "I've always had a love affair with actors. To me, they are the babies, the mistreated babies of the industry," Alonzo said in 1997. Cort recalled, "Every morning, first thing on the set, John would walk up, and he would just stare at my face; he would walk around me, he would do like a perfect 180 degrees, and he would look and see what was happening." When Cort cut himself shaving one day and had a large wound on one side of his face, Alonzo took care to shoot the other side. Cort said, "It wasn't just with me, it was with Ruth. [Alonzo] made us feel very special." Alonzo also came to

9. The Rosecourt

very much admire Pickles. "She was totally oblivious to the camera. It seemed like she was on stage, not on camera, and she played it out where the audience is supposed to be."[21] Jeff Wexler, however, recalled that, while Alonzo was nice to him, he could sometimes be unkind to his crew and also "was a little full of himself."[22]

At the end of this eventful week, Friday, February 12, and Saturday the 13th, the moviemakers were at the 520 Office Building at 520 El Camino Real in San Mateo, filming the scenes with G. Wood as Harold's psychiatrist. Like Cort, Wood was a veteran of the movie *MASH*. Their *Harold and Maude* scenes together are memorable for their deadpan humor. According to Mulvehill, costume designer Bill Theiss came up with the idea of having Harold and the psychiatrist dressed exactly alike in all their scenes. The film gives no explanation to the audience for this odd fact, but a reason can perhaps be found in an early note that Colin Higgins wrote about the psychiatrist: "[He] tries to appeal to hippie youth by wearing their clothes and affecting their mannerisms."[23] This seems as logical an explanation as any. Since Harold is going to his mother's psychiatrist, she may just have gotten on the phone before each appointment and told him what clothes Harold would be wearing when he comes to the appointment, so that the psychiatrist can wear the same clothes and be ready for him. For whatever reason, having Harold dressed as a weird doppelgänger for his psychiatrist works, and adds to the film's black comic tone.

Although the crew was seven days behind schedule due to weather problems and various unforeseen delays, for the most part Ashby felt the shoot was going smoothly. Around this time, he received a telegram from an elated Peter Bart: "[H]aving viewed rushes, must tell you I am elated by film. Quality of acting is solendid [*sic*]. Also wish to congratulate you on bringing off real turnaround in terms of schedule despite earthquakes."[24] However, on Monday, February 15, when Ruth Gordon returned to the set, there would be an accident that would put the film even further behind schedule and derail, again, plans to shoot the scenes with the motorcycle cop.

10

The Motorcycle Cop, the Ambulance and the Railcar

At six-foot-five, Bill Lucking cut an imposing figure. The actor had been working in television, mostly Westerns due to his size. Born in 1941, he had attended UCLA, graduating with a degree in theater and literature. Like many up-and-coming actors in the late 1950s and 1960s, Lucking had attended the Pasadena Playhouse and worked with acting coach Jeff Corey, a well-known character actor in films and television who had turned to teaching when he was blacklisted for supposed Communist activities and failure to name names before HUAC.[1] Corey was highly influential in the career of another young actor, Jack Nicholson, and later had a small part in *The Cincinnati Kid*, the first film that Ashby edited for Norman Jewison.

Cast as the motorcycle cop who stops Harold and Maude on their way to replant the tree, Lucking was getting ready for his first shot on Monday, February 15. The shooting of this scene had been rescheduled from the previous month, when it had been called off because of bad weather. The scene was set to take place on the east side of the Dumbarton Bridge, the southernmost of the San Francisco Bay's three main east-to-west bridges and, at 1.63 miles, the shortest. The Dumbarton had been selected over the San Mateo and the Bay Bridge because it had considerably less traffic and would be easier to close for filming.

In the first shot, Harold and Maude drive past in a pick-up truck with the little tree in the truck bed. The shot called for Lucking to jump on his motorcycle and chase after them at a high speed. Lucking assured Ashby that he was well versed in riding a motorcycle and so could do it himself instead of using a stunt double. But Lucking, in his excitement, unfortunately forgot to put the motorcycle kick stand up

10. The Motorcycle Cop, the Ambulance and the Railcar

before taking off and, after he went around the first curve, the kickstand glanced off the highway, causing a total wipeout. Lucking ended up in the shallow waters of the bay, moaning in excruciating pain.

At 11:05 AM, the injured actor was taken by ambulance to Washington Township Hospital in Fremont, on the east side of the Bay (not, as Ruth Gordon remembered in her biography, to Peninsula Hospital in Burlingame). Dr. Webb administered Demerol to reduce the pain. The orthopedic surgeon who treated Lucking noted that he had suffered a "comminuted fracture of his right tibia and fibula, compound and sequestrated."[2] Lucking would eventually make a full recovery, but for now he was incapacitated and would need several months to recover. His participation in *Harold and Maude* was over, including all the dialogue scenes that had not yet been filmed.

Feeling guilty about what had happened, Lucking wrote Ashby a February 29 letter saying, "Sorry I screwed up your schedule ... the doctor tells me my leg will heal with no complications."[3] On March 25, Ashby replied to Lucking, assuring him that it had been no problem and thanking him for his participation.

With no motorcycle cop for the time being, the crew had to again reschedule the shooting of the bridge shoot. Now the production shifted to scenes set in Maude's home. In Higgins' original script, Maude lives in an apartment, but one of the most important early decisions on the film was made from a suggestion by production designer Michael Haller, that Maude's apartment be changed to a home in an old abandoned railcar, located by the side of the road on Oyster Point Boulevard in South San Francisco. South San Francisco is an industrial area (its famous sign, written into a hillside says "South San Francisco ... the Industrial City"); other scenes would be shot in the vicinity, including several of the junkyard and automotive demolition scenes.

Ashby and Mulvehill thought that they had made a great decision to place the railcar in South San Francisco, as it is a five-minute drive to the San Francisco Airport and would expedite the process of getting the photographed film off to Los Angeles for processing. With the tight schedule they were on, even a few minutes could make the difference in getting the film out on time. But, to their chagrin, the filmmakers realized later that the proximity to the airport would mean constant plane noise as jets took off and landed, making sound recording difficult. Still, they managed to get the shoot finished without needing any additional voiceover recording, or "looping" as it is known, a process that Ashby hated.[4]

The decision to shoot near the San Francisco International Airport resulted in an interesting theme of vehicles and modes of transport emerging in the film. With planes flying everywhere overheard, the world that Harold and Maude live in appears to be a modern world that has gone slightly out of control. This is contrasted by the Cat Stevens music and songs like "Miles from Nowhere" and "On the Road to Find Out" that suggest that, with all our emphasis on fast motion, we only are able to make any actual progress by spiritual movement. Harold and Maude are also often seen driving; in one scene, Maude drives down a road, wildly out of control, passing a bewildered pair of

The interior of Maude's railcar home as it looks today. The ornate glass and carpeting is still in place. The railcar's narrow width made filming difficult.

10. The Motorcycle Cop, the Ambulance and the Railcar

hippie hitchhikers. When the scene cuts back to the interior of the car, Maude shrugs and says, "Power steering!" But Maude's inability to drive well (made further ironic by the fact that Ruth Gordon wasn't actually driving at all) suggests that she is out of place in the modern world that requires speed and precision to get along. Maude appears to be much more at home in her abandoned railcar, an abode that is classically beautiful and whimsically furnished but quite a bit out of time and place. It's a perfect metaphor for Maude's own life.

For the railcar, an arrangement was made to rent Western Pacific "Feather River Solarium" Lounge Car #653 from the Bay Area Electric Railroad Association, for a fee of $250. The car was built in 1913; in 1931 Pullman rebuilt it into a buffet lounge car with solarium for the Western Pacific Railroad. It was used starting in 1939 on the "Exposition Flyer" train between Chicago and Oakland, during a period in which train travel was still the most common way for people to cover long distances. Replaced by the California Zephyr in 1949, the car was never modernized; its 1931 luxury interior was still in excellent condition in 1966 when it was donated to the Western Railway Museum in nearby Suisun City, near the scenic Napa Valley wine country.

After arrangements were made to rent the car, it was determined that there was pitting in the wheels and the car would have to be sent to Sacramento for repairs to make it safe for use. According to Bill and Roger of the Western Railway Museum, the repairs took longer than anticipated and were just being finished by the time the call came in January that the railcar was needed for the film. A special diesel engine had to be rented to bring the railcar back from Sacramento in time to put it on its siding in South San Francisco, at a cost to the studio of $7000. When filming was completed, the car was returned to the Western Railway Museum, where you can still see it today. It still has the floral print carpet seen in *Harold and Maude*, as well as the ornate glass that separates the front of the car from the back.

With the railcar in place, production designer Haller and assistant Steve Silver went to work decorating it to make it look like a place that Maude would live. In contrast to the Chasen home, which is filled with fancy artwork and priceless antiques, Maude's home contains offbeat bric-a-brac and unique items whose value was entirely personal. The car was 85 feet in length, which was plenty long, but it was narrow. In 1972, Ashby noted that shooting in the railcar was "very cramped. A

The railcar used as Maude's home has been at the Western Railway Museum in Suisun City, California, since 1966.

lot of stand on your head and back into the wall. I didn't think anybody was going to be able to breathe. It was very tough shooting in the railway car."[5] A fake fireplace was installed to give the railcar a homey feeling, particularly for the scene when Harold talks about his first "death." The painters apparently had difficulty matching the color of the railcar interior, which was stained by years of smoking. A piano, some plants, tables and two unique paintings completed the decor.

The paintings hung in the railcar, "The Rape of Rome" and "Rainbow with Egg Underneath and an Elephant," were by the multi-talented Steve Silver. Haller and Silver also took the time to fill the drawers of Maude's home with various small items like spools of thread that, although they would not be filmed, would give anyone who looked in them the sense that someone actually lived in that place, thus making it all more realistic for the actors.[6] The railcar also included a number of props that had to work properly, including the trap shooting arm which Maude used to shoot out bird seed. When the device malfunctioned, prop master Jeff Wexler had to scramble to get it working properly.

Filming at the railcar actually began back on January 19, when the scene in which Harold drives Maude home after the funeral was shot. On February 16 and 17, the lengthy sequence in which Maude shows Harold her home for the first time was filmed in its entirely. Maude's home is filled with objects that emphasize gratification of several of the senses, including the visual (her paintings), hearing (the piano), smell (the "odorifics" machine) and taste (ginger pie and oat straw tea). But ultimately, Harold finds Maude's home to be quite sensual, as it is dominated by a large wooden sculpture that appears to be in the shape of the female vagina. Maude even encourages Harold to touch the sculpture and, when her back is turned, he cannot resist but try to thrust his head into it. As *Harold and Maude* is very much a film about change and rebirth, this action can be seen as either an attempt to return to the comfort of the motherly womb, or to escape from it and thus be reborn. Contrary to popular belief, this was one scene in which Cort did not improvise; in fact, the head thrust into the wooden sculpture is carefully described in Higgins' script.

Although most of the scenes were filmed as Higgins had written them, the screenwriter-producer did do some rewrites, and occasional improvisation was allowed. In one of the scenes slightly altered from the script, Harold and Maude picnic in a meadow and discuss their philosophy of life. Maude comments, "You can't let the world judge you too much," as she and Harold act crazy, somersaulting in the grass and letting out yodeling sounds. This scene began filming on February 18 in Menlo Park and was finished near the end of production, on March 11, but it was decided that Harold and Maude wouldn't have an actual picnic; instead, they just are relaxing on a blanket, talking about God and life. Cort recalled that Gordon was understandably concerned with injuring herself doing some of the stunts, however minor, and so stunt double Pamela Bebermeyer performed the somersaults and in an improvised scene in which Harold gives Maude a piggyback ride.

Bebermeyer, an athletic Californian who loved outdoor sports like water skiing, was only 20 when she worked in *Harold and Maude*. She had done some earlier stunt work but *Harold and Maude* would be her first credited film. Her long career would include such later films as *Animal House, The Blues Brothers, Hooper, Smokey and the Bandit* and *National Lampoon's Vacation*. Now retired and residing in Idaho, she but has fond memories of her time on the *Harold and Maude* set.

The evening of the 18th was taken up with the filming of Harold's most emotional scene, back at the railcar in South San Francisco. This was the scene that was used for the audition of Cort and the other five actors, and it contains Harold's emotional description of the chemistry building explosion and his mother's dramatic breakdown at the thought of his death. Cort built the scene to a suitable pitch, coming to tears as he tells Maude that he suddenly realized he "enjoyed being dead" and began his habit of committing fake suicides for his mother's benefit. When the scene was finished, the crew burst into applause and an wrought-up Ashby was in tears, but director of photography John Alonzo was embarrassed: Halfway through the dramatic speech, the camera had run out of film. Alonzo later noted, "I don't know why we ran out of film. The assistant didn't know it was going to run that long or something." Ashby took Cort aside to tell him about the filming gaffe and, after getting a pep talk, the actor returned and did the scene again. Amazingly, on the next take, it was even better.[7]

February 19 involved a reshoot of the Emeryville Marina scene in which Maude makes her Dreyfus speech. The next day, Marjorie Eaton was on hand to shoot her scenes at Maude's home as Madame Arouet. On Saturday the 21st and Monday the 23rd, the lengthy scene at Maude's home was shot in which Maude tells Harold about her background in Europe and fighting for the "big issues. Liberty. Rights. Justice. Kings died and kingdoms fell." This scene would be completed on the second to last day of filming, March 12, to include Ruth Gordon appearing to play the piano while she sings a song provided for the production by songwriter Cat Stevens, recently brought on board by Ashby. The song is "If You Want to Sing Out, Sing Out" and it encapsulates many of the themes of the movie perfectly.

Venerable stage actor Cyril Cusack was on hand for three days, beginning February 24, to shoot his scenes as Glaucus, the elderly ice sculptor who lives near Maude and enjoys sculpting her in the nude. The scenes were shot at an abandoned warehouse at the Southern Pacific Railroad Bayshore Yard in Brisbane, near South San Francisco.

10. The Motorcycle Cop, the Ambulance and the Railcar

The weather was blustery and, according to Mulvehill, the scenes took "forever to shoot." Additionally, Cort had also developed strep throat at this point and was doped up on cold medication during the shoot. To make matters worse, during a rehearsal, Cusack cut his hand rather badly with an ice chisel. Ashby recalled that Cusack—the ultimate pro—carried on with the scene, not wanting to stop and ruin the other actor's rehearsal. Sadly, it was later determined that most of Glaucus' scenes were not particularly relevant to the plot and seemed to slow down the flow of the narrative, so only one short scene remains in the film's final cut.[8]

On February 27 and March 1, the final scenes in Maude's railcar home were shot, including the birthday celebration which ends in disaster for Harold, as well as the sex scene. Higgins' script suggests Harold and Maude have finally had sex by a montage of shots including the exploding fireworks at the arcade, a pan of the fireplace full of smoking ash, and a shot of Harold and Maude in bed, with Harold smoking a post-coital cigarette. Ashby knew that the studio would not allow him to show actual nude shots of Cort and Gordon, but he did get some film of them kissing nude in bed. One of these shots was eventually used in one of Pablo Ferro's trailers, which the shocked Paramount executives would never allow to be shown. The film ended up with a sequence that is similar to the one described in the script, although in the movie Harold is not smoking, he is dreamily blowing bubbles (emphasizing his still child-like ways, despite having just participated in a very adult act) while Maude sleeps contentedly beside him.

The nighttime shots of Maude being taken by ambulance to the hospital were shot late on March 1 and 2. On March 2 and 3 the crew was at Peninsula Hospital in Burlingame (now Mills-Peninsula Hospital) to shoot the sequence of Maude arriving at the hospital and being admitted, as well as Harold's long nighttime wait. The sequence apparently did take all night to film, with Ashby employing some of the actual hospital staff as extras. Higgins' brother Barry, an early candidate to play Harold, appears in this sequence in the small part of a hospital intern seen while Maude is being admitted. Ashby would later write Higgins to complement him on his participation in the film: "[Y]ou really are an excellent actor."[9]

Although the Peninsula staff was mostly cooperative, Ashby was slightly annoyed when personnel objected to the depiction of hospital procedures during the scene. The director was told that, had an old woman actually been wheeled in from an ambulance, they would have never asked her to sign all those forms and paperwork before she was admitted. Ashby knew they *were* taking a degree of artistic license. His annoyance turned to anger when he himself suffered a cut on a trailer door and needed some treatment; the first thing hospital personnel had him do was begin filling out forms. Eventually he was treated, but the hypocrisy of the bureaucracy bothered the already overworked and stressed-out director.[10]

With the film already nearly two weeks behind schedule, the crew rushed to complete the rest of the scenes. They headed farther south to the seaside town of Santa Cruz, known for its great surfing—the annual "Mavericks" surf competition is held nearby—and home to U.C. Santa Cruz, as well as the Santa Cruz Beach Boardwalk. Here they shot for two nights, March 4 and 5. The Santa Cruz Beach Boardwalk, which has been in operation since 1907, is the only major seaside amusement park remaining on the West Coast, offering a unique combination of classic and modern rides, a sandy mile-long beach, and a variety of attractions.[11]

Jeff Wexler recalled the circumstances of the Santa Cruz Boardwalk shoot:

> It was a night shoot and we were all transported down to Santa Cruz on the upper deck of the Cinemobile. Arrived fairly early in the afternoon and many of us had a little too much time on our hands before actually having to prepare for the night's shooting. A bunch of us, Hal included, walked out onto the pier, smoked a little weed, got the munchies big time, ate a lot of fresh shrimp, crab followed by snow cones, cookies and so forth, by the time we had to actually go to work we were pretty blissed out.[12]

The crew had fun filming stock shots of the merry-go-round, rides and the arcade games. Ashby got into the act himself, playing with the electric trains and even filming a cameo of himself operating the trains while Harold and Maude watch. Then they shot the pier scene of Harold and Maude holding hands and watching the fireworks. According to Mulvehill, the fireworks "expert" they'd hired failed to provide impressive

10. The Motorcycle Cop, the Ambulance and the Railcar

explosions and so later they had to resort to using stock footage of fireworks, much to everyone's disappointment.[13] Still, as the Santa Cruz filming ended and they headed into the final week of filming with two major sequences to go, they could see the light at the end of the tunnel.

Behind schedule by this point in the production, Ashby was also over-budget. Although he wrote to his attorney's secretary Lois Ulrich "Everything is going beautifully here," he faced enormous challenges in finishing the picture.[14] Evans, Bart and others at Paramount felt that Ashby had fallen behind because he was smoking too much pot and not running a tight ship. Looking back on *Harold and Maude* in 2002, Bart noted, "Ashby was smoking a lot on the set, and we're not talking Lucky Strikes.... At one point I flew to San Francisco where they were shooting and handed Hal a one-way ticket back to L.A. I told him that if he kept on getting stoned and losing days, he might as well use the ticket 'cause he wasn't going to stay on the movie."[15] (I could find no evidence that Paramount ever seriously considered firing Ashby.)

The old disagreement about putting Chuck Mulvehill on the film—the studio regarded him as nothing more than a mouthpiece for Ashby—surfaced again. In 1972, Ashby noted that Paramount had accused him of falling behind because he didn't have a strong producer, to which he answered, "For Christ's sake, we're moving all over the place, two or three times a day sometimes, and all the things that go with it."[16] In truth, the crew was tremendously efficient, given the number of locations and the time constraints they faced. Later in his career, Ashby would justifiably be accused of unnecessary filming delays, but it certainly was not true on *Harold and Maude*. In early 1972, looking back on the experience of making the film, he commented, "We tried to get people who were really interested in film, for instance, Bob Stein, who did our makeup. When we were cleaning up at night after working somewhere he would be lugging cable—which I would do too. What the hell, we had to help everybody move out so everybody could get some rest. So everybody would kind of chip in and help everybody that way. We didn't get into one of those things where everyone said, 'This is my job and this is his job'—which is usually what happens."[17]

Ashby was understandably worried about the continued interference from the studio while on location, which went back to an incident that happened during the first week that the film was in production. At one in the morning, Ashby was roused from bed by a phone call from one of the film's production managers, who had just been awoken himself by a call from Paramount executive Jack Ballard with a complaint about something that had happened with a driver on the location. No one was clear exactly what it was about, but it was certainly not something that warranted a phone call in the middle of the night. The production manager was so upset and tired of the unnecessary oversight that he was packing up to leave the film. Ashby and Mulvehill had to hurry over to the motel to mollify him.

Ashby told him, "Listen, whatever you say, I'm behind you, even with mistakes, because I know one goddamn thing, I know you're trying to do the best thing for the film and if you make a mistake, you make a mistake—we all make mistakes, but they're not intentional, they're not malicious—they're just mistakes. So I am behind you and don't leave." Ashby turned to Mulvehill and told him to call Paramount and tell them that if one of the executives "telephones this goddamn set one more time I'm not going to shoot, and if they want to have another director come up and shoot it, fine."[18] Ashby was infuriated that his staff was being harassed about minor issues at a time when they needed to rest and get ready for another long day of shooting ahead. After he put his foot down, the nitpicking stopped, but the second-time director was still sensitive to the way he and his crew were being treated.

On March 8, as most of the country was getting ready for the Joe Frazier-Muhammad Ali championship fight in New York City, Ashby and crew were attempting to finish the motorcycle cop sequence that had bedeviled them the entire production. With William Lucking unavailable, Ashby had to find another actor to play the cop. By a stroke of good fortune, Ashby's friend, actor Tom Skerritt, was available and agreed to fill in and take the part. In 1970, Skerritt had gotten his big break playing Duke Forrest in *MASH* (a film that featured three actors, Skerritt, Bud Cort and G. Wood, who all ended up in *Harold and Maude*). Skerritt had already done a considerable amount of TV work in Westerns such as *Death Valley Days*, *Gunsmoke* and *The Virginian*, as well as getting some experience playing a cop in *The Fugitive* and *The F.B.I.* Skerritt was also an aspiring writer, and Ashby was trying to help him get one of his scripts sold. On May 14, 1971, perhaps as

10. The Motorcycle Cop, the Ambulance and the Railcar

thanks for playing the motorcycle cop part, Ashby forwarded two of Skerritt's scripts to Peter Bart for his consideration. He also sent two scripts by Pablo Ferro, saying that all the scripts "have merit and most certainly the men involved do."[19]

Not wanting to take credit for a part he got under such unusual circumstances, Skerritt would forego an on-screen credit, instead going under the pseudonym "M. Borman"—a reference to Martin Bormann, Adolf Hitler's chief secretary and one of the architects of the Holocaust. Given that Maude's character is a victim of a Nazi concentration camp, the name was apt, and in hindsight it adds to the hilarity as she gives the hapless motorcycle cop fits. To disguise himself, Skerritt wore a fake mustache, even turning the mustache upside down during one scene to make it appear the wind had blown it that way. Ashby later told his friend, film critic Michael Dare, that it was one of the only shots he'd ever left out of a film because it was too hilarious. Ashby said later, "One of the funniest things that happened on that film was when I got Tom Skerritt as the motorcycle cop. Tom is a very loose actor, but whatever he would say, Ruth would still say her lines. She was a stage actor, and those were her lines, and if those were the lines, that's where she was going. She was everything about that role that should have been there." The disconnect between the two actors (and characters) makes the scene even funnier.[20]

Still, the Dumbarton Bridge scenes could not be completed without some problematic incident. On March 10, while shooting the scene in which Harold and Maude flee from the cop after planting the little tree, Cort had to run back to the pick-up truck, grab the shovel and return to hop on the back of the motorcycle with Gordon. But as he ran towards the motorcycle, the shovel he was carrying slipped and banged him in the side of the head. Following the example of Cyril Cusack, Cort kept going despite the pain so that the take wouldn't be ruined, and this ended up being the shot that was used in the film. Watching the film, one can see Cort wince as the shovel connects. The injury turned out to not be a serious one. The scene ends hysterically, as Skerritt's motorcycle cop pulls out his revolver as Harold and Maude drive off on his motorcycle. His attempt to shoot them ends as his empty gun clicks impotently. At last, the motorcycle cop sequence was finished.

The final two days of filming, March 12 and 13, were spent completing a couple of earlier scenes and then the climactic car crash, as Harold drives madly towards the coast after Maude dies. On March 12 the crew was back at the Oyster Point location in South San Francisco, attempting to finish up the scene where Maude plays the song on the piano, when a gust of high wind toppled the accident-prone Ashby and caused him to briefly lose consciousness. The Bay Area is prone to high winds, and the area in South San Francisco was located at a spot where these winds occurred frequently. Nick Dawson noted in his Ashby biography that, every time Ruth Gordon finished a take and "stopped singing, [Ashby] had rushed outside to throw up."[21] Despite this, the next day—March 13, the final day of filming—Ashby had to pull off the most complicated shot of the film and one of the most complicated of his career, the scene in which Harold drives his car off the cliff.

At one point, Ashby had considered changing Higgins' script and having Harold die in the car crash, but after consultation with Higgins he ultimately realized this would be too downbeat an ending. They ended up filming the scene the way Higgins had written it, with the car plunging off the cliff and then a shot tilting up from the wreck to Harold standing at the top of the rugged cliff. He puts on the banjo and walks off into the distance, picking the strings and playing the tune Maude taught him, no doubt with a determination to "go out and love some more."

This complicated sequence of shots was filmed at Mori Point in Pacifica, a coastal town north of the Half Moon Bay and Santa Cruz areas where earlier scenes had been shot. As the mini-hearse would be destroyed going over the cliff, the crew would have only one chance to get it right. In 1976, Ashby recalled what happened:

> [T]hat was singularly one of the most horrendous takes I've ever gone through in my life, because we set up a lot of cameras, we had this ramp built over the ledge, we had only one car.... I was [sorry to see it go] but I didn't know any other way to do it. It was an old one anyway. So we had this thing going and we had all these cameras set up—a slow-motion camera and one down below; we must have had six cameras set up—and we yelled, "Roll it," and when we yelled, "Roll it," somebody was on the walkie-talkie and the guy on the other side of the hill was out of the shot; they've got the car jacked up with the wheel going like this, and the idea is that they drop that out and it goes up the ramp, that it doesn't go crazy and go off at an angle so that nobody sees it and down the other side of the hill—you're hoping for all that—and you say, '"Okay, roll it. Let the

10. The Motorcycle Cop, the Ambulance and the Railcar

car go." And as soon as they say, "Let the car go," the guy on the high-speed camera about 20 feet from me says, "I've got a jam." So then you yell, "Cut, cut, stop everything, stop everything," and you think, "My God." And you see the car going over the ridge and you're saying, "Holy Christ, if they cut, that's it." Well, everybody else kept rolling. You know, everybody else was so wired that they didn't even hear people yelling, "Cut," or doing anything like that. Of course, we didn't get the slow-motion shot. The other one that they fucked up on was inside the car where we had a camera. The guys never really taped it up. I said, "Tape it in," but I thought that they would just normally tape that magazine—they had a little Bell & Howell in there—and the magazine popped off and film was everywhere. It was gone.[22]

In the end, only one camera had a good closeup shot of the car going over the cliff, and Ashby had to settle for that. And because that camera didn't get rolling in time, he had to save the shot by inserting a still frame (that he thought was "cheesy") in order to get the shot to the length that it needed. But as the wrecked car was cleaned up from the beach, the director could take one thought with him: The film, despite being finished two weeks behind schedule, was finally in the can.

A look at the film's budget indicates how well Ashby and company had kept costs under control. Cast costs rose slightly, to a final total of $101,644, about $9000 over budget. Camera costs were $71,164, quite a bit over the initial budget of $46,100, due to Ashby's tendency to allow his actors to do numerous takes. With minimal set construction needed, total costs for set design and construction was only about $25,000, just barely above budget. Living expenses stayed at a modest $26,430, which was $1500 under budget, although other location expenses ballooned to $345,000, which was over $100,000 over budget (in part due to the delays and the schedule going two weeks beyond what was expected). The only other significant cost overrun was in editing, as Ashby spent $134,285 to complete the film against an initial budget of $81,800.

The final budget figure for finishing the production of *Harold and Maude* was $1,566,889, about $280,000 over the initial budget prepared on January 8, 1971. Compared to other films of the day, *Harold and Maude* was inexpensive. *Dirty Harry*, another 1971 film shot on location in San Francisco, cost Warner Bros. roughly four million, more than twice that of *Harold and Maude*. The 1971 James Bond film *Diamonds Are Forever* came in on a budget of 7.2 million. So you can see that, all in all, *Harold and Maude* was not an enormous investment for a studio such as Paramount, and concerns about cost overruns and schedule delays did not end up being a problem for the studio.

In 1997, director of photography John Alonzo recalled Ashby's accomplishment at finishing *Harold and Maude* so efficiently under the circumstances. Unlike filmmakers today, Ashby had "no storyboards. No video assist." Cort noted, "Toward the end of that movie, John and I and Hal were so in sync ... and that's because we were all living that film moment to moment."[23]

With filming complete, a wrap party was thrown at the San Francisco home of production assistant Steve Silver. Ruth Gordon remembered it thusly: "Everybody looked dazed. It was over. A way of life was over. The breakup." Gordon recalled that Cort came to her trailer and put a square package in her hand, saying, "I love you. See you at the party." The blue leather box from Shreve's in San Francisco contained a violet pansy with a diamond dewdrop set on a petal. She pinned it on and, with Garson Kanin, went to the wrap party.[24]

Gordon recalled that Silver had spent weeks preparing for the party, with elaborate decorations everywhere in sight. The house was strung with icicles; there were snow banks in every corner, wet slickers and umbrellas here and there. A sign said, "Over here for your ginger pie and oat straw tea" and another sign read "Organic hashish." Cat Stevens music played in the background while partygoers smoked a hookah pipe. Gordon also noted the message on the back of the pin that Cort gave her: "I love you, Maude. Harold." While the two had worked together professionally for the course of the film, Cort had apparently developed a sincere affection for his older co-star.[25] In November, when Gordon was featured on the TV show *This Is Your Life*, Cort made the effort to return from England to be there to honor her.

With 13 weeks of madcap filming behind them, the crew and cast went their separate ways. Ashby was headed back to the place that he had called "the best school for a director," the place that he was most comfortable: the editing room. Here, the film would either be ruined or made.

11

Cat Stevens

Even before Al Jolson sang "Mammy" in *The Jazz Singer* in 1927, music had always played an important part in filmmaking. But from the 1930s through to the 1960s, music had primarily been a background technique used for accent and mood, except for the lavish movie musicals that featured music front and center. That began to change in the era of the "New Hollywood" that began in the later 1960s. As early as 1964, the Beatles' *A Hard Day's Night* had set the tone for the importance of music by incorporating the Beatles songs as an essential part of the narrative. *Easy Rider* used previously recorded music by a variety of artists, none of whom were in or otherwise associated with the movie, to create a diverse soundtrack that made the movie more appealing (and helped the soundtrack album sell very well). The song "Everybody's Talkin,'" which had been recorded a year or two earlier by Harry Nilsson, became a massive hit when featured in the 1969 movie *Midnight Cowboy*.

But the best analogy for the use of music in *Harold and Maude* is to compare it to Mike Nichols' *The Graduate*. At first, Nichols wanted original music to be written by Paul Simon and recorded by Simon & Garfunkel. Simon modified a song that he was working on, "Mrs. Roosevelt"—a nostalgic paean to the 1940s—to become "Mrs. Robinson," which fit in nicely with the film's themes, and also provided "Punky's Dilemma" and "Overs" for use in the movie. Nichols didn't particularly care for the latter two songs, and as he edited *The Graduate*, he used music from Simon & Garfunkel's two previous albums to edit several of the sequences. By the time he had finished editing, Nichols was so in love with the way songs like "The Sounds of Silence" and "Scarborough Fair/Canticle" worked in the film that he decided that, aside from "Mrs. Robinson," he wouldn't need any more music from Simon & Garfunkel. When the film was released, not only was it a big hit, but the soundtrack album, featuring the earlier songs by Simon & Garfunkel as well as the one new song and some additional background music by David Grusin, sold very well.[1]

Eventually Ashby would take the same tack in *Harold and Maude*. First, though, he had to settle on a singer-songwriter to provide his soundtrack music, and initially it seemed that it would be Elton John. As late as December 1970, Ashby was still considering John but knew that, since "he is fast becoming a superstar," it was not likely they would get him.[2] But although John did not end up working on *Harold and Maude*, he did suggest to Ashby a logical alternative: Cat Stevens.

Born on July 21, 1948, Steven Demetre Georgiou, who would take the stage name Cat Stevens, was the son of a Greek Cypriot restaurant owner and Swedish mother. He grew up living above the family business in London, near the heart of the West End, a place full of excitement, lights, sounds and music. The young boy developed a natural love for art and music, taking up the guitar at age 15. Stevens drifted towards folk music instead of rock'n'roll because it was simpler and easier to play and sing alone, without the accompaniment of drums, piano and other instruments. He was something of a loner, and on most evenings in the busy London of the early 1960s he would climb to the high rooftops and gaze at the noisy city below, allowing for moments of peaceful and elevated detachment under the night sky.

While studying at Hammersmith Art College, Georgiou took the stage name Cat Stevens (he later said he couldn't imagine anyone coming into a record store and asking for the latest Steven Demetre Georgiou album) and was signed to a record deal by producer Mike Hurst and selected by Decca Records to launch the new Deram label, which also signed new British talent such as David Bowie and the Moody Blues. Stevens was something of an overnight sensation, with his first single "I Love My Dog" reaching number 28 on the U.K. charts in November 1966 and his next single, "Matthew and Son" going to number 2. "I'm Gonna Get Me a Gun" was almost as successful, reaching number 6, and Stevens found himself rich and famous. Now clean-cut, in sharp black velvet Carnaby Street suits, he appeared to be a prime '60s recording artist at a time when the music business was in its infancy and singers were not heavily targeted to any one audience. While his

11. Cat Stevens

material at this time had a distinctive orchestrated sound, combined with easy-to-remember, quirky lyrics, Stevens began to lean towards Celtic-influenced folk music as his preferred style, anticipating the singer-songwriter trend that would come into vogue in the early 1970s.

Stevens' attempts to change his style to a less pop-oriented, more personal approach was met with resistance by his record company. To make matters worse, his second album flopped. His whirlwind lifestyle and smoking habit finally took its toll, and in the winter of 1968, what began as a cold quickly turned into tuberculosis and a collapsed lung. Once on the verge of superstardom, the young singer now hovered near death in a Sussex hospital.

The nearly year-long convalescence offered Stevens a chance for peace and mediation, and ultimately it probably saved his life. As he remembered on his website bio: "To go from the show business environment and find you are in hospital, getting injections day in and day out, and people around you are dying, it certainly changes your perspective. I got down to thinking about myself. It seemed almost as if I had my eyes shut." When Stevens emerged healthy in 1969, he was a changed man and had gone through a transformation that was not just personal, but also musical. He began to write a string of deeply inspiring songs meditating on age, change, life and death. In a 1973 *Rolling Stone* interview he told writer Paul Gambaccini: "In the old days, I was more concerned with melody. Now it's what I have to say. I do realize I am using more words. And sometimes I stop the melody, I stop singing ... and make a statement."[3]

After signing with a new manager, Barry Krost, and a new record label, Island Records, Stevens was ready to restart his career. Krost teamed him with producer Paul Samwell-Smith, formerly of the Yardbirds, and in April 1970 he released a new album, *Mona Bone Jakon*. It featured the madrigal-inspired "Lady D'Arbanville," which went to number 8 on the *Billboard* charts and began to get Stevens attention in America. With curly black hair and a trim beard, Stevens replaced his sharp '60s style suits with jeans and t-shirts, placing himself firmly among the emerging breed of singer-songwriters such as James Taylor, Joni Mitchell, Carole King and Paul Simon.

Tea for the Tillerman was released in December 1970, and Stevens was ready to reclaim his superstar status as the album went gold. Not only that, but songs such as "On the Road to Find Out" and "Where Do the Children Play?" with their contemplation of life and death, endings and beginnings, fit perfectly into the themes of *Harold and Maude*. The timing was good for Ashby, who was trying hard to find someone he could count on to provide music for his movie. Ashby wrote to Evans on December 7 that he was considering jazz composer Johnny Mandel, who had done the score for the 1965 film *The Sandpiper* and had written the music for the *MASH* theme song.[4] But Mandel, who would later work for Ashby on *The Last Detail* and *Being There*, could not possibly bring to the table everything that Stevens brought, including songs with great lyrics and his status as a popular singer-songwriter with a career on the rise. After Jeff Wexler gave him a copy of *Tea for the Tillerman*, and Ashby listened to the wonderful combination of self-contemplative ballads, thoughtful rockers and English- and Celtic-influenced folk tunes, he knew that he had found the right person for his film

But as usual, his boss at Paramount had some different ideas. In a January 15 telegram, Evans wrote Ashby, "Haven't been able to speak to you all week to compliment you on great dailies. Have heard Cat Stevens music and think extremely good, however I gather James Taylor also available and he could be an excellent choice. Let's discuss this and several other important matter [*sic*] if you call, that is, over the weekend."[5] Although Stevens' music is so interwoven with the film that it is hard to imagine Ashby even contemplating anyone else, apparently the final decision was not made until about a week later when, on January 21, Ashby sent a telex to Stevens and manager Krost, requesting they come to San Francisco to meet with the director and discuss the use of Stevens' music in the film.

Inspired by his background growing up in London's theater district, Stevens had at first thought he might actually want to write a musical of his own. When contacted by Ashby, however, he realized that using his music as a film soundtrack would be a fulfillment of this ambition and so was very interested. After reading the *Harold and Maude* script on the flight to California, Stevens had some reservations. The film was a black comedy and, especially at this point in his life, Stevens was taking his music very seriously and was not sure that this would be a good match.[6]

11. Cat Stevens

Ruth Gordon and Bud Cort engrossed in conversation at the Sutro Baths with the Cliff House on the hill behind them.

On January 23, while the sequences at the Sutro Baths were being shot, Stevens and Krost arrived in the Bay Area. Stevens was taken aback when he first met Ashby, noting that Hal looked like a "guru ... not a proper film director!" But Stevens felt a synergy with the strange, sadistic dark humor of the film; in 2011, he commented that, by committing his mock suicides, Harold is trying to "get as close as possible to the edge of life."[7] This idea clearly appealed to Stevens, who felt he had cheated death when he survived tuberculosis, and who had recently taken to studying eastern religions as part of his new, philosophical approach to life.

After watching rushes of the funeral procession synced to his song "Miles from Nowhere," Stevens was sold on *Harold and Maude* and agreed to be involved. Some have speculated that Stevens has a cameo in the film as the bearded man in front of Maude at the Holy Cross Cemetery funeral; however, as those scenes were shot on January 11 and 12, and Stevens did not arrive in California until the 23rd, it would be impossible for him to have been in this particular scene. The man standing in front of Maude is just an extra who happened to resemble Stevens. In fact, while all agree that Stevens did visit the set of the *Harold and Maude* shoot, nobody—even the singer himself—can remember exactly when he was present during the filming.

Ashby had been "living with" *Mona Bone Jakon* and *Tea for the Tillerman*, listening to them constantly as he worked on the film. When sending the dailies to Los Angeles, Ashby told his editors to have the two albums converted over to mag tape and instructed them to insert music randomly into any part of the film that didn't have dialogue. But as Stevens later remembered, "He wanted some other songs that were unique to the film, that's why I went off to do those other two songs."[8] On February 12 Stevens returned to the Bay Area while the production of the film continued. Mulvehill recalled having the odd experience of picking Stevens up at the airport and, while driving him to the set, hearing one of Stevens' latest hits begin playing on the car radio. *Tea for the Tillerman* was taking off in America, and its popularity would soon limit the amount of time Stevens could contribute to the project.

On his return, Stevens played Ashby and Mulvehill the two new songs he had been working on for the movie, "If You Want to Sing Out, Sing Out" and "Don't Be Shy." Although he was still tweaking the lyrics—handwritten notes indicate that at the last minute, Stevens changed the words with the original version: "If you want to LIVE high, LIVE high" changed to the current version where LIVE is substituted with BE, which substantially changed the meaning—when Stevens played the songs for the filmmakers, they were blown away by them.[9] On February 17, a letter from William Stinson, the Paramount executive handling the music, to New York attorney Nat Weiss, outlined the terms that Paramount wished to offer Stevens for his participation in the movie. Stevens would be paid $10,000 for services rendered, which would include two periods, the current February period in which he would provide "instrumental music or songs required for photography of the motion picture," as well as a later period "when the motion picture has been edited and is ready for Stevens to compose the music or songs for the background score." Paramount also reserved the right to release a soundtrack album of the music and stipulated the terms by which Stevens would be compensated for that album. (Ultimately it was not released in the U.S. until many years later.) Although a finalized

11. Cat Stevens

contract for the music would not be signed until September 30, Ashby felt confident enough about Stevens' desire to be involved in the film to have Ruth Gordon sing "If You Want to Sing Out, Sing Out" on March 12, when the film was near wrapping (with backing piano, recorded earlier by Stevens himself).

Ultimately, Stevens' participation in the film would be limited to his contribution of the two original songs as well as the previously recorded music taken from *Mona Bone Jakon* and *Tea for the Tillerman*. On his February trip, it was decided that Stevens would record the two original songs in a form that Stevens viewed purely as a "demo" recording, with the intent of re-recording them later. Stevens was booked into Wally Heider's studio at 245 Hyde Street in the San Francisco Tenderloin; the well-known studio was opened in 1969 by Heider, who had trained as a sound engineer in Hollywood but felt that the native Bay Area artists (such as Jefferson Airplane, Grateful Dead and Creedence Clearwater Revival) needed a quality recording studio in their home town. Some of the greatest albums of the time, such as *Volunteers*, *Green River* and *Tupelo Honey*, were recorded at Heider's.

Although Stevens felt that the songs he recorded in San Francisco were only for demo purposes and would be re-recorded more "properly" at a later time, that time never came. In a 2011 interview, Stevens (now Yusuf Islam) claimed that he was "a little bit upset" when the film came out without him having a chance to re-do the songs[10]; however, a review of the evidence shows that Stevens was actually given substantial consultation on the film soundtrack as it progressed and ultimately he agreed that the songs be used as they were a couple of months before the film was released.

In the months that followed the filming, Stevens was quite busy touring and promoting *Tea for the Tillerman*, as well as working on his next album *Teaser and the Firecat*, which would be released in the fall of 1971. Feeling that he was too busy to give the film the attention it needed, Stevens called Ashby in July and told him he was quitting. Ashby took the trouble to fly to Paris on July 30 to meet with Stevens to allay his concerns; the director spent two days talking to the singer, explaining to him in detail how he (Ashby) planned to use the music that he already had in the movie. Mollified, Stevens agreed to continue on the project. Paul Samwell-Smith, Stevens' producer, came to Hollywood from October 5 to 13 to work with Ashby on integration of the songs into the soundtrack.

The songs ultimately used in the film included some of Stevens' best-known songs from the period, as well as others that were not as familiar. Ashby used the organ part that comes at the end of "On the Road to Find Out" to transition from the scenes in which Harold purchases the hearse to the first funeral scene. Two other songs from the *Tea for the Tillerman* album, "Miles from Nowhere" and the album's brief title track, were used during the rainy outdoor funeral sequence.

The folk-oriented "Where Do the Children Play?"—also from *Tea for the Tillerman*—begins to play during the daisy fields sequence and ends with the transition into the scene in which the little tree is discovered. The upbeat rocker "I Think I See the Light," from *Mona Bone Jakon*, is used to suggest Harold's elation during the sequence that tran-

Ruth Gordon and Bud Cort during the rainy funeral sequence shot at Holy Cross Cemetery in Colma, known as the "city of souls" because there are so many cemeteries there.

sitions from the Santa Cruz fireworks to the morning after lovemaking at Maude's home. "I Wish, I Wish," also from *Mona Bone Jakon*, is used during the scene in which Harold arrives home driving the hearse, shocking his mother and her friends. And "Trouble," from *Mona Bone Jakon*, is memorably used during the film's penultimate scene, in which Harold is told of Maude's death and drives from the hospital to the coast in his car.

On October 23, Stevens, Krost and Samwell-Smith viewed a cut of the film with the music in place at the Paramount Projection facility in New York. According to a December 16 memo from Mulvehill, after the screening Krost phoned from New York to say, "Cat was ecstatic and that he would now allow us to use his vocal on the two new songs" Samwell-Smith "also told us how happy he was with the screening and the use of the new songs in question." Mulvehill noted that, although Stevens and Samwell-Smith thought "If You Want to Sing Out, Sing Out" worked perfectly as is, they would try to go into a studio in New York to see if they could get a better recording of "Don't Be Shy." However, on Monday, October 25, they called back and told Chuck that they were not going to re-record the song as they felt "that it couldn't be substantially improved and also that he was sending us a tape of 'Don't Be Shy' that Cat Stevens had recorded at some point in London (while drunk). After listening to the tape, we elected not to use their version."[11]

Final contracts were signed for the music on September 30, although the details on a few points remained fuzzy until closer to the film's release. Ashby had originally intended to use the song "Pop Star" from *Mona Bone Jakon*, but once he began editing, he decided "I Wish, I Wish" worked better and substituted it. In a November 29 letter to Krost, William Stinson also noted that Paramount was relinquishing its rights to the two original songs recorded for the movie except for synchronization licenses for their use in the picture. He concluded by writing, "As soon as you return the license for 'I Wish, I Wish' along with a letter signifying that the basic agreement between B.K.M. (Barry Krost Management) and Paramount dated September 30, 1971, covers the use of the ten Cat Stevens recordings we are using in the motion picture, including 'If You Want to Sing Out, Sing Out' and 'Don't Be Shy,' then the final payment will be made to B.K.M. immediately."[12] As Mulvehill wrote in his December 16 memo, "The bone of contention, as explained to me by Barry Krost, over this matter was strictly Cat Steven's [sic] reluctance to use his vocal on 'Don't Be Shy' and 'If You Want to Sing Out, Sing Out,' as he had originally written them for a female singer."[13] With Stevens' management company retaining the rights for the two new songs, the chances of a soundtrack album were essentially killed. In 1972, a soundtrack album for the movie was released in Japan but it only contained the already available Stevens songs, *not* the two new ones—plus several of Stevens' other popular songs such as "Morning Has Broken" and "Wild World" that were not used in the film. This album also included the non-Stevens songs "Greensleeves" and Tchaikovsky's "Piano Concerto No. 1," which were used as background music in several scenes. In 2007 a full soundtrack album was finally released on a limited edition vinyl disc.

Stevens' ultimate compensation for the music ended up being a little under $57,000, which turned out to be a great investment, even without a soundtrack album. In 1984, "If You Want to Sing Out, Sing Out" and "Don't Be Shy" finally ended up being released on *Footsteps in the Dark, Cat Stevens' Greatest Hits Vol. 2*. Incomplete demos or not, people loved those songs, which ended up being an integral part of not only Cat Stevens' oeuvre, but also of the legacy of *Harold and Maude*.

12

Editing the Film

With 13 weeks of intense work behind him, Ashby took a little time off after the completion of the shoot. On March 20, Cort wrote Ashby, calling him a "genius" and signing it "Your humble servant, Harold Parker Chasen, 1st."[1]

Ashby, who was at the time involved in a minor feud with Irving Klein, Norman Jewison's business manager, wrote to Jewison on March 29,

> For whatever reasons, I have really been on the longest down bummer of my life for the past month. I guess it has a lot to do with the film. I really felt as if I was running out of time during the last two weeks of shooting, but I'm not sure now if it was not having enough time to get all my ideas on film, or if I was just running out of life time in general. At any rate, it has deteriorated to the point where I'm convinced the only reason anybody is to see what they can get from me, or some such thing. I really am confused, and don't know. God knows, there isn't much to get, so why should they even bother.[2]

During the shooting of the film, Ashby had difficulty with the printing of his dailies by Technicolor, which was moving its lab from Hollywood to the San Fernando Valley. On March 18, Skip Nicholson of Technicolor wrote Ashby a letter apologizing for the problems and offering to "share, in some way, a portion of the expense of certain rephotography" that might be needed to fix the problems. He suggested that it would be difficult for Ashby to have a new lab "accurately intercut with existing daily prints." Nicholson assured Ashby that all post-production printing would be done at their Hollywood plant and supervised personally.[3] On March 25 Ashby replied, "I won't rehash any of the many problems which led me away from Technicolor. Let's just say I've never ever been as disappointed in the almost disrespectful way a lab handled film. It really went beyond my comprehension." Ashby told Nicholson he was aware of the potential trouble in trying to get the

MGM lab to make reprints which would intercut with Technicolor's but "I'm more prepared to suffer these troubles, than I am to go along with the constant fear that my negative will undergo even more damage than it has already."[4]

At around the time *Harold and Maude* was being edited, the technological landscape was changing for American film editors. For years, the Moviola, an upright 35mm film editor, had been the dominant machine used by editors. Then in the late 1960s, two editing systems that had been developed in Germany in the 1930s came into use in America, the Steenbeck and the KEM. Francis Ford Coppola was one of the first people in America to realize the superior ability of flatbed "tabletop" editing equipment, which worked much faster and more smoothly than the upright Moviola. Coppola's 1969 road film *The Rain People*, edited by Walter Murch on a Steenbeck, was the first Hollywood film completed on equipment of this type. The Steenbeck was favored by editors in the east, but West Coast editors worked more frequently on the KEM, and this was the system used to edit *Harold and Maude*.[5]

One of the results of Ashby's penchant for allowing actors to improvise on the set was that he shot and printed an unusually high amount of film; this had been the case on *The Landlord* and would continue throughout Ashby's career. Jane Fonda, who starred in Ashby's *Coming Home* in 1978, noted, "He would do 30 or 40 takes of each scene, not saying very much to the actors about what they should do differently each time—and he'd print all of them."[6] *The Landlord*, however, was made at United Artists, a company well known for not meddling with the filmmaking process and allowing the director to complete his work as time allowed. On *The Landlord*, Ashby worked with editor William A. Sawyer and brought on Edward Warschilka to do some additional cutting. He would work with this duo again on *Harold and Maude*. In January 1972 at the American Film Institute Seminar, Ashby admitted that he had finished the final cut of the film himself, though it was "something I want to break away from, because I've been into editing and I don't like to do that."[7]

As time went on, Ashby found that he was encountering what he felt was unusual interference from Paramount executives Peter Bart

12. Editing the Film

and Robert Evans, who wanted a definite say in how the film was cut. After Evans and Bart insisted on seeing the film, Ashby said,

> What I used with them was a kind of reverse psychology. I wouldn't even go down and run the film with them the first time myself, but they had to look at it before I thought the film was ready for them to look at. So I told them, "Okay, if you have to look at it, but it's long and it'll bore the hell out of you." But they said, "No, no, we've been around film long enough." So they were very uptight and upset that I didn't show up, and at the end of the thing they said, "Gee, it's fine, it's working, but isn't it a little long?"

Ashby finally consented to attend a screening of the work in progress at Evans' house.

> I thought, okay, I'm going to sit down and they're going to run through the picture and we're going to talk about individual cuts. But I knew intrinsically there would always be much more that I would be unhappy about with the film than anybody else was, I just knew that by nature. So I just started out with reel one and I said, "I'm going to do this and I'm going to do that"–and they said, "Wait a minute, gee, that's working pretty good" and by the time we got to reel three I had about 15 times more things than they were ever prepared to talk about. So it took the edge off of where in hell they were going with it, and we ended up boiling it down to just a couple of areas that way.[8]

Because of the capabilities of the KEM, Ashby was able to complete a cut of the first half of the picture before leaving for Europe in late July to consult with Stevens on the music. Bart sent a congratulatory telegram, "That was the first half of the best movie I ever saw," to which Ashby replied on August 4, "The movie has managed to take over my heart, soul and time for the present."[9] Still, the first complete cut of the movie was an intolerable three hours long, and Ashby knew it would need considerable editing to get it down to a manageable length. He would need to trim some of the repetitive scenes and arrange the film in an order so that the audience would not get impatient for Maude to show up, or lose interest in her during some of the lengthy parts that she is not on-screen. It was quite a challenge.

Ashby shortened many of the scenes featuring Maude and rearranged the order of some of the scenes. In the original script, the pool "suicide" comes much earlier, after the first scene in the psychiatrist's office. In a note to Evans, Ashby said, "I am continually concerned about too much time going by before we really get Harold and Maude together."[10] In order to get Maude in the picture earlier, Ashby moved the pool scene back so that it comes after the first meeting with Uncle Victor and after we have first seen Maude at the outdoor funeral. Ashby wisely eliminated many of the cutaway shots of demolition yards and construction work that punctuate the scenes with the psychiatrist, letting the black humor in these sequences stand on its own. He also cut much of their dialogue, including eliminating Harold's revelation to the psychiatrist that he blew up the chemistry building. This way, when Harold emotionally admits this to Maude later in the film, it is the first time the audience has heard about this event and the result for us is much more powerful than if it had been revealed earlier. In addition, Ashby eliminated the church funeral scene in which Maude borrows Harold's pen and puts smiles on the saints, thereby tightening up the way this important sequence played.

The scene in Harold's room, right before Mrs. Chasen tells him that she has lined up some computer dates for him, was cut entirely, as was the scene with Maude's neighbor Madame Arouet, whose appearance was not essential to the plot. Although Ashby struggled with cutting the scenes with Glaucus so they were shorter and could still be used, he eventually eliminated three of the scenes in Glaucus' studio entirely, leaving only the short scene where Harold comes in and finds Maude modeling in the nude for the sculptor. A lengthy scene in which Harold tells Maude about his mother's plans to induct him into the Army was removed completely, but Ashby was afraid "we are a long time away from Maude without it"[11] and so the scene was re-inserted with a shot of the outside of Maude's railcar home and their dialogue heard in voiceover. (Madame Arouet was in this scene, and since they were eliminating her character they could not use the scene as filmed.) The scene with Sunshine Dore, which occurs in the screenplay before the sequence in which Harold and Maude fool Uncle Victor, was moved back to occur just before the arcade sequence and was shortened slightly.

Two bones of contention between Ashby and Evans were the inclusion of the "Fuck War" sculpture in the waterside scene and the shot of Harold and Maude kissing and caressing as a prelude to their sexual encounter. Ashby had to remove "Fuck War" because it put the film in danger of an R rating, which had to be avoided if the movie was to have any chance of commercial success. When it came to the foreplay scene, Ashby later told an audience,

12. Editing the Film

I did have a scene in *Harold and Maude* where—well, I didn't have them really balling, making it—but I did have a scene where they got very much into the preliminaries of making love and, Christ, Paramount just went crazy. They said, "Oh my God, you just can't do that." That was the part where I was trying to shoot some young flesh and old flesh and do something pretty with that too, because I figured an audience would get into that.... I knew I could turn around and say, "Goddamn it, it was going to be that way." But in the end, I know somewhere along the line it's going to be turned over to them, and when it's turned over to them they'll just whack it out. So what I did in that case, I said, I know what it's going to arrive at, so what I'd better do is take it out and still make my film work with my own cut and they don't just say, Wham! and take it out there and you look at it and say, "Oh my God."¹²

The shot was removed but left in the film's trailer, which resulted in the firing of Pablo Ferro and in Paramount's decision to quash the trailer entirely. Ferro, who was to be paid $9500 for the trailers and had received a $1500 up front payment, eventually had to threaten Paramount with legal action to get the balance paid.¹³

The final cut of the film ended up being a tidy 91 minutes. Ashby had waded through many scenes that were overly long and had reduced much of Maude's dialogue in order to keep the audience from becoming weary of her earthy proclamations. The result was a movie that was not only enjoyable and eminently watchable, but would be, in fact, life-changing for many.

The film opens with a shot of a door opening, through which comes a pair of feet. At first there is no music, only ambient sound. A man moves across the room with the camera following his feet. He stops to place a record on a turntable; the song that begins playing is Cat Stevens' "Don't Be Shy." He then continues walking, stopping briefly to sit at a small table and write a name tag for himself. Impatiently, the man walks over to a small step stool, steps up on it and then steps off quickly. His feet swing out in the air and we, the audience, realize with horror that he has hung himself. The camera cuts to a quick overhead shot showing the audience the full room and the man swinging from a rope.

Harold and Maude is a film that at first emphasizes ambiguity and a search for identity. The audience never got a clear view of the face of the person who has hung himself. When we finally see his face, due to Bud Cort's youthful looking appearance (Robert Downey referred to him as "a bar of Camay with eyes") we are not sure if he is a grown man or just a boy, and it turns out that he is somewhere in between. Because he stopped and wrote a name tag (for no apparent reason) it appears that the man who has hung himself is also in some kind of a search for his own identity.

Once Harold's mother enters and does not offer a discernable reaction to the hanging, the audience begins to realize that they have been the victim of a hoax, and the film begins to take on another theme: Appearances are often deceiving and belie the reality of the situation. On the surface, Harold appears to be a well-adjusted young man, not a hippie or malcontent like many others in his generation. In fact, as we will see, he is badly damaged psychologically and in need of help, which he will not get from his psychiatrist, the priest or family members. The help that Harold needs can only come from Maude and, fortunately, in the course of the movie he gets that help and finally learns how to live and love.

In the next scene, we see Harold having dinner with his mother and her friends. Harold's mother treats her son with brusque condescension, speaking to her friends about him as if he is not even there. She then tells him to eat up his food, as if he were a child instead of an adult. Harold's mother, in her imperious manner and behavior, appears to belong to a wealthy class of people, a modern-day form of the aristocracy of the type that had ruled Great Britain and other European countries. By placing the Chasen home in a setting as distinctive as the Rosecourt, surrounded by the expensive and rare artwork acquired by the wealthy George Cameron and his wife, and featuring the family butler in the film (Higgins' script makes no reference to a butler or household servant), Ashby emphasizes that Mrs. Chasen is living in a world in which she views herself as a privileged aristocrat, ready to be waited on and catered to by her underlings. Ashby further encouraged this notion in the dinner scene by adding a harpist, who sits in the corner playing the song "Greensleeves" (one of the rare times in the film that Cat Stevens' music is not used). "Greensleeves" is a traditional English folk song written in the 16th century, and thus ties the Chasens to a world of traditional manners, mores and aristocracy. Furthermore,

12. Editing the Film

the Christmastime lyrics that are frequently associated with this song ("What Child Is This?") suggest the childlike way Mrs. Chasen treats her son, as well as Harold's search for his own identity separate from his mother.

As Harold's mother regards herself as an aristocrat, a member of the privileged ruling class defined by wealth, education and supposed good manners, she believes that her son will continue in this tradition and carry on in the manner prescribed by his birth. But Harold seems to have different ideas. By the late 20th century, this system of aristocracy and privilege had been falling apart for many years. Harold doesn't want to conform to his mother's world, in which he is compelled to act, dress and live in a way prescribed by his mother. Harold's rebellion is somewhat different than the typical hippie rebellion of the time (which mostly entailed growing long hair and doing drugs) but is nonetheless quite devastating to his mother. He can't become what she wants him to be, but at the beginning of the film he can only express this rebellion by embracing death and acting out in a manner that is designed to shock and upset his mother, such as performing his mock suicides or by transforming her gift of a sports car into a pseudo-hearse.

When Harold meets Maude and begins to find out who she really is, she offers an interesting contrast to his mother. Maude identifies herself as originally coming from an aristocratic, European background of the type that Harold's mother seeks for herself. She relates to Harold a story about being taken to a garden party in Vienna as a little girl, and assuming that she would marry a soldier when she got older. When Harold asks Maude about this, she replies that she doesn't regret that the kingdoms have fallen, but that she does miss the kings. While at first this might seem surprising for someone who is as anti-materialistic as Maude, it reveals that she still has a reverence for the large, domineering personalities that were present in royalty, as well as showing her occasional nostalgia for the past.

Maude is part of a sort of "anti-aristocracy" in the sense that she is freed from the materialism of the past by owning nothing and by not even respecting the ownership rights of others. Espousing the philosophical beliefs of Theosophy that Higgins had discovered, she believes totally in living her life to the fullest each day, in being in life and in the world of organic nature, and so she has shed the shackles of the past. By casting American Ruth Gordon as Maude (and by contrast the classically trained Vivian Pickles as Mrs. Chasen), Ashby successfully highlights the difference between the two women, one of them stuck in the world of the long-ago past and the other living in the present.

Religious iconography is used frequently in the film, particularly in the funeral sequences. The St. Thomas Aquinas Church scene, for instance, begins with a closeup on the stained glass window at the front of the church, then the camera pulls back as we hear funeral organ music play. The solemn tone is interrupted several times by Maude's clumsy attempts to get Harold's attention, much to the irritation of the priest. When Maude does get Harold's attention, she begins by offering him a piece of black licorice. The black licorice is particularly foreboding, and Harold does indeed note later in the film that he is "picking up on vices" since meeting Maude. In Higgins' original script, Harold's first view of Maude is sitting off alone in the distance during a funeral, having a picnic; but in the film, Harold first sees Maude sitting by herself eating a piece of fruit, which is much more suggestive of sexual temptation.

One can't help but think that Ashby was using these appearances to suggest that Maude appears to Harold as a form of temptress, offering him a bite of the tempting but potentially ruinous things in the world. When Harold is first introduced to Maude's railcar home, the scene is filled with imagery bursting with physical sensations that suggest sex. She shows him a picture of "The Rape of Rome" which features the image of Leda and the Swan (a story from Greek mythology in which the God Zeus takes the form of a swan and rapes a woman, who bears him two children). Maude says slyly, almost to herself, that this image is a "self-portrait." Harold is so excited by the tactile sensations of Maude's home that he can't help himself and tries to force his head into the suggestive wooden sculpture that resembles a vagina. But in the end, the film makes Maude out to be a character of such benign grace that we can only make the assumption that Ashby is suggesting that Harold needs a few vices in his life to give him the opportunity to live a little, and that Maude's character is helping to liberate him sexually so he can go on to have a normal sex life.

Ashby does not attempt to give realistic explanations as to how impossible or inexplicable events happen in the film, and in this sense the film begins to enter into the realm of absurdity or even a fairy tale. For instance, in Higgins' script there is a brief scene explaining how

12. Editing the Film

Maude survived being thrown into the reservoir (she wore a scuba mask). Ashby did away with this scene, cutting to Harold and Maude sitting contentedly on a blanket, offering no explanation as to how Maude survived plunging through a hole and falling into the ocean. There are also several other examples of things that happen in the film that can only be described as surreal. When Maude sings and plays the Cat Stevens song on her piano, she at one point stands up and begins to dance around the room, and the piano simply continues to play without her. The dance was apparently somewhat improvised by Gordon who, according to Ashby, "got up and danced around and we just kept the music going." Ashby said it struck him funny when she did that, and he left it in with no explanation necessary.[14]

These unexplainable things are not limited to what happens to Maude. When Harold has his date with Candy Gulf and lights himself on fire, he appears behind her almost immediately after going up in flames. Again, no explanation is given. In the final scene, Harold's car hurtles over the cliff and onto the beach below, but when the camera tilts up, we see him standing at the top with his banjo in his hand. It would seem to be impossible for Harold to leap out of the speeding car as it travels towards the edge without seriously hurting himself and, in fact, some have speculated that Harold does die in the crash and the final shot of him walking away playing the banjo is purely fantasy. But in the context of previous events which rise to the point of being surrealist, it is likely that the filmmakers merely wanted to dramatize Harold's rebirth into a new life of love and music in the most dramatic and climactic way possible, through his "miraculous" escape from the car.

Ashby created an extraordinary sequence to illustrate Maude's worldview to Harold in the clearest way. As he begins to fall under her spell, they go to a greenhouse where Maude walks amongst the plants extolling the virtues of life and all its living things. Next comes the scene in the daisy field, where Maude tells Harold that the daisies should not be treated as one large group of flowers, but instead should be considered as individual flowers with all their own peculiar differences taken into account. The film then cuts to show Harold and Maude sitting in a grass field, and now the camera begins to pull back, revealing that they are not in a daisy field any more; they are seated in a massive graveyard. As the camera zooms out, we see them from a far distance, and now the white gravestones in the green field appear to be, in fact, daisy petals! Harold and Maude have been transformed so that they are now sitting in a daisy field of tombstones. While *Harold and Maude* for the most part avoids political statements, this amazing shot suggests visually the devastating consequences of war and the death that it causes in a way that has no parallels in the written word.

But Ashby's most courageous and bold move was to re-edit the final sequence in which Harold and Maude arrive at the hospital. Harold waits through the night for the determination that Maude has died and then drives his car crazily to the coastline, ultimately sending the vehicle over the cliff. In Higgins' script, this sequence is written as a straightforward linear narrative, including dialogue at the hospital where the admitting nurse and an intern attempt to question Maude about her condition and insurance, while Harold demands that they attend to her immediately. Ashby cut the sequence instead as an impressionistic montage, eliminating the dialogue and setting the sequence to the Cat Stevens song "Trouble." The scenes of their arrival at the hospital are edited together with shots of the doctor walking down the hall to give Harold the news, as well as images of Harold driving, his face looking alternately blank, shocked and even a little blissful. The effect is disorienting, particularly on a first viewing when we are unsure what happened to Maude, but in the end this technique heightens our awareness of Harold's emotional ordeal by cutting up time into non-linear pieces, building the sequence together in a rhythm that culminates when the car goes over the cliff.

This brilliant editing shows not only Ashby's awareness of but his willingness to employ more complex filmmaking techniques that were being put to use by bold and experimental filmmakers such as John Schlesinger, Mike Nichols and Arthur Penn, all of whom had used music very effectively in their recent films. It also is an early indication of the way that Ashby was tuned in to the power of the marriage of images and music, which he would use to great effect in several of his later films, particularly in the *Coming Home* sequence in which Bruce Dern's character commits suicide by walking into the ocean (Ashby told friends that he himself had considered suicide in this manner and, in fact, several of his other films—including *Being There* and *Eight Million Ways to Die*—end near bodies of water). Bold and compelling, the final sequence of *Harold and Maude* goes from fairly routine story-

12. Editing the Film

telling to one of the most powerful moments in contemporary American film.

———∞∞———

In August of 1971, Lippincott & Sons published Higgins' novelized version of the screenplay. It received mixed reviews. Eventually the story would also be turned into a stage play, which was how Higgins had envisioned it when he first wrote the script for the film. In 1972 the play began running in France (where the film had fared much better than in America) and continued to run for many years after. In 1980, a Broadway production closed after a short run.

A look at Higgins' novel compared to Ashby's film reveals interesting differences in the way the writer and the director approached the material. The novel is told mostly from Harold's point of view, which put Higgins in the sometimes uncomfortable position of having to get into Harold's head. Ashby, meanwhile, was able to sit back and show us Harold's mostly impassive face, which revealed very little. Readers of the novel learned that Harold's father was named Charlie and that he died while photographing parrots in Polynesia, though the details of the elder Chasen's demise are left out of the book. Uncle Victor's missing right arm was attributed to an accident during training maneuvers in Fort Jackson, South Carolina. Higgins did away with the pool drowning scene in the novel, although he did have Harold describe the event to the psychiatrist (named Dr. Harley in the novel) in some detail. Other scenes deleted from the film for length, such as the painting of the smiles on the statues of the saints and the mannequin of Harold created for an unrealized suicide, were back in the book.

The film and its locations seemed to have had an influence on the novel. During the church funeral scene, the novel mentions the stained glass window of St. Thomas Aquinas, which has to have been an inspiration from the prominent shot used in the film. (When he wrote the novel, Higgins had seen the dailies but not the finished film.) But Higgins departed from the film when it suited him, describing Maude as having a slight British-European accent and white hair, nothing like Ruth Gordon. Maude's formal name is changed from Marjorie to Mathilda and her home is not an old railcar but a small cottage with a walnut tree in the front yard, although descriptions of many of the home furnishings match the ones in the film. Maude's neighbor Madame Arouet, condemned to the editing room floor by Ashby, was back in the story. In addition, Higgins filled in more details about Maude's husband Frederick, including the fact that he was captured and shot, in Maude's words, "trying to escape. At least that's what they told me later. I guess I never will know the real story."[15] This detail lends credence to the idea that Maude and Frederick were imprisoned at some point in a World War II concentration camp.

Later in the novel, Higgins adds an interesting element that doesn't exist in the film, but is included in the original script. Harold notices that all of the picture frames in Maude's homes have no pictures or photographs in them, and asks her why. She responds simply, "They mocked me. They were representations of people I dearly loved, yet they knew these people were gradually fading from me and that, in time, all I would have left would be vague feelings—but sharp photographs. So I tossed them out. My memory fades, I know. But I prefer pictures made by me, with feeling, and not by Kodak with silver nitrate."[16] This passage suggests that Maude is suffering from some kind of dementia or the early stages of Alzheimer's Disease and that, even worse, she is aware of it. Instead of having the pictures mock her fading memory, she gets rid of them.

In summarizing the novel for his publishers, Higgins noted, "Harold is a man constantly examining whether life is really worth living ... he is bound to life. He cannot end it but he cannot live it." Maude, meanwhile, "has lived life fully. She is finished with the world now and ready for the next. In coming to terms with death, she has come to terms with life."[17] Higgins' published novel fills in more details about the characters, but ultimately it leaves one with a feeling of dissatisfaction. The film, meanwhile, only sketches in the character of Maude, but the less we seem to know about her and her past, the better. There is an element of mystery to Maude in the film and this works in favor of her character and the story as a whole.

With Stevens, Krost and Samwell-Smith on board with the music after their October screening, the film was ready to be previewed in early November, with the running time cut down from three hours to

12. Editing the Film

a concise 91 minutes. On November 12, 1971, it was previewed at the Varsity Theatre in Palo Alto (the church funeral sequence had been filmed in Palo Alto ten months earlier) to an audience of largely college students, and with Robert Evans and Peter Bart in attendance.[18] Ashby gave Evans some handwritten notes before the preview, indicating recent changes he had made and saying, "As usual I'm rushing around like a maniac trying to get the film in as presentable condition as possible before the preview."

The film still had some changes to go through at this point, as one of the Glaucus scenes was in place that would later be cut, as well as the scene in which Maude adds the smiles to the statues. Ashby agonized over the inclusion of the Glaucus scene, telling Evans that he had "looked at the film three times with the Glaucus scene out, and it just didn't work as a transition." The scene in which Harold tells Maude about the plans to induct him in the army was not in the film at this point. Ashby also had changed the final shot of the film, eliminating the part in which Harold does a little jig as he walks away from the camera playing the banjo; the director noted to Evans that the reason for this was the final shot was now a "little more serious." Ashby went on to make the interesting observation that "the Happy Happy always seemed to lessen [Harold's] real feelings for Maude."[19] In the end, the jig was added back to the final shot, and the whimsical feeling that this brings to the film's conclusion is worth diminishing the seriousness of the tone of the scene.

Ashby also complained to Evans about the lack of communication regarding the Technicolor printing of the film: "As a result, all kinds of technical problems were thrown at us, and we're unable to go to preview with a print that I'm happy with.... Aside from that, let's hope we have some good luck tonight."[20] Apparently they did; in Bart's 2002 book he recalled, "At the end, more than half the audience got to its feet and applauded. I'd never seen that at a preview. I literally shook with excitement, then hugged Hal, who was in shock. The kids in the audience followed us outside and wanted to talk about the movie. They wouldn't quit."[21] Of 360 review cards, 300 said the film was "right on."

A week later, the film was previewed at the Camelot Theatre in Palm Springs. Ashby was still tweaking the film. Notes indicate that he was adjusting the Foley mix, had made the final decision to drop the Glaucus scene before Harold and Maude are stopped the first time by the motorcycle cop, etc. Furthermore, Ashby had finally decided to drop the scene where Maude paints the smiles on the statues, so the film cuts from the casket being put into the hearse directly to Maude introducing herself to Harold on the church steps. Although this was a bit of an abrupt jump, it was the only way to eliminate a scene that Ashby now felt was wholly unnecessary to the development of the characters and their relationship.

With the opening and closing titles completed by Pablo Ferro, *Harold and Maude* was previewed on December 6 in Los Angeles. The film was now finished and ready to go. A few months earlier, when Colin Higgins had filled out a questionnaire for his publisher, he noted, "Paramount considers the film this year's *Love Story*. I dunno if lightning strikes twice."[22] Could lightning, in fact, strike twice? *The Hollywood Reporter* noted on December 8 that Evans was beaming with happiness at *Harold and Maude*'s Directors Guild screening, certain that it would be a big hit.[23] A Paramount executive told Mulvehill that *Harold and Maude* had previewed as well as any of Jerry Lewis' films, which meant they expected it to be a huge success. Anticipation was high. The film was set for a Christmastime release: December 20, 1971.

Harold and Maude was ready for the public ... but ... was the public ready for *Harold and Maude*?

13

Dropping a Bomb and Rising from the Ashes

While the finished cut of *Harold and Maude* showed promise, the post-production process had been problematic and the studio made a series of decisions that inevitably ruined the picture's chances for box office success. The first cut of the movie that Bud Cort saw was "horrifying, it was a disaster. All the delicious moments were on the floor. Ashby said, 'I totally agree with you. But they won't listen to me.' Shortly after that they asked me to come to New York, to the top floor of the Gulf+Western building." Cort told the Paramount public relations people "'Gentlemen, until this film is recut, not only to my specifications, but to Mrs. Gordon's and Mr. Ashby's, I am not available for any publicity on this film. Thank you very much. Good day.' And from that moment on I've been persona non grata over at Paramount."[1] To some extent, this story is emblematic of Cort's naïveté at this point in his career; neither he, Gordon or Ashby had the clout to influence a studio like Paramount in the editing or handling of the film.

Cort did participate in one bit of publicity, although his feelings for his co-star may have been the reason. On November 21, 1971, Ruth Gordon was featured on the television show *This Is Your Life*, and Cort, according to host Ralph Edwards, flew in from London to appear on the show. Cort gave Gordon a handful of daisies in homage to the use of the flower in *Harold and Maude*, and spoke sincerely and lovingly of how she had affected him as an actor. His tribute was returned by Gordon, who seemed overwhelmed at the affection she received from her young co-star. This was the beginning of a warming of the relationship between the two which, during the filming, had been mostly on a professional basis. The airing of the *This Is Your Life* episode was the perfect opportunity to make the public aware of the film and to promote its release the following month.

Around this time, Cort's father passed away quite prematurely (age 50) from multiple sclerosis. In 2014, the actor told the London *Guardian* that this event finally brought him close to his *Harold and Maude* co-star. The morning after his father died, Gordon called Cort and said, "Oh, honey, let me tell you about the day my father died." Cort noted that, from this moment on, "suddenly we were the characters we had played." He added that his relationship with Gordon "was one of the most important friendships I've ever had. She was a great woman."[2]

The Paramount publicity department had some interesting promotional ideas. They considered "sending motorcycles with sidecars with an old lady in the sidecar, driven by a young man on opening day" of the film, noting this "would cost $200 per unit. Motorcycles would carry 'Just Married' signs and play information." This idea was wisely dropped. Additionally, it was contemplated that "we could have Ruth Gordon plant a tree in central location for an ecology tie-in."

"If approved, we would like to have invitations to the film printed like a Valentine." Other possibilities included local tree plantings through block associations and civic improvement groups, a botanical garden and local flower shop tie-in, senior citizens arts festivals and an ice sculpture contest. For media, it was thought radio and TV talk shows could discuss the theme "You needn't grow old" and also offer an essay contest looking for the most humorous reply to the question "How to stay young?"[3] While most of these ideas were clearly just being offered to have something to kick around, the nature of them seems to indicate that the p.r. department didn't really understand what the film was really about.

The release date of the film was also an issue. Not exactly a Christmas movie, *Harold and Maude* nonetheless had its world premiere on Monday, December 20, 1971, at the Coronet Theater at 59th Street and Third Avenue in New York. Paramount had expected its highly anticipated *The Godfather*—the film that Ashby lost cameraman Gordon Willis to—to be ready to open by Christmas and had planned a release

13. Dropping a Bomb and Rising from the Ashes

strategy accordingly. According to Higgins, "We opened at the Village Theater in Westwood at Christmas, and the reason we had all these large, large theaters across the country was that *The Godfather* wasn't ready, and Paramount had booked *The Godfather* into all these theaters for Christmas. These theaters had nothing to play. Paramount told them, 'We've got this little comedy called *Harold and Maude*' and the theaters had no choice. It was a real treat for me to go to the Village in Westwood and see *Harold and Maude*, but you can't hold that theater with such a small film, and once it leaves, it's gone."[4] *Harold and Maude* was rated GP (Parental Guidance Suggested), which meant there were no age restrictions.

Higgins hated the advertising for the film: "If you've seen the original poster for *Harold and Maude*, you know that it's a disgrace. Just blank letters on white: *Harold and Maude*, starring Ruth Gordon. It looked like it was done on a hand-press."[5] Ashby felt the same. Just weeks after the film came out he told a USC audience,

> I couldn't get [Paramount] to go along with anything as far as the relationship between the 21-year-old boy and the 80-year-old woman being in love. And we backed off enough in the film itself. But they said, "No, we don't want to go for that." I'm not crazy about too much stuff in advertising, but I did feel that was important to be provocative in that sense. Business was not good anywhere, I mean what I thought was good and they thought was good, except in Baltimore. In Baltimore it was doing sensational business. So I said, "Why the hell is it doing good in Baltimore? Are they just all freaks in Baltimore, or what is it?" That seemed a little unreal bit to me. So they found out when the exhibitor or the theater owner involved got his advertising kit, which are his radio plugs and his ads, his allocation for the money to spend for the ads, said, "No, I don't like that," and he made his own ads, and they were on the other thing—the provocative thing—she's 80 and he's 20 and they're in love. And it's been holding up just fine in Baltimore.[6]

Aside from the "blank letters" poster that Higgins found uninspiring, the other poster that seems to have been the most widely circulated (particularly in Europe) pictured Gordon and Cort riding a motorcycle with daisy flowers for wheels. While this poster captures the whimsy of the film, it is a bit confusing and does nothing to reveal the essence of the story. The two trailers created by Pablo Ferro were considered unsatisfactory by the studio and were never circulated (you can find them as supplemental features on the DVD release of the film). Tag lines such as "This is Harold. His hang-ups are hilarious" didn't help much, although "They met at the funeral of a perfect stranger. From then on, things got stranger and stranger" was pretty funny.

Reviews ranged wildly from enthusiastic to disgusted, but most critics seemed to not like the film or at least to not understand the points it was trying to make. Roger Ebert, who had praised *The Landlord*, wrote a negative review, giving the film 1.5 stars and concluding: "And so what we get, finally, is a movie of attitudes. Harold is death, Maude life, and they manage to make the two seem so similar that life's hardly worth the extra bother. The visual style makes everyone look fresh from the Wax Museum, and all the movie lacks is a lot of day-old gardenias and lilies and roses in the lobby, filling the place with a cloying sweet smell. Nothing more to report today. Harold doesn't even make pallbearer."[7]

Vincent Canby in the *New York Times* hated the film:

> As Harold and Maude, Bud Cort and Ruth Gordon are supposed to appear magnificently mismatched for the purposes of the comedy. They are mismatched, at least visually. Mr. Cort's baby face and teenage build look grotesque alongside Miss Gordon's tiny, weazened frame. Yet, as performers, they both are so aggressive, so creepy and off-putting, that Harold and Maude are obviously made for each other, a point the movie itself refuses to recognize with a twist ending that betrays, I think its life-affirming pretensions.[8]

Ruth Gordon was so outraged at this review that she immediately penned a reply to Canby by mail, a letter she later published in her autobiography. Pauline Kael seemed ambivalent, praising parts of the movie but faulting Ashby's direction and the cinematography for viewing the actors at a great distance. (This was actually Ashby's style and he would return to it again and again in subsequent films.) Kael complained about the technical quality of the sound level, which she felt varied enough to make some of the voices inaudible. According to *Variety*'s scathing review, "*Harold and Maude* has all the fun and gaiety of a burning orphanage!"

But a few critics liked the film. Charles Champlin praised it in the *L.A. Times* and Judith Crist, seizing on Gordon's performance as Maude, wrote a favorable review and suggested that the film was something of a modern fairy tale. By and larger, however, the critical assessment was not good, and did not help the word of mouth for a film that

13. Dropping a Bomb and Rising from the Ashes

was a bit of a hard sell to begin with. Initial box office receipts were bad in almost all major markets. In Los Angeles, for instance, *Harold and Maude* only grossed $8500 during its first week, in comparison with $75,000 for Jewison's *Fiddler on the Roof* and $40,000 for *Dirty Harry*.[9]

A 1974 *New York Times* article noted, "With hindsight, most people connected with *Harold and Maude* feel that the crucial error was not the advertising campaign but the timing."[10] Aside from *Fiddler* and *Dirty Harry*, *Harold and Maude* was competing against a slate of acclaimed films with adult themes that opened in late 1971, such as Kubrick's *A Clockwork Orange*, Sam Peckinpah's *Straw Dogs*, John Schlesinger's *Sunday Bloody Sunday* and Arthur Hiller's *The Hospital*, the latter with a brilliant Paddy Chayefsky screenplay. There was also a new Sean Connery-James Bond movie to contend with, *Diamonds Are Forever*. Mulvehill commented later,

> You couldn't drag people in. The idea of a 20-year-old boy with an 80-year-old woman just made people want to vomit. If you asked people what it was about, ultimately it became a boy who was fucking his grandmother. We were devastated, couldn't believe it, and the scripts and phone calls that had been coming in just stopped. It was as though somebody had taken an ax to the phone lines. It was a really rude awakening. It was a big, big shock to Hal."[11]

A week after the film was released, Paramount pulled it from most of the theaters. Several fans who had seen and liked it wrote letters to Paramount, expressing their surprise that it was yanked so quickly. In 1972 Gordon and Cort were nominated for Golden Globes for their performances, but neither won.

Although his basic pessimism caused him to doubt the film's success anyway, Ashby felt, "Jesus, I don't want to spend a year of my life making that film and not have anybody see it."[12] In Marilyn Beck's January 25, 1972, *Evening Bulletin* article "Director Charges Studio Was Afraid of Maude," Ashby commented, "Paramount has gone out of its way to see there's been no mention in ads of the fact that this is a love affair between an 80-year-old woman and a young boy." He again cited the Baltimore example to illustrate the point that a different ad campaign might have resulted in a different box office result.[13] Ashby later told Richard Cuskelly of the *Los Angeles Herald Examiner*, "I can't blame Paramount. They did everything they knew how to promote the picture. It was their project from the beginning after all. I was brought in much later." But Ashby had a premonition that ultimately all was not lost with *Harold and Maude*. He added this telling comment: "I'm proud of what is up there on the screen and I think later the film will find an audience or at least the attention it deserves."[14]

Moviegoing and film exhibition had undergone a period of enormous transition by the early 1970s. Attendance had dropped radically in the postwar years from a peak of about 78 million per week in 1946 to about a quarter of that by 1966, due mostly to suburbanization and the advent of television. In 1948 the U.S. Supreme Court issued the Paramount decree, an anti-trust ruling which forced the studios to begin to divest themselves of theater ownership, so large chains such as Paramount's Balaban and Katz and MGM's Loew's Theaters had to be sold. Movie theaters also re-tooled in the 1950s to handle Cinema-Scope, VistaVision, Todd-AO and other widescreen formats that the studios implemented to battle the competition of television. By the mid–1960s, with audiences shrinking and production and exhibition costs rising, many of the film studios and theaters found themselves in terrible financial condition.

In the early 1970s, Hollywood was beginning to take a new approach to the release of its major films. Instead of releasing a picture in major markets first and then sending them out to smaller markets and rural areas some time later, the studios began opening films such as *The Godfather* (1972) and *The Exorcist* (1973) in hundreds of theaters at a time. While this practice is common now, with big-budget movies typically opening on thousands of screens during their debut weekend, at the time it was revolutionary. However, by the time *Jaws* was released to over 400 theaters in the summer of 1975, this "blockbuster" approach was becoming more of a standard practice.

One of the results of this was, simply put, a demand for more movie screens. Some single-screen theaters began evolving into multiplexes, with many movie screens at a single location, showing different films. The owners of many small theaters, however, could not afford to remodel their theaters into multiplexes (or didn't want to or were unable to for some other reason) so they were faced with a choice:

13. Dropping a Bomb and Rising from the Ashes

either turn their theater into a bowling alley (or something else) or continue as a single-screen theater, running "art" films, foreign releases or movies that had already had a theatrical release. Audience of the 1970s also continued to evolve and become more sophisticated; as Pauline Kael noted, not only had the standard film audience started to shrink, but it was also sharply divided between the "art-house crowd" and the "old-fashioned, entertainment-seeking moviegoers."[15] With the home video revolution still a decade away and the popularity and availability of foreign films by directors such as Truffaut, Antonioni, Wertmuller and Herzog, many of the older movie theaters decided to go in the direction of the art house cinema. By and large, these were the theaters that embraced *Harold and Maude* between the years 1972 and the mid–1980s and turned it from a box office dud into a cult hit.

The Westgate Theater in Edina, Minnesota, was one of those theaters. Edina is a small but affluent town of about 47,000 people, located southwest of Minneapolis. The Westgate was a small neighborhood theater at 3903 Sunnyside Avenue, opened in 1937 in the town of Morningside, which was later annexed by Edina.[16] According to the Edina Historical Society, the Westgate "began the strategy of finding a market to stay alive in a time when multiplex theaters took most of the movie business from small single-screen operations."[17] Part of this strategy was playing cult movies that would attract consistent repeat business. *Harold and Maude* opened at the theater in mid–1972 and was so popular that it played for an astounding 1957 consecutive showings. Ruth Gordon was invited to the theater for the June 1973 one-year anniversary of its run, and the next year she appeared at the two-year anniversary, this time accompanied by Bud Cort. The run at the theater would eventually gross almost a half-million dollars by itself.[18]

After 114 consecutive weeks, the run of the film was beginning to wear thin. In pictures taken of Cort and Gordon at the two-year anniversary show, local residents can be seen in the background carrying picket signs requesting that the theater show some different films. Shortly thereafter, the showings of *Harold and Maude* came to an end. Like many small, independent theaters, the Westgate was eventually bought by a large chain, General Cinema Corp., and was closed in late 1977 when it ceased to be profitable. Today the theater building is home to the Edina Cleaners and Launderers.[19]

Just as *Harold and Maude* was ending its record Edina run, Paramount was breathing more life into the film. Buoyed by the increasing box office receipts from rentals at theaters like the Westgate, Paramount made new prints and gave it a limited re-release in the summer and fall of 1974. A May 26, 1974, *New York Times* article noted that Paramount was reopening the film at the Thalia, a theater near Columbia University which had a reputation for having "an audience of American film buffs who appreciate classic American films as well as foreign ones." Paramount vice-president of marketing Charles O. Glenn noted that he could not remember the studio ever re-releasing a film that was a failure on its initial run. Although the New York opening was something of an experiment, eventually the film opened wider; I first saw it in St. Louis a few months later, in the fall of 1974.[20] In 1976 it was re-released again. *Harold and Maude*, the onetime box office bomb, was becoming a hit in slow motion!

Ashby, of course, was pleased about the ongoing screenings of *Harold and Maude* and its growing cult reputation. In 1976 he told Larry Salvato and Dennis Schaefer in *Millimeter* magazine that it was "probably the most gratifying film I've ever made." Regarding its late-in-coming success he said, "I think it's because of what it has to say. It's the idea of the young and the old, the love thing, what she has to say, the statements and the way the thing is presented."[21]

For Colin Higgins, *Harold and Maude* brought success in different ways. The film did very well in France, and in 1972 a stage version opened in Paris and ran for three years. The play had long runs in 20 other countries, although the 1980 Broadway version flopped. In 1979, after Higgins had achieved some other film successes, Paramount again gave the film a limited re-release, printing posters that stated that *Harold and Maude* was from "the creator of *Silver Streak* and *Foul Play*." But that same year, at an AFI seminar, Higgins told the audience, "After *Harold and Maude*, I couldn't get a job in this town." He added that the film "has never made a dime to this day for me. No, for the studio it's probably made a lot.... Hal and I and Ruth Gordon have points and deferrals, and they've never been paid off."[22] Indeed, a 1977 audit of the film still revealed that it was not in the black for the studio.

13. Dropping a Bomb and Rising from the Ashes

Movie studio accounting has long been suspect, and sometimes films that seemed to do well at the box office are painted as financial duds by their makers for purposes of avoiding taxes or residual payments. The financial fortunes of *Harold and Maude*, which at first were horrible, changed considerable as the decade of the 1970s wore on. In 1973, it was still in the red by $1.65 million, meaning that in its initial release the movie did not even make back the studio's costs for advertising, promoting and distributing it, much less production costs. After re-releases in 1974 and 1976, it was doing better, but was still underwater by $871,000. But by the beginning of the 1980s, Paramount was now saying that *Harold and Maude* was only $210,000 in the red and was close to breaking even. Higgins' accountant George Gelles wrote to Higgins on September 30, 1980, "*Harold and Maude* should be in the black by about $6,000 at this time next year." He added, rather ruefully, "All this is assuming that Paramount reports all the receipts and doesn't find additional expenses to charge the picture."[23]

After more than a decade, in March 1982, Paramount could no longer deny that *Harold and Maude* was finally a moneymaker. That month, checks began to be sent out to the participants who had a cut of the profits under their original agreements. Higgins received from Paramount a check for $78,276 that was divided between himself and Mildred as part of the long-defunct Lewis-Higgins Productions, which also went on to receive a residual check of $93,313 in 1984. In 1985 the total was $63,746 and in 1987 they received $42,764. Once a flop, it was paying off big time for those who had a back end payday.

In the 1983 *New York Times* article "After 12 Years, a Profit for *Harold and Maude*," Aljean Harmetz wrote, "Twelve years later, profit checks have been sent to *Harold and Maude's* director, Hal Ashby; its author, Colin Higgins; and its star, Ruth Gordon." The article noted that Gordon almost threw her $50,000 check away. "I thought it was one of those sweepstakes from the *Reader's Digest*," she said. The article quoted Barry London, Paramount's vice-president of distribution, as saying, "We ship it to college campuses and repertory theaters. Most pictures don't mean anything 12 years later but a new generation of college students is finding this one." London further noted that in the last 12 months alone, *Harold and Maude* had played in 646 theaters and rented halls.[24] As people connected with the characters in the film, they returned to see the movie over and over again.

The article went on to make this interesting point about *Harold and Maude* and its status as a cult picture: "Unlike *The Rocky Horror Picture Show*, another box office failure that has become a cult film, *Harold and Maude* has not primarily earned its money playing midnight shows on Saturday nights." The phenomenon of the cult midnight movie had started about a year before the release of *Harold and Maude* when the Elgin Theatre in New York's Chelsea district began playing Alejandro Jodorowsky's surrealist Western *El Topo*, a film made in the style of Sergio Leone's spaghetti Westerns of the 1960s, but featuring considerably more fake gore in its special effects. The showing of the movie at midnight attracted a fanatical following, selling out every night for months, until the Beatles' John Lennon—a fan who had seen the movie several times—actually arranged for the purchase and re-release of the film.

The "midnight movie" trend caught on, not just at the Elgin but at numerous movie theaters in urban areas that were beginning to find themselves outdated by the new trend towards multiplex theaters. Several older films, such as Tod Browning's 1932 *Freaks* and the 1930s "anti-drug" message film *Reefer Madness,* were picked up and turned into cult favorites due to their bizarre content and unintentional humor, which appealed to the pot-smoking audiences of the midnight movies. George Romero's low-budget gorefest *Night of the Living Dead* (1968) also became a cult hit and spawned several sequels which were released through more conventional distribution channels. John Waters' *Pink Flamingos* and several of Andy Warhol's movies, known more for their prurient content, also became successes due to showings at midnight movie screenings.

But by far the most successful of these films was *The Rocky Horror Picture Show*, a sex parody of old horror movies that was released to mediocre box office business in the fall of 1975. Revived as a midnight movie about a year later, it took on a life of its own, with theaters showing it at midnight and encouraging audience members to come in costume, shout out dialogue from the movie in unison, and hurl rice and other objects at the movie screen. Made on a low $1.4 million budget (and launching the careers of several actors, including Susan Sarandon),

13. Dropping a Bomb and Rising from the Ashes

Rocky Horror ended up grossing over $140 million, thus becoming not only one of the most successful independently produced movies of all time, but the greatest cult success in the history of the cinema.

Harold and Maude's success did not come via midnight screenings. The people who embraced the film did so because they loved the characters, their situations, the catchy dialogue and the beautiful way the film was shot and edited. A 1973 *Box Office* article noted that 22-year-old fan Doug Strand had already seen the film 138 times, even though it had only been in release for a little over a year. *Harold and Maude* had an unusual story line—one that was strange enough to chase away box office success on its original release—but, compared to midnight movies like *El Topo* and *Pink Flamingos*, the film is downright conventional. So while *Harold and Maude* did not get caught up in the midnight movie phenomenon, it certainly did become a cult success in its own way and ended up generating a huge audience that loved it, and loved it on its own terms, and not as a cultural oddity or group phenomenon. As the *New York Times* noted in 1974, "The fanatics who have seen *Harold and Maude* three, six, nine times speak of it as a 'regenerative thing' or 'like getting your battery recharged.' It is not the comedy but the philosophy that sends people plunging back into the darkness of the theater again and again."[25]

14

After *Harold and Maude*: Hal Ashby

Although the phone was not ringing as much for Ashby after *Harold and Maude* flopped, he still had a few options for his next project. While on location in Northern California, Ashby had separated from his wife Joan Marshall, but eventually he and Joan reconciled. In the spring of 1972, while Hal planned his next move, the couple was living at the Appian Way home with Joan's daughter as well as two black Persian cats named Booker T. and Priscilla. Marshall, a moderately successful actress, had played the original Lily Munster (named "Phoebe Munster") in the pilot of *The Munsters*, but it was decided that in her costume she looked too much like Carolyn Jones' Morticia Addams, and the part was re-cast with Yvonne DeCarlo as Lily. Marshall and Ashby would be on again, off again for several years before separating for good after *Shampoo* came out in 1975. The director purportedly used some of the Hollywood gossip that Marshall had told him in confidence in the script of *Shampoo,* and this infuriated his ex-wife (although he did give her a small part in the film). Sad to say, Ashby was not highly successful in his close interpersonal relationships with women, and Joan was his fifth and final wife. Marshall died in Jamaica in 1992 at the age of 61.

While making *Harold and Maude*, Ashby met Jack Nicholson at Robert Evans' home, and the two hit it off. Nicholson, a former "B" actor, was riding high after playing a supporting part in *Easy Rider* and starring in the hits *Five Easy Pieces* and *Carnal Knowledge*. He had seen *The Landlord* and liked it, and had heard of Ashby's great reputation with actors and wanted very much to work with him. The first project they considered was a remake of the 1946 Lana Turner–John Garfield film noir, *The Postman Always Rings Twice,* which was to be

14. After Harold and Maude: Hal Ashby

called *Three-Cornered Circle* and was to be produced at MGM, which had made the original film and owned the rights. However, as discussions about the project proceeded, Ashby ran into difficulty with MGM when he wanted to cast Nicholson's girlfriend, former Mamas and the Papas singer Michelle Phillips, in the Lana Turner part. MGM refused Ashby's request to cast Phillips, as well as one other actor, and eventually the whole deal fell apart.[1] Nicholson eventually did do a remake of *The Postman Always Rings Twice* in 1981 (Bob Rafelson directed) with Jessica Lange. The film was a flop.

Ashby and Nicholson still wanted to work together, and Nicholson had another project at Columbia Pictures, a film version of Darryl Ponicsan's novel *The Last Detail*. (Ashby had been sent the script earlier, but had passed on it, but with Nicholson on board was now interested.) Nicholson's longtime friend, screenwriter Robert Towne, was working on the adaptation as a vehicle for Nicholson, who would play Navy lifer Billy "Badass" Buddusky. Buddusky and another lifer, "Mule" Mulhall, are assigned to take an 18-year old seaman first class, Larry Meadows, to the brig for a eight-year sentence after Meadows was caught stealing $40 from a cashbox for the base commanding officer's wife's favorite charity. The film covers a period of several days while Mule and Badass transport Meadows to the brig, during which time they have a series of adventures in order to give the young prisoner a taste of life's experiences before he has to serve his unfairly lengthy sentence. Towne modified the novel a bit, eliminating its depiction of Buddusky as a closet intellectual, and modifying the ending. (The film ends after Mule and Badass have dropped Meadows off at the Portsmouth Naval Prison. In the novel, the two are so distraught at having to take Meadows to prison that they go AWOL and are eventually killed. Ashby and Towne did not think this ending was realistic.)

Columbia was reluctant to hire Ashby to direct, having heard that he often fought with studios and was hard to control. But Nicholson insisted and had enough pull to carry the day. As the film was critical of the Navy, the U.S. Navy was not interested in allowing filming on their bases, so Ashby went to Canada for his locations. In the summer of 1972, while going through customs in Toronto, Ashby was busted for marijuana possession. He was eventually pardoned by a Canadian court, but in the meantime, to appease a nervous Columbia, Ashby trimmed his hair and shaved his beard in order to clean up his act a bit.

The Last Detail went into production with a budget of $2.6 million. There was a delay when Rupert Crosse, the actor cast as Mule, developed terminal cancer just before the scheduled start date. Ashby pushed production back a week, but Crosse eventually had to withdraw and Otis Young stepped in.[2] Randy Quaid and a young John Travolta were the finalists for the crucial part of Meadows (Nicholson wanted singer John Denver, but to no avail), but in the end Ashby chose Quaid, whom Ashby had seen in *The Last Picture Show*; he had "a naïve quality" that the director liked.[3] With his 6'4" frame towering over Nicholson's Buddusky, Quaid fit the part of the kleptomaniac oddball Meadows perfectly.

Along with Beau Bridges' Elgar and Bud Cort's Harold, Quaid was the latest incarnation of Ashby's vision of tainted youth, crushed by lost innocence and problematic parental relations. While both Elgar and Harold have mothers who dote and interfere too much, Meadows suffers from the opposite, parental neglect. When Mule and Badass take Meadows to his mother's home to say goodbye, they find the small, rundown house deserted and a mess, filled with trash and empty booze bottles. It becomes clear that Meadows' sad background has contributed to his problems with theft and melancholia, and the scene is the first one in the movie in which Mule and Badass begin to realize that their efforts to show Meadows a good time are destined to fail.

In the December 5, 1976, *New York Times*, Ashby was interviewed by film writer Aljean Harmitz. The article ends with this interesting comment: "Ashby describes himself most often as 'naïve.'"[4] Indeed, it is this naïve, almost innocent quality that holds together the protagonists of Ashby's best films. Certainly Elgar Enders, Harold Chasen and Larry Meadows have it. From Ashby's later films I would also include George Roundy from *Shampoo*, Woody Guthrie in *Bound for Glory*, Luke Martin in *Coming Home* and Chance from *Being There* as other examples of this tendency. In the 1980s, when Ashby got away from featuring "naïve," somewhat innocent and "lost" type of characters, his films seemed to suffer.

The Last Detail is a somber film shot in muted colors, as different in tone and style from the brown and green earth tones of *Harold and*

14. After Harold and Maude: Hal Ashby

Maude as possible. A road film populated with lovable misfits seeking to soak up life's experiences, it functions as a wry commentary on the confusion of American life in the early 1970s, particularly amongst young people. Meadows, Mule and Badass go from one crazy situation to the next, beginning by getting drunk and eventually going to a whorehouse (so Meadows can lose his virginity) and finally stumbling upon a group practicing a recent trend, Transcendental Meditation. But in the end, no great insight into life is gained by the adventures they experience; it can't change the sad reality of Meadows' lengthy prison sentence, or even of Badass and Mules' own "sentence" as lifers in the Navy, as they are confronted by the officious Marine Duty Officer (Michael Moriarty) who berates them for their handling of Meadows in transit, and for not getting their orders filled out properly. In the end, Mule and Badass go their separate ways, vowing only to see each other back at the base, and cursing the Navy for giving them "this damn lousy detail!"

As would become his habit, Ashby took longer editing the film than the studio wanted. He fired his first editor and hired Robert C. Jones, who became a regular associate of Ashby. The first cut of the film received an R rating due to the profanity. Columbia released it on a limited basis in December 1973 to qualify for Academy Award consideration. Nicholson, Quaid and Towne were Oscar-nominated, and Nicholson won the best acting award at the 1974 Cannes Film Festival, while the movie was nominated for the Palme d'Or. Released wide in the spring of 1974, *The Last Detail* received good reviews and did solid business, taking in $10 million domestically. Hal Ashby had his first hit on his hands.

Screenwriter Robert Towne helped Ashby land his next project, which ended up being his biggest commercial success. Towne and Warren Beatty were both working on scripts about a Hollywood hair stylist of the late 1960s who was loosely based on Beverly Hills hairdresser Gene Shacove, with elements of Jay Sebring, Vidal Sassoon and Warren Beatty himself thrown in. Beatty intended to write, produce, direct and star in the film, but Towne convinced him to bring in Ashby as director and to help them merge their two scripts into one. For six days in November 1973, the three men plus a secretary worked frantically at a Hollywood hotel on the script. Ashby suggested that the film be set on Election Eve 1968, when Richard Nixon defeated Hubert Humphrey in a divisive election that was too close to call until the morning. The film, called *Shampoo*, eventually went before the cameras in the spring of 1974, with Beatty as the protagonist George Roundy. Julie Christie played Jackie, his longtime love who is now the mistress of Lester Carpf, played by Jack Warden. Roundy is sleeping with Lester's wife Felicia (Lee Grant again) while also trying to maintain his relationship with girlfriend Jill, played by Goldie Hawn.

Shampoo overcame its soap opera elements with incisive humor to become a devastating commentary on the shallowness of the lives of the rich and famous in America in the late 1960s. Audiences loved the film upon its release in the spring and summer of 1975, just at a time when the country was trying to overcome the effects of the traumatic Watergate scandal. *Shampoo* ended up being a massive hit with both the public and film critics alike, pulling down $49 million and ending up as one of the top-grossing films of the year.

Michael Douglas wanted Ashby to direct the forthcoming film version of *One Flew Over the Cuckoo's Nest*, but producer Saul Zaentz didn't hit it off with Ashby and, as he was the man writing the checks, the job eventually went to Czech director Milos Forman.[5] Despite the *Cuckoo* disappointment, Ashby next took on an ambitious project, the Woody Guthrie biopic *Bound for Glory*. Starring David Carradine as Guthrie, the film was released in late 1976 and, while not a commercial hit, was critically lauded and Oscar-nominated for Best Picture. Cinematographer Haskell Wexler won for an Oscar for the film, which (along with *Rocky*) is generally credited with being the first film to use the steadicam, a camera-balancing device that allowed for very smooth handheld traveling shots.

In 1977, Ashby directed *Coming Home*. It was about the Vietnam War and its effects on life at home, with a script by Nancy Dowd. Waldo Salt had taken over the writing of the film (Ashby never even saw the Dowd script or heard about her work on the film until much later) and John Schlesinger was set to direct at one point. Ultimately Schlesinger backed out, feeling that it was inappropriate for a Brit to direct a film so critical of the American war effort in Vietnam, and so Ashby signed on the project. Ashby originally intended to cast Jack Nicholson as Luke Martin, the paraplegic Vietnam War veteran who is befriended by Jane Fonda's Sally Hyde when she volunteers at a hospital for dis-

14. After Harold and Maude: Hal Ashby

abled vets. Jon Voight was to play Bob Hyde, Sally's officer husband who goes to fight in Vietnam believing it is a righteous cause, only to return home (having shot himself "accidentally" in the leg) to find his marriage in ruins along with his view of the world. But Voight really wanted to play Luke, and when Nicholson dropped out due to scheduling problems, Ashby quickly shifted Voight's role to Luke and brought on outstanding character actor Bruce Dern to play Bob Hyde.

Coming Home returns to the anti-war message depicted humorously in *Harold and Maude*, but it does so in order to show the tragic consequences of an unjust war on the lives of young men and even women. Ashby used actual injured Vietnam War vets in several scenes, including the opener in which Voight is playing pool with a group of men who discuss the war and its effect on them. Ashby had cameraman Haskell Wexler shoot the intimate scenes from a distance, with a long lens, in order to "give the scenes a sense of beauty and voyeurism, as though the audience were looking through a keyhole at something intensely private and real." Jane Fonda noted, "The improvisational nature of our acting added to this feeling of cinema verité." Ashby's ability to select the perfect music also helped the film succeed. According to Fonda, the music "was all Hal. He wallpapered the film with the essential music of the '60s, and all of us who had lived through it were transported back to the rage, the existential angst, the desperate idealism of the time."[6]

Coming Home was nominated for Best Picture of 1978, Ashby for Best Director and Dern and Penelope Milford for Best Supporting Actor and Actress. They didn't win, but Jane Fonda and Jon Voight took home Oscar statuettes for Best Actor and Actress. In addition, the film won a Best Original Screenplay Oscar for Dowd, Salt and Ashby editor Robert C. Jones, a Vietnam vet who stepped in to work on the script after Salt suffered a heart attack.

In 1978 Ashby entered into a three-picture deal with Lorimar Pictures, a production company known for television shows such as *Dallas*. Although Ashby's first film released by the company, *Being There*, was highly successful, the deal ended up being a turning point in his career ... and not in a good way. Based on a novel by Jerzy Kozinski, *Being There* had long been planned as a project for Ashby and Peter Sellers, who would play the gardener Chance. Chance has lived his entire life in the confines of the home of his wealthy employer and only knows about the outside world by what he has seen on television, but once the employer dies, Chance—the ultimate innocent and naïve Ashby character—is cast out into a world with which he is not familiar. At once confused, bemused and banal, Chance eventually works his way into the home of rich industrialist Ben Rand and his wife Eve, who falls in love with him. Despite his lack of education, after a series of bizarre incidents, Chance becomes thought of as a brilliant economic advisor to Rand and, after the old man dies, Chance seemingly takes his place as heir to the Rand empire.

Sellers and Ashby worked perfectly together. Ashby's willingness to allow actors to improvise was right up Sellers' alley; Ashby shot take after take of the English actor to get the best from him. A hit when released in late 1979, *Being There* turned out to be Sellers' last completed film as he died in the summer of 1980.

Ashby's second film for Lorimar, *Second Hand Hearts*, didn't work out so well. Based on a script by Charles Eastman called *The Hampster of Happiness* that had been bouncing around for several years, the film had a troubled production when Ashby and star Robert Blake did not get along well. It was bogged down for two years in post-production; Lorimar finally sold it off to Paramount, which gave the film a very limited release in only six markets in the spring of 1981. A meandering road film featuring the type of lovable losers who had previously seemed so appealing in Ashby's films, *Second Hand Hearts* was panned by critics and ignored by the public, and turned out to be Ashby's first outright failure.

Ashby's career really hit a snag with his final film for Lorimar, *Lookin' to Get Out*. Based on an original script written by a friend of Jon Voight's, it told the story of gambler Alex Kovac (Voight) and his friend Jerry Feldman (Burt Young) who leave New York to escape a gambling debt that Alex owes. In Las Vegas they end up at a casino run by Bernie Gold (Richard Bradford), who has taken up with Alex's former love Patty Warner (Ann-Margret). When Feldman is mistaken for a high roller with the same name, the casino comps Alex and Jerry a suite and line of credit, which Alex uses to try to raise the money to pay his gambling debt while at the same time trying to woo back Patty.

14. After Harold and Maude: Hal Ashby

In the end, Alex gets the New York gamblers off his back but must agree to leave Las Vegas and Patty, even after meeting his young daughter (played by Angelina Jolie, Jon Voight's real-life daughter, in her first screen role) for the first time.

Lookin' to Get Out went wildly over budget and schedule, eventually costing $17 million. As usual, Ashby took months trying to edit the film to a releasable length. Whereas he had rescued several films in the past, unfortunately this time he couldn't pull it off. *Lookin' to Get Out* was finally taken from the director by Lorimar and recut, and was eventually released in the fall of 1982. It was pulled from theaters after only a short run and box office receipts of just over a million dollars. In the meantime, Ashby had taken so long editing the film that he missed a chance to direct *Tootsie*, the hilarious Dustin Hoffman cross-dressing comedy that became one of the biggest hits of the year. The double whammy badly damaged Ashby's career.

The 1982 *L.A. Times* article "Whatever Happened to Hal Ashby" said it all: Ashby's career was considered on the wane and there was speculation that drug use was contributing to his unreliability. The truth is that Ashby was working harder than ever, but his continued battles with studio heads were now undercutting him when the films he was making did not turn out well. A concert film of the Rolling Stones, *Let's Spend the Night Together*, shot during their 1981 tour and released to moderate success in early 1983, did little to reverse Ashby's downturn. His next film was a comedy based on a script by Neil Simon, *The Slugger's Wife*, starring Michael O'Keefe and Rebecca De Mornay. It was not a good fit for Ashby and died a quick death at the box office. The film that followed it, *Eight Million Ways to Die* with Jeff Bridges and Rosanna Arquette, showed much more promise but Ashby was inexplicably fired before he had a chance to edit the film and it too flopped.

Taking a break from the studio politics of feature films, Ashby directed the pilot for a TV series called *Beverly Hills Buntz* in 1987 and the following year he went to England to direct *Jake's Journey*, a proposed TV series with Monty Python member Graham Chapman.

Many of Ashby's contemporaries also suffered severe career downturns in the early 1980s, as audience tastes seemed to quickly change and move from personal films featuring offbeat characters to movies that were more conventional and a throwback to earlier times. Robert Altman, after directing a series of critical and commercial hits in the early '70s, went into a slump following the success of 1975's *Nashville*. After *Popeye* (1980), a difficult and troubled production that went far over budget, he stopped making features and for most of the 1980s directed either very small productions or TV movies, before he staged a comeback with the 1992 hit *The Player*. Roman Polanski totally disappeared from the scene after *Tess* (1979), finally returning with *Pirates* (1986), an enormous flop. His follow-up, 1988's *Frantic*, was also a critical and commercial disappointment, and Polanski did not really return to the limelight until *The Pianist* was a success in 2002. Francis Ford Coppola did not fare well after *Apocalypse Now* was released to acclaim in 1979. His 1982 film *One from the Heart* was such a box office catastrophe that Coppola had to declare bankruptcy and spent years trying to repair the financial damage the film caused him. Later films like *The Cotton Club* (1984), *Gardens of Stone* (1987) and *Tucker* (1988) were all commercial flops for the director of *The Godfather*.

What these directors had that Ashby didn't was the time and opportunity to eventually make a comeback. After *Jake's Journey*, Ashby pursued several projects, including the English film *Vital Parts* and Richard Brautigan's *The Hawkline Monster*, a longtime project that appeared to be on the verge of fruition.

In 1988, Ashby, not been feeling well, saw a doctor on the advice of Warren Beatty. The news was devastating: pancreatic cancer had set in, and the odds for a recovery were long. Despite emergency surgery at Johns Hopkins, Ashby could not overcome the disease and he passed away on December 27, 1988, at the age of 59. Three days after his death, a memorial service was held at the Directors Guild, organized by old friends from *Harold and Maude*: Bud Cort, Pablo Ferro, Mike Haller and Jeff Wexler. Acquaintances, work associates—and even actors who had never worked with Ashby, such as Sean Penn—spoke of him in glowing terms.[7] Later, Ashby's ashes were scattered in the Pacific Ocean right across from his home in the Malibu Colony by Wexler, Jeff Bridges, Jerry Hellman and another Ashby family member. His friends and associates were stunned at the director's early death.[8]

Due to his collaborative nature and unassuming style, Ashby had never gained the reputation of the other hot young directors of the

14. After Harold and Maude: Hal Ashby

"New Hollywood" period. The success of *Shampoo* and *Coming Home* were largely chalked up to the films' stars, Warren Beatty and Jane Fonda, respectively. This combined with Hal's late career downswing and relatively early death—with no chance for a career resurgence—resulted in Ashby becoming a victim of critical neglect. It took over 20 years for a biography about Ashby to appear: Nick Dawson's *Being Hal Ashby: Life of a Hollywood Rebel*, published in 2009. Finally directors such as Wes Anderson, Judd Apatow, the Coen brothers and David O. Russell began to acknowledge the influence of Ashby's style of personal filmmaking on their own efforts.

The man who once directed the ultimate cult film, Hal Ashby, now appears to have become something of a cult figure himself. The "cult of Ashby" has grown surely and steadily over the few years since the publication of Nick Dawson's book. In hindsight, Ashby appears remarkably fresh with the passing of time. His long hair and casual dress made him an unusual figure in Hollywood, even during the 1970s, but now it seems like a great badge of honor, something that he wore proudly. His commitment to making films about iconoclastic and individualistic anti-heroes now makes him an even more refreshing figure and adds to his appeal in the rear view mirror of time. And the fact that he crashed and burned in the somewhat more conservative 1980s is now far from being a drawback; in fact, it is a credit to his endearing style and persevering mentality.

Ashby's battles against "the suits," the people he regarded as his enemies, the studio executives who watched the budgets and worried about the marketing of films, were eventually his downfall. Orson Welles called moviemaking a "terribly expensive paint box" and it is; when all was going well for Ashby, when his movies were connecting with his audiences and making money, he could afford to be the somewhat contradictory artist, uncompromising and unrelenting, thinking of the film first and nothing else second. But when it began to go against him, whether it was changing audience tastes or a decline in the quality of his films, it went against him hard and it went against him badly. His fall from grace was quick and merciless, and his untimely, early death made sure there would be no recovery.

But the story of Hal Ashby is more than a Shakespearean tragedy. Fans now admire him because his style was gentle and collaborative, and his approach to filmmaking broke the mold of the hard-driving

Hollywood studio director. At times he could explode in anger and frustration, but he took the opinions of many into account when making his films, from the actors to the lowliest technician in the background. It was a group process at its best, and though it was clear that he was in charge, he made everyone feel like they had some kind of say. Anyone who has made films knows that this is the best way to do it, though it might make the process somewhat more difficult, gut-wrenching and lengthy. Despite all this, Ashby directed 12 films in 15 years, so his output was high, and the results were mostly very good.

Many of Ashby's co-workers are still around and making films, and their comments about Ashby have helped people who never met him understand him better. Beau and Jeff Bridges, Jack Nicholson, Randy Quaid, Warren Beatty, Goldie Hawn, Jane Fonda, Jon Voight and Shirley MacLaine have all continued acting well into the 21st century, and their high opinion of Ashby and his style have added to the status and mystique of the man. With a major biography of Ashby already published and a documentary film on the way, a new generation can now get to know and love a filmmaker who truly deserves the attention.

Norman Jewison once told Ashby: "We must always maneuver and cope with the realities of life—both personal and business—and continue to try and create beautiful and meaningful films, no matter what the cost to pride and emotional frustration."[9] There is no doubt that Ashby lived a sometimes tumultuous personal life that caused him problems at times, and that he often raged at the system of filmmaking that he was forced to work within. Nonetheless, when one looks at Ashby's career, it is amazing that he turned out the marvelous films that he did, and that he did it over a relatively short period of time.

Ashby's work as a director and moviemaker, who bucked the system and stretched at every opportunity to get the freedom to make the films he wanted, has finally been embraced by a younger generation. He is now remembered as one of the great directors of the "New Hollywood" era, a filmmaker whose works are a tribute to him, someone to admire and hold in highest esteem.

15

After *Harold and Maude*: The Rest of the Cast and Crew

Harold and Maude's box office failure didn't really affect the career of Ruth Gordon. At 75, she continued to work regularly, mostly in television. She was pleased that *Harold and Maude* continued to grow in reputation, attending both the one- and two-year anniversaries of the movie at the Westgate Theater in Edina. In 1983, reflecting on the legacy of her part as Maude, she told Aljean Harmitz: "If I'd never gotten a profit check, it would have been worth it. People stop me in the street. In Paris, they say, 'C'est Maude!' They send presents, gifts to share with me like a painting of something the giver loves. Yesterday I was leaving the house, all dressed up in my pink dress, when the tour bus came to the end of my street. 'And there she is,' the people on the bus shouted and they started to applaud."[1]

In 1978, she co-starred as "Ma" in Clint Eastwood's comedy hit *Every Which Way But Loose*, and reprised the role in the 1980 sequel *Any Which Way You Can*. These appearances plus a part in the 1980 hit *My Bodyguard* kept Gordon in the eye of the filmgoing public well into her 80s. Her last major film appearance was as the landlady, Mrs. Lavin, in the 1985 comedy *Maxie* with Glenn Close and Mandy Patinkin. The film, set in San Francisco, was the story of the ghost of a 1920s flapper who takes over the body of a woman named Jan.

In *Harold and Maude*, Gordon had noted that by age 85 you are "just marking time." Gordon had made it past that age, but eventually time caught up with her, and on August 28, 1985, she passed away from a stroke in Edgartown, Massachusetts, not too far from Quincy, where she had been born 88 years earlier.

Being the least established of the major figures associated with the film, Colin Higgins had the most to gain from *Harold and Maude* being a success and so, when the film appeared to flop, he also had the most to lose. He noted later, somewhat tongue-in-cheek, that his career did not immediately take off after the film came out. In 1972, Higgins wrote a made-for-TV movie, *The Devil's Daughter*, that he described as "just a job." Also that year, he was commissioned to write a stage version of *Harold and Maude* by French director Jean-Louis Barrault. As noted before, the play ran in Europe for seven years in repertory and is still revived around the world. He continued to work in the theater for a time, and in 1974 adapted for the stage an anthropological study of a displaced African tribe. British director Peter Brook's company toured that play, *The Ik*, which Colin co-wrote, throughout the U.S. during the 1976 Bicentennial Year as a gift from the French government to the American people.

Higgins considered a number of different story ideas in the years following *Harold and Maude*, including at one point the idea of a film about the first 30 years of the life of Christ. Higgins also thought about making a movie about American history totally from a Native American point of view, as well as a kid's film called *Flunk, the Flunky Dragon*. Other ideas that ran through his ever-creative mind were *The Man Who Looked Like Lenin*, a satire on MGM musicals, a three-part Western and a horror film called *The House of Dr. Pretorious*.

In 1976 Higgins returned to Hollywood with a script for a movie that was eventually called *Silver Streak*, an homage to director Alfred Hitchcock's 1959 film *North by Northwest* as well as Hitch's earlier (1938) *The Lady Vanishes*. Starring Gene Wilder, Jill Clayburgh and rising comedian Richard Pryor, *Silver Streak* was deftly directed by veteran Arthur Hiller and proved to be a major hit when it was released, eventually grossing over $50 million. Now on the map in a big way, Higgins was tabbed to write and direct Goldie Hawn and film newcomer Chevy Chase in his 1978 film *Foul Play*, another Hitchcock-influenced movie, this time set in San Francisco. *Foul Play* was a second major hit for Higgins, well received by critics and audiences alike.

In the wake of his success, Higgins considered writing a sequel, as well as a prequel, to *Harold and Maude*. According to an August 6, 1978, article by Marilyn Beck, "Higgins eyes *Harold's Story*," he wanted to write a film "that would focus on Harold's life without Maude" and that he would like to work with Bud Cort again. Beck suggested that

15. After Harold and Maude: Cast and Crew

the sequel would be appropriate in the wake of Paramount's decision to make a sequel to its 1970 hit *Love Story*, entitled *Oliver's Story* (the film was made with Ryan O'Neal and Candice Bergen, and it flopped).[2] Higgins and Cort had remained friendly and stayed in touch after *Harold and Maude*. In 1974, Cort sent Higgins a note inquiring about his plans for the future and mentioning that he was going to see Ruth Gordon soon and was planning to take her to dinner to introduce her to singer Bette Midler.

The Beck article also mentioned that Higgins was interested in doing a prequel to *Harold and Maude* called *Grover and Maude*, pairing Ruth Gordon with Richard Pryor's *Silver Streak* character, Grover Muldoon. The story was to take place in the 1960s in San Francisco, where Grover is a civil libertarian Black Panther whose life is consumed with hate until he meets Maude. Under the influence of Maude, Grover's life begins to turn around as he sees things from her point of view. But Maude gets one important thing out of the relationship: Grover is a thief and he teaches her how to steal cars, something that she puts to good use later in life. Recalling, perhaps, the extent to which Pryor had ad-libbed and improvised his way through his scenes in *Silver Streak*, essentially re-writing the character of Grover as he went along, Higgins decided that he did not want to pursue the idea of making *Grover and Maude*.[3] Neither it nor *Harold's Story* ever ended up seeing the light of day as a film project.

With his next film, *Nine to Five* (1980), Higgins broke out of the mold of Hitchcock imitator and crafted a funny and compelling film about three women, Judy, Doralee and Violet (Lily Tomlin, Jane Fonda and Dolly Parton) who work in an office with the boss from Hell, Franklin Hart (Dabney Coleman). The women wrongly believe they have accidentally killed Hart, then end up kidnapping him to keep him quiet while they take over the office and implement their ideas on improving the workplace. When the ideas work, the newly freed Hart quickly takes credit, but eventually ends up promoting the women and going along with their changes. A groundbreaking film, *Nine to Five* addressed the issues of sexual harassment and workplace inequality—and it didn't hurt that it was a huge success, grossing over $100 million.

Higgins had another hit in 1982 with an adaptation of T*he Best Little Whorehouse in Texas* with Dolly Parton and Burt Reynolds, but the 1980s would ultimately not be kind to him. Higgins contracted AIDS in 1985, years before medical treatments were developed for the disease, and he passed away its the effects on August 5, 1988. Higgins was aware that the disease was fatal and, in order to leave a legacy and help others, he established the Colin Higgins Foundation. Dedicated to supporting LGBT youth in underserved communities, the Foundation annually awards the Colin Higgins Youth Courage Awards for bravery in the face of discrimination, intolerance and bigotry based on sexual orientation and/or gender. Since 1993, the Foundation has awarded over 341 grants totaling over $3 million to further the humanitarian vision of Colin Higgins.[4]

Not surprisingly, Bud Cort found himself somewhat typecast. In *Brewster McCloud* and *Harold and Maude* he played oddball parts in box office flops, not a promising career start. Cort did not make a movie for another five years, concentrating on Broadway instead; he appeared in the play *Wise Child* in 1972. In 1975 he was offered the role of Billy Bibbit in the film of *One Flew Over the Cuckoo's Nest*, but Cort was sensitive to the fact that Bibbit's character is not only in a mental institution, but is a mama's boy who commits suicide at the end. Having had enough of that kind of role, Cort decided to pass on it, not wanting to typecast himself further, and the part went to Brad Dourif. In 1977 he appeared in the Canadian film *Why Shoot the Teacher?* with Samantha Eggar, which went on to become one of Canada's highest grossing films. *Why Shoot the Teacher?* got a belated U.S. release in the early 1980s.

An interesting sidebar to Cort's life was his friendship with Groucho Marx. Cort met Marx at a party shortly after completing *Harold and Maude* and someone mentioned that he'd just done a movie with Ruth Gordon. Always ready to shock, Marx immediately said, "She had the hots for Harpo." After that, the two hit it off and Groucho invited Bud to have lunch with him the following week. Cort lived as a houseguest of Marx's for several years in the 1970s, becoming a close friend and caregiver to the great comic actor, who passed away in 1977 "in my arms," according to Cort.[5] However, Cort's career was severely disrupted in 1979 when he was in a near-fatal Hollywood Freeway acci-

15. After Harold and Maude: Cast and Crew

dent. Cort was driving at night, returning from a Frank Sinatra concert, when he rear-ended a car that had been abandoned on the freeway without warning lights or flashers; he endured suffer years of surgeries, operations and physical therapy. He eventually recovered, but facial scars and disfigurement caused him to lose jobs and a lengthy lawsuit

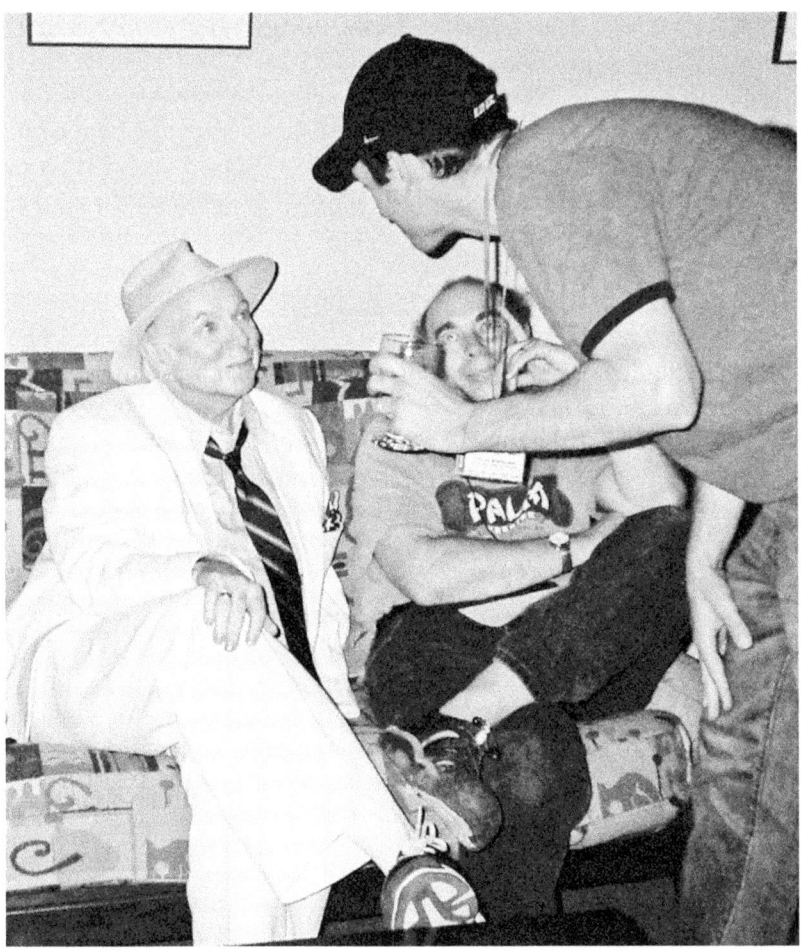

Bud Cort (seated left) greets a fan at the Maine International Film Festival in 2007. Cort found himself typecast after *Harold and Maude*, and a serious automobile accident in 1979 also slowed his career. In the last 15 years, though, he has found steady film and TV jobs and also voice work (courtesy Tiwanna Ellerbe).

against the driver of the other car further distracted Cort from getting his career back on track.

Eventually Bud began to work again in television, returning to feature films in the late '90s in *Dogma, Coyote Ugly* and *Pollock*. In 2004, he had a featured role in the Wes Anderson film *The Life Aquatic with Steve Zissou* with Bill Murray and Owen Wilson.

Cort has been reluctant to speak much about *Harold and Maude*. During a 2000 appearance on the *Roseanne* talk show, he even taped his mouth shut in an effort not to speak about the role that made him famous. Understandably annoyed that he has never received any additional payments from Paramount despite its eventual financial success, Cort is unwilling to discuss his role as Harold. He continues to act regularly, including a voice-only appearance in *The Little Prince* with Rachel McAdams.

Vivian Pickles returned to England after *Harold and Maude*, appearing in Lindsay Anderson's 1973 film *O Lucky Man!* with Malcolm McDowell and his 1982 *Britannia Hospital*. She appeared frequently on British television, starring with Judi Dench in the 1980 mini-series *Love in a Cold Climate*. She continued to act regularly in England through the 1990s. Pickles was married to New Zealand actor Gordon Gostelow for 43 years until his death in 2007, and they have a son who, as far as I know, has never tried to commit suicide for his mother's benefit.

Charles Tyner was a regular Hollywood character actor throughout the 1970s and '80s. His most memorable part came in Robert Aldrich's 1974 prison comedy *The Longest Yard* as Unger the murderous prison snitch. Alfred Hitchcock loved *The Longest Yard* and cast several of its actors in his next film *Family Plot* (1976), including Tyner as the headstone maker Wheeler. Tyner went back to the stage in 1977, and in 1981 had a recurring role on the weekly television drama *Father Murphy*. Now past age 90, Tyner is retired from acting.

Eric Christmas, the frustrated priest, acted frequently in character roles in films throughout the 1970s and '80s. He eventually turned to parts in television and continued to act until 1998. In 2000 he passed away at age 84. George Wood, the psychiatrist, also passed away in 2000 at the age of 80. Tom Skerritt, who played the motorcycle cop, has continued to work often in film and television, including a regular role on the 1990s TV series *Picket Fences*.

15. *After* Harold and Maude*: Cast and Crew*

Two of Harold's computer dates acted infrequently in the years following *Harold and Maude*. Judy Engles (Candy Gulf) did several voices in the X-rated animated film *Fritz the Cat*, then went on to write for *ABC Afterschool Specials* in the 1980s. Shari Summers (Edith Phern) married producer Chuck Mulvehill, and had her most notable later part as the wife of Vic Morrow's baseball coach in the 1976 hit *The Bad News Bears*. Ellen Geer (Sunshine Dore) acted frequently throughout the years following *Harold and Maude*, including a regular part on the TV show *Desperate Housewives*. In 1978, upon the death of her father, she took over as the Artistic Director of Will Geer's Theatricum Botanicum, an outdoor amphitheater in Topanga, and turned it into a major cultural institution. A theatrical version of *Harold and Maude* was performed there in 2000, with Ellen taking over the part of Maude. Also a playwright, Geer penned a 1995 play about her father's 1950s blacklisting. In addition to all of her other work, Geer somehow found time to teach acting at UCLA for many years.

Ellen Geer had a wonderful experience working on *Harold and Maude*. She described the time to me as "coming into that world of talented strangers" and that she "was in awe of the film power all around me." She said, "The ideas and love that flows from the script makes this film one that will survive for a long time to come. Love and acceptance matter at any age ... between people in any combination. Despite ridiculous society rules." She was particularly proud of the fact that her performance as Maude at the Theatricum Botanicum seemed to have a strong effect on one young audience member who was troubled and struggling with issues; and through seeing what Harold went through in the play, he had an epiphany that it was okay to be different. *Harold and Maude* has certainly been a life-changing experience for many people, and this is just one example of such an occurrence.[6]

Cat Stevens was at the height of his popularity when *Harold and Maude* debuted, with both *Tea for the Tillerman* and *Teaser and the Firecat* connecting with his audience in a big way. His follow-up album *Catch Bull at Four*, released in the fall of 1972, was one of his most popular, topping the *Billboard* charts for three weeks. Although his next album, *Foreigner*, was a commercial disappointment, he bounced back in 1974 with *Buddha and the Chocolate Box,* and his 1975 *Greatest Hits* collection was a huge seller.

In 1976 Stevens had another near-death experience, as he had when he contracted tuberculosis in 1968. This time he was at a friend's Malibu home when he decided to go for a swim in the Pacific Ocean. The current was stronger than he expected, and he found himself being pulled farther and farther away from shore. Tiring, Stevens realized that the pleasure swim was turning dangerous and that he was at risk of drowning; struggling, he began to pray and asked God to save him, promising that if he did, the singer would dedicate his life to the Lord and away from the earthly pursuits that had preoccupied him for most of his life. As if by a miracle, a moment later the current changed and Stevens was swept back in to the shore.

Shortly thereafter, Stevens' brother David gave him a copy of the Quran, the Islamic book of faith. Always a mystic and searcher for truth, the singer found himself fascinated by the book and the Islamic faith. In 1977 he converted and by 1978 he had released his final album as Cat Stevens and left the music world entirely, becoming totally devoted to Allah and taking a new name, Yusuf Islam. In 1979, he entered into an arranged marriage with a Muslim woman, Fawzia Ali. Deciding that all forms of music were against the faith, he sold all of his guitars and refused to record for many years. The public only heard of him when he was involved in controversies. In 1989, for instance, he made comments that were interpreted to be supporting the Ayatollah Khomeini's death sentence of writer Salman Rushdie; and after the 9/11 attacks he was placed on a "no fly" list that prevented him from entering the United States.

But Yusuf Islam eventually decided that turning his back totally on his Cat Stevens persona was wrong, and he slowly began to return to the world of music where he had achieved his great fame. He released a new album in 2006 to positive reviews, and he began to again record music. In 2009 he participated in a tribute to Hal Ashby in Los Angeles, and in 2011 he was interviewed for the Criterion Collection release of *Harold and Maude*. In 2014 he released the new album *Tell 'Em I'm Gone* and undertook his first worldwide tour in many years, including stops in the United States. Embracing and being embraced by the music world again after a long absence, he was finally inducted into the Rock and Roll Hall of Fame, also in 2014.

15. After Harold and Maude: Cast and Crew

Peter Bart left Paramount and moved on to be vice-president of production at MGM, then president of Lorimar, where he worked with Ashby during his troublesome tenure there. In 1989 Bart returned to his original calling, journalism, when he became *Variety*'s editor-in-chief. Bart also wrote a number of books on Hollywood and, in 2003, he began co-hosting an AMC series about the movie industry, *Shootout* with Peter Guber.

Robert Evans stayed on as Paramount head of production until 1974, the year that he branched out as an independent producer and made *Chinatown*. Directed by Roman Polanski and written by Robert Towne, *Chinatown* is now considered a masterpiece of the "New Hollywood" era. Evans decided to move into independent production fulltime and leave his position as Paramount chief, fearing there would be a conflict of interest. The move served him well for a while, as he produced the hits *Marathon Man* and *Urban Cowboy*, but in the '80s and '90s he lost his Midas touch as his productions *The Cotton Club*, *The Two Jakes* and *Sliver* all bombed. Evans' best-selling biography *The Kid Stays in the Picture* was turned into a documentary several years later, and he remains a legendary figure in the landscape of Hollywood filmmaking.

Chuck Mulvehill went on to work on several of Ashby's later films including *The Last Detail, Bound for Glory* and *Being There*. A producer in the 1980s and '90s, he worked on a variety of interesting films including the remake of *The Postman Always Rings Twice, The Godfather Part III, Dracula, Dolores Claiborne* and *The Last Samurai*. In the 1975 Antonioni film *The Passenger*, Mulvehill played the dead man that Jack Nicholson trades places with (the same age as Nicholson, Mulvehill bore a striking resemblance to the actor).

John Alonzo photographed some of the best-known films of the '70s and '80s including *Chinatown, The Bad News Bears, Blue Thunder* and *Steel Magnolias*. He passed away in March 2001 at 66. Production designer Michael Haller also passed away prematurely in 1998. He worked on a number of Ashby's films in the 1970s, including *Coming Home*, as well as Ashby's last feature, *Eight Million Ways to Die* and a handful of other films.

Working on *Harold and Maude* ending up being a life-changing experience for production assistant Jeff Wexler, who prior to the job had not intended on following his father's footsteps into the movie industry. Beginning in 1972, Jeff began working in film as a sound recorder and mixer, providing sound mixing and design on dozens of features including six for Ashby. When Colin Higgins was looking for a sound mixer for his first directorial effort, *Foul Play,* Ashby told him that Wexler had begun working in the field and, as the two had developed a friendship and good working relationship during *Harold and Maude,* Colin hired Jeff for *Foul Play* and for his next film, *Nine to Five.* Wexler has been nominated for two Academy Awards and a prime time Emmy Award and won a BAFTA Film Award in 2001 for *Almost Famous.* He certainly owes much of the career that he has had to the little movie that he worked on back in 1971, as well as the relationship that he formed with Hal Ashby.

16

The Legacy of *Harold and Maude*

Harold and Maude has had a long-lasting and enduring legacy. Aside from its eventual cult success, the film has also been transformed into a novel and a play, and in 1978 was turned into a made-for-TV movie in France. In February 1980, the play came to Broadway, opening at the Martin Beck Theater, with film veteran Janet Gaynor playing Maude and Keith McDermott as Harold. Unfortunately, the play was not as successful on Broadway as it had been in Europe, and it closed on February the 9th after only four performances. Critics commented that what had been endearing on film seemed corny and unconvincing on the stage.

Unwilling to die, the play was revived as a regional theater musical in 2005 at the Paper Mill Playhouse in New Jersey, with well-known actress Estelle Parsons playing Maude. Veteran librettist Tom Jones ("The Fantasticks") and scoring partner Joseph Thalken did the music. *Variety* was not particularly kind, the reviewer commenting, "The new incarnation has several points in its favor, chief among them two engaging leads, but still seems a long way from finding a robust commercial form."[1] The West Coast premiere of the play, now called *Harold and Maude: An Intimate Musical*, took place later in 2005 in the Bay Area in Palo Alto at the Lucie Stern Theatre.

Harold and Maude was released on VHS home video in the 1980s, and a DVD version was released in 2000. In 2012, just after its 40-year anniversary, the Criterion Collection issued a restored, hi-def Blu-ray which includes a booklet on the film, a newly shot interview with Yusuf Islam (Cat Stevens) and audio excerpts of Hal Ashby and Colin Higgins' comments about the film during AFI seminars in 1972 and 1979 respectively. The Blu-ray also contains an audio commentary by Ashby biographer Nick Dawson and producer Chuck Mulvehill.

Ruth Gordon was initially surprised when Hal Ashby hesitated to cast her, but the two got along wonderfully during the filming.

Harold and Maude stayed firmly in the hearts and minds of movie fans, resulting in its high ranking in polls. In June 2008, the film was ranked #9 on the American Film Institute's list of the ten greatest films in the genre "Romantic Comedy." In 2000, during a televised special, the AFI listed the film as #45 on its list of *AFI's 100 Years ... 100 Laughs: America's Funniest Movies*. Additionally, the film was listed #89 in the

16. The Legacy of Harold and Maude

2006 special *AFI's 100 Years ... 100 Cheers: America's Most Inspiring Movies*. In 1997, it was selected for preservation by the National Film Preservation Board.

For fans of the movie, as well as fans of Bud Cort, Ruth Gordon, Colin Higgins and Hal Ashby, the movie *Harold and Maude* lives on in a big way. In 1997 "The Unofficial *Harold and Maude*" homepage was launched by fan Mike Sullivan. The site contains a number of interesting entries: trivia, pictures, history, reviews and a very comprehensive guide to the Bay Area locations used in the film (some of which were helpful to me as I went "in search of" *Harold and Maude* locations for my own edification). The website also features entries from fans of the film who were invited to share their love of *Harold and Maude*. Correspondence to the site came from fans from all over the world, from as far away as England, Wales, Germany and Austria, to as close to home as New Jersey, Philadelphia, Omaha and San Francisco. Fans shared their deep love for the movie, including memories of the first time they saw it, how it affected them, and the way that the film and its various positive and uplifting messages helped them cope with personally tragedies and challenges in their lives.

Elsewhere on the web, there are tributes to *Harold and Maude* on film sites such as Rotten Tomatoes, where the film has a 86 percent "Tomatometer" rating and an audience rating of 93 percent who liked the film. On the Internet Movie Database the film has an 8.1 out of 10 ranking and it was reviewed by 285 users from places as far away as Australia, Ireland and Brazil. The TCM website offers a page on *Harold and Maude* with the following observations:

> Not all cult movies age gracefully ... but after more than thirty-four years *Harold and Maude* holds up much better than other cult films of its era such as that other repertory favorite, Philippe de Broca's *King of Hearts* (1966), in which the inmates of an insane asylum escape and take over a French village during World War II. Although both films celebrate the unconventional and individuals who march to the beat of a different drum, *King of Hearts* now seems unbearably cloying and self-indulgent while *Harold and Maude* continues to impress with its lighthearted juggling of such usually grim themes as death, suicide and lives not lived.[2]

While on some levels *Harold and Maude* might seem the ultimate hippie film, the movie really is not. Certainly some of the world views that Maude holds—rebel against authority, the unimportance of possessions, here today and gone tomorrow—were embraced by hippies and the hippie movement. But seeing the film again in the context of later years, it is surprising how "undated" the film feels. *Harold and Maude* is simply a call for people to act out their individual wills and to fight for their own identities and their own personalities, a theme that recurs frequently in Ashby's films. While Harold may appear to hate his mother, expressing the view that many young people felt about their parents' generation in 1971, he really is just venting his hatred of a society that has marginalized and isolated him and kept him from expressing his own unique and individualistic personality. Maude frees him from this trap, and that is one of the things about the film that is so rare and exciting.

Since its release, *Harold and Maude* has influenced many films that feature offbeat, personal characters and "odd couple" relationships. Wes Anderson's 1998 film *Rushmore* features an alienated youth, Max Fisher (Jason Schwartzman), who is very much like Harold Chasen and becomes infatuated with a teacher at his school; he enters into a problematic relationship with a disillusioned industrialist (Bill Murray), who is also in love with the teacher, and the conflict results in a battle of wills between the two. Like *Harold and Maude*, *Rushmore* failed at the box office on its release but has since developed a substantial following and has appeared on several "Best of" lists.

Other recent films such as *Juno* by Jason Reitman and Judd Apatow's *Knocked Up* and *Superbad* feature characters who enter into odd or conflicting relationships, but see them through and learn some life lessons in the bargain. Apatow is an avowed devotee of Hal Ashby and has called him a big influence on his career. Apatow and his wife, actress Leslie Mann, even named their oldest daughter Maude in honor of Ruth Gordon's character. Maude Apatow, now 16, has appeared in three of her father's films, *Knocked Up*, *Funny People* and *This Is 40*. Even Ashby's mentor, Norman Jewison, got into the act when he had a hit with *Moonstruck* (1987), in which an older woman, Loretta (Cher), has an unlikely romance with a younger man, Ronny (Nicolas Cage).

Director David O. Russell, another noted fan of Ashby's films, started off his career with the indie *Spanking the Monkey* (1994), about

16. The Legacy of Harold and Maude

an incestuous mother-son relationship. Later films such as *Flirting with Disaster* and *I Heart Huckabees* indicated that Russell's style would be offbeat movies featuring troubled characters and unusual situations. More recently, his films *Silver Linings Playbook* and *American Hustle* have struck a resonant chord with audiences, indicating that the Ashby style has come back in a big way. Other filmmakers who seem to have been influenced by Ashby's highly personal style include brothers Joel and Ethan Coen, whose films *Barton Fink*, *The Big Lebowski* and *A Serious Man* include the kind of irreverent and unusual characters frequently found in Ashby's works.

Oscar-winning writer-director Cameron Crowe, whose films include *Almost Famous, Vanilla Sky* and *Jerry McGuire*, is also a big fan of *Harold and Maude*. Crowe has commented that the film is "the greatest capsulized story and it's done with music that scratches at your soul." He notes that the film is done very "rock and roll." Crowe enjoys the way the film has a stripped-down style that is very effective and "the movie holds up to this minute."[3]

Ashby has finally begun to be appreciated for the work that he did at crafting so many great films in the 1970s, including *Harold and Maude*. The same year (2009) as Nick Dawson's biography of the director, film scholar Christopher Beach published a comprehensive critical study of Ashby's films. In 2010, Dawson edited *Hal Ashby: Interviews*, a compilation of major interviews and stories written about Ashby. And in 2014, filmmaker Amy Scott began to work on the first full-length film documentary about Ashby's life and films. Entitled *Once I Was: The Hal Ashby Story*, it is supported by a number of significant members of the film industry and is also officially sanctioned by the Hal Ashby estate, and thus has at its disposal a large amount of material that would otherwise be unavailable. It will also feature interviews with a number of people who were important to Ashby's career, such as Jane Fonda, Haskell Wexler, Jon Voight and Pablo Ferro.

The light is also being shined on others who contributed to *Harold and Maude*, particularly its author and creator, Colin Higgins. In 2016 the major documentary *Celebrating Laughter: The Life and Films of Colin Higgins* was completed by Nicholas Eliopoulos. Eliopoulus, who had previously completed a documentary about silent film star Mary Pickford, had also worked on several Higgins films, including *Nine to Five* as supervising sound editor and *The Best Little Whorehouse in*

Texas as a film editor. His documentary features interviews with Fonda, Gene Wilder, Goldie Hawn, Bud Cort and Ed and Millie Lewis, who discuss working with Higgins on his original script for *Harold and Maude*.

On June 25, 2009, the Academy of Motion Picture Arts and Sciences held a major tribute to Ashby at the its Samuel Goldwyn Theater in Beverly Hills. The event, hosted by Peter Bart and Cameron Crowe, featured a panel of actors and technicians who had worked with Ashby, as well as more current members of the film community who had been influenced by Ashby and wanted to express their admiration for his films. Actor-writer Seth Rogan noted that he had seen a poster for *Harold and Maude* at the home of director Judd Apatow and decided, "I had better see this movie!" He watched it as a prelude to writing the script for *Superbad* and, after laughing and crying profusely, he decided, "This Hal Ashby guy is onto something!"[4] After watching *The Last Detail*, Rogan realized that it is possible to inject a raunchy comedy with real emotion, and he used this idea in writing *Superbad*. The film was a major success.

Haskell Wexler was on the panel that night, and noted that as a cinematographer working on a film with Ashby, he didn't talk about the look of a film with Ashby, whom he referred to reverently as not just a director, but "a filmmaker."[5] Jon Voight spoke about the making of *Lookin' to Get Out*, saying "at that time, Hal was *the guy*." He noted that everyone wanted to work with Hal during this period because he set up a very nurturing atmosphere on the set and everyone loved that feeling, which was how he got such great performances. The film screened at the theater that night: *Harold and Maude*, of course.

Why do Ashby's films, and his life, have such resonance with not only his contemporaries, but also with these young performers and film buffs? A key may lie in a comment that Bruce Dern made on the documentary *Hal Ashby—A Man Out of Time*, which appears on the DVD of *Coming Home*: "He would cry ... he cried when I was at the lifeguard stand ... he held on to me maybe 15, 20 seconds." Dern said that Ashby made sure that Dern took off his wedding ring before he waded into the ocean to commit suicide. Ashby conveyed these deep

16. The Legacy of Harold and Maude

emotions to his actors, and those emotions come through and appear on the screen and now, years later, these emotions are still evident and coming through to a new generation of actors and writers.

If this work can make any contribution to the legacy of Hal Ashby as a director, it is to show the many ways that Ashby's creative ideas made *Harold and Maude* a unique film. Not to lessen the contributions of others such as Colin Higgins, but every step of the way Ashby made important decisions that contributed to the creation of the film. From shooting in the San Francisco Bay Area, to casting Ruth Gordon and Bud Cort in the lead roles, to the music of Cat Stevens, to the final editing and preparation of the film, Ashby put his signature on the movie in every possible way. Without him, *Harold and Maude* would surely have been a much different film and thousands of people would not have come to appreciate it for what it is: a rare and wonderful look at life, living and love. Even without *Harold and Maude*, Ashby's legacy would be assured by films like *Shampoo* and *Being There*, but *Harold and Maude* is a major work and one that must be considered first and foremost when contemplating the directorial career of Hal Ashby.

My wife and I were dining recently at a local pizzeria restaurant with our friend Jennifer. We had ordered a family-sized salad that we were going to split, and when it arrived I noticed that one part of the salad had beets. Not being a fan of beets, I suggested to the others that I would be more than happy to pass on the beets if they wanted extra.

Jennifer chuckled to herself. "Beets!" she said. "Ha! *Harold and Maude!*"

She was referring to the scene in which Harold's mother imperiously commands him to eat his beets, and he gobbles them up quickly in order to appease her. My wife and I looked at each other in shock and amazement: Jennifer had no idea of my interest in the film or the fact that I was writing a book about it. It all came up as a total coincidence.

I tell this anecdote in order to illustrate a point about the movie: So many people who have seen *Harold and Maude* feel so personally about the film and equate it to their own life, even many years later. It is a testament to the power of the compelling story that Higgins wrote and Ashby filmed so well. For those fans of *Harold and Maude*, it seems that the film is always with us, in our hearts and our minds, and we are ready to bring it out and revisit it whenever we find the need.

Over 40 years later, *Harold and Maude* is remembered by many as a unique and wonderful journey through the changes that life and love bring. It has a history that is almost as unusual as is the film. Made in a unique period in film history by the "New Hollywood," it was almost killed off many times, but survived and saw the light of day. Although not at first embraced by the public, it became a hit over time, a cult success of major proportions, a film that would not die. It's one of a kind, like many of the people involved in making it. *Harold and Maude* remains the one unalterable and totally rare moment in their careers: a film that gets better with age and is loved and loved some more. In the unforgettable words of Maude: "It's all memorabilia, but incidental and not integral, if you know what I mean." In the case of *Harold and Maude*, the film is not incidental and is certainly integral and not just memorabilia … if you know what I mean!

Chapter Notes

Unless otherwise noted, all letters and other primary source documents are held at the Margaret Herrick Library, Los Angeles.

Chapter 1

1. UCLA website, http://www.tft.ucla.edu/about/history/.
2. Colin Higgins Biography, Higgins papers, UCLA Library Special Collections.
3. Colin Higgins, "The Influence of My Childhood Reading," Higgins papers, UCLA Library Special Collections.
4. *Ibid.*
5. Expo '67 website: www.cinemaexpo67.ca, "Films" page.
6. Colin Higgins Biography, Higgins papers, UCLA Library Special Collections.
7. Edward Lewis biography, http://stanley_kubrick.enacademic.com/126/Lewis,_Edward.
8. Susan, Ed and Mildred Lewis, interview by James Rogers of the Colin Higgins Trust, June 7, 2001.
9. Colin Higgins, AFI Harold Lloyd Masters Seminar, Jan. 10, 1979.
10. *Ibid.*
11. Colin Higgins, "Project Three Proposal," Higgins Papers, UCLA Library Special Collections.
12. Colin Higgins, "Thesis Proposal," Higgins Papers, UCLA Library Special Collections.
13. John Poppy, "Why We Need a New Religion," *Look* Magazine, Jan. 13, 1970.
14. John Gordon Melton, "Theosophy—Religious Philosophy," Encyclopedia Britannica. www.britannica.com.
15. Charles J. Ryan, "What Is Theosophy? A General View for Inquirers," Section 1. www.theosociety.org.
16. Colin Higgins, "Harold and Maude—New Notes to Use," Higgins Papers, UCLA Library Special Collections.
17. *Ibid.*
18. Colin Higgins, *Harold and Maude* screenplay, May 29, 1970.

Chapter 2

1. Colin Higgins, *Harold and Maude* screenplay, May 29, 1970.
2. *Ibid.*
3. *Ibid.*
4. Colin Higgins, "To Whom It May Concern" (summary of Sandra Lowell's work on the *Harold and Maude* script), Higgins papers, UCLA Library Special Collections.
5. Written comments on "Full Length Draft," Colin Higgins, Higgins papers, UCLA Library Special Collections.
6. Written comments on "Harold and Maude, 4-10-70 Draft," Colin Higgins, Higgins papers, UCLA Library Special Collections.

Chapter 3

1. Interview with Ed Susan and Mildred Lewis by James Rogers, June 7, 2001.
2. Aljean Harmitz, "Harold's Back and Maude's Got Him," *New York Times*, May 26, 1974.
3. Scott Saul, *Becoming Richard Pryor*

(New York: HarperCollins Publishers, 2014), pg. 273.
4. Robert Evans biography, website: www.imdb.com.
5. Robert Evans, *The Kid Stays in the Picture: A Notorious Life* (New York: HarperCollins Publishers, 2013), chapter 23.
6. John Hiscock, "I Broke Every Rule," London *Daily Telegraph*, Sept. 21, 2002.
7. May 26, 1970 contract between Paramount Pictures and Lewis-Higgins Productions, Inc.,.
8. Evans, *The Kid Stays in the Picture: A Notorious Life*, chapter 23.
9. Colin Higgins, "To Whom It May Concern," Nov. 10, 1970, Higgins Papers, UCLA Library Special Collections.
10. Ibid.
11. Letter from Ludwig H. Gerber to Robert Evans, Oct. 17, 1970, Higgins Papers, UCLA Library Special Collections.
12. National Enquirer newspaper article, "19-Year-Old Weds Woman, 80 ... Says Love Brought Them Together," Higgins Papers, UCLA Library SpecialCollections.
13. Michael Shedlin, "Harold and Maude," *Film Quarterly*, fall, 1972.

Chapter 4

1. Jane Fonda, *My Life So Far* (New York: Random House, 2006), pg. 367.
2. Nick Dawson, *Being Hal Ashby: Life of a Hollywood Rebel* (Lexington: The University Press of Kentucky, 2009), p. 5.
3. Ibid., p. 13.
4. Norman Jewison, *This Terrible Business Has Been Good to Me: An Autobiography* (New York: St. Martin's, 2004), p. 98.
5. Mark Harris, *Picture at a Revolution: Five Movies and the Birth of the New Hollywood* (New York: The Penguin Press, 2008), pg. 218.
6. Hal Ashby, "Breaking Out of the Cutting Room," *Action* 5.5 1970. Reprinted in *Hal Ashby Interviews* (Jackson: University of Mississippi Press, 2010), edited by Nick Dawson.
7. Interview with Mike Hale, September 19, 2007, *New York Times*, http://www.nytimes.com.
8. Ashby, "Breaking Out of the Cutting Room."
9. Roger Ebert, Oct. 21, 1970 review posted on: http://www.rogerebert.com/reviews/the-landlord-1970.
10. Nick Dawson, commentary track on *Harold and Maude*, 2012 Criterion Collection blu-ray.
11. Letter from Charles Mulvehill to Patrick Palmer, Sept. 23, 1970.

Chapter 5

1. Robert Evans, *The Kid Stays in the Picture: A Notorious Life*, chapter 14.
2. American Film Institute Seminar with Hal Ashby, March 12, 1975; Interview by Rochelle Reed. From Nick Dawson's chapter notes on *Being Hal Ashby*.
3. Letter from Hal Ashby to Robert Evans, December 1, 1970.
4. Paramount Pictures Corporation Production Budget for *Harold and Maude*, Nov. 21, 1970.
5. Hal Ashby, AFI Seminar at USC, Jan. 11, 1972.
6. Ibid.
7. Letter from Charles Mulvehill to Patrick Palmer, Sept. 23, 1970.
8. Steve Toy, "Director Hal Ashby's Office Is a House with Psychedelic Walls," *Variety*, December 24, 1972, reprinted in *Hal Ashby Interviews*.
9. Letter from Hal Ashby to Dame Gladys Cooper, Dec. 4, 1970.
10. Nick Dawson, *Harold and Maude* chapter notes from *Being Hal Ashby: Life of a Hollywood Rebel*.
11. Letter from Hal Ashby to Robert Evans, December 1, 1970.
12. Website, http://www.bayareacensus.ca.gov/bayarea70.htm.

Chapter 6

1. John Rubenstein biography, www.imdb.com.

2. Bud Cort biography, www.imdb.com.
3. Ruth Gordon, *My Side* (New York: Harper and Row, 1976), pg. 389.
4. Dame Edith Evans biography, www.imdb.com.
5. Hal Ashby casting notes.
6. Aljean Harmitz, "Harold's Back and Maude's Got Him," *New York Times*, May 26, 1974.
7. Ashby travel itinerary, Oct. 21–26, 1970.
8. Harmitz, "Harold's Back and Maude's Got Him," May 26, 1974.
9. Dave Itzkoff, *Mad as Hell* (New York: Times Books, 2014), pg. 16.
10. Ruth Gordon biography, http://www.rottentomatoes.com/celebrity/ruth_gordon/biography.php.
11. Leticia Kent, "A Boy of Twenty and a Woman of Eighty," *New York Times*, April 4, 1971.
12. Handwritten note, Edith Evans to Hal Ashby, Nov. 12, 1970.
13. Hal Ashby, letter to Dame Gladys Cooper, Dec. 4, 1970.
14. Vivian Pickles interview, "Being in Harold and Maude," www.criterion.com.
15. Vivian Pickles biography, www.wikipedia.com.
16. Vivian Pickles interview, "Being in Harold and Maude."
17. Charles Tyner biography, www.imdb.com.
18. Charles Mulvehill, commentary on *Harold and Maude*, 2012 Criterion Collection, Blu Ray release.

Chapter 7

1. Letter from Hal Ashby to Robert Evans, December 1, 1970.
2. *Ibid.*
3. *Ibid.*
4. *Ibid.*
5. *Ibid.*
6. Ashby letter to Robert Evans, Dec. 7, 1970.
7. John Alonzo, interview with Bud Cort and James Rogers of the Colin Higgins Trust, Feb. 5, 1997.

8. Alex Simon, "Life in the Court of Bud," *Venice* Magazine, May 2005.
9. Bob Balaban biography, www.imdb.com, Bob Balaban page.
10. Nick Dawson, chapter notes on *Harold and Maude* for *Being Hal Ashby: Life of a Hollywood Rebel*.
11. Gordon, *My Side*, pg. 395.
12. Colin Higgins, Jan. 10, 1979 AFI Masters Series Seminar.
13. Jeff Wexler, e-mail interview with the author, August 24, 2014.
14. Charles Mulvehill, commentary on *Harold and Maude*, 2012 Criterion Collection, Blu Ray release.

Chapter 8

1. Charles Mulvehill, commentary on *Harold and Maude*, 2012 Criterion Collection, Blu Ray release.
2. Gordon, *My Side*, pg. 388.
3. Valley News article, April 17, 1977.
4. Alex Simon, "Life in the Court of Bud."
5. Jeff Wexler, e-mail interview with the author, August 24, 2014.
6. Letter from Ann Nolan to Hal Ashby, March 21, 1971, Nick Dawson chapter notes on *Being Hal Ashby*.
7. Edward Vasgerdsian, telephone interview with the author, April 12, 2014.
8. Gordon, *My Side*, pg. 402.
9. Gordon, *My Side*, pg. 403.
10. City of Coma website, www.colma.ca.gov; Holy Cross Cemetery website, www.holycrosscemeteries.com.
11. Sir Thomas Aquinos Church website, www.paloaltocatholic.org.
12. Charles Mulvehill, commentary on *Harold and Maude*, 2012 Criterion Collection, Blu Ray release.
13. Jeff Wexler telephone interview with the author, August 23, 2014.
14. Ellen Geer, e-mail interview with the author, May 2, 2015.
15. Golden Gate National Recreation website: http://www.nps.gov/goga/historyculture/sutro-baths.htm.
16. Edward Vasgerdsian, telephone interview with the author, April 12, 2014.

Chapter 9

1. Helen M. DeYoung Cameron profile, www.findagrave.com/.
2. "Family Feud," American Journalism Review, Nov., 1999.
3. Listing for 10 Stacey Ct., Hillsborough, CA, www.zillow.com.
4. Northern California and Northwest Previews Newsletter, August, 1970.
5. Marilyn Beck, "Director Charges Studio Was Afraid of Maude," Evening Bulletin, January 25, 1972.
6. David DeMarco letter to Scott Milne, Feb. 1, 1971.
7. Beck, "Director Charges Studio Was Afraid of Maude."
8. Letter from Alan Fox to Charles Mulvehill, Dec. 23, 1970.
9. John Morrison, interview with Ann Brebner for TV magazine "Aspect Ratio," April, 2011.
10. Alex Simon, "Life in the Court of Bud."
11. Charles Mulvehill, commentary on *Harold and Maude*, 2012 Criterion Collection, Blu Ray release.
12. Jeff Wexler, e-mail interview with the author, August 24, 2014.
13. Charles Mulvehill, commentary on *Harold and Maude*, 2012 Criterion Collection, Blu Ray release.
14. Paramount press book for *Harold and Maude* from Nick Dawson's chapter notes.
15. Ellen Geer, e-mail interview with the author, May 2, 2015.
16. Charles Mulvehill, commentary on *Harold and Maude*, 2012 Criterion Collection, Blu Ray release.
17. Bill Royce, "The Big Boys Are at Work," The Daily Cal Arts Magazine, Feb. 19, 1971.
18. Michael Shedlin "Harold and Maude," Film Quarterly, fall 1972.
19. Alex Godfrey, "Bud Cort: 'Harold and Maude' Was a Blessing and a Curse," *The London Guardian*, July 10, 2014.
20. "Bud Cort and John Alonzo" interview with James Rogers of the Colin Higgins Trust, Feb. 5, 1997.
21. *Ibid.*
22. Jeff Wexler, e-mail interview with the author, August 24, 2014.
23. Colin Higgins, "Old Notes on Harold and Maude," Higgins Papers, UCLA Library Special Collections.
24. Peter Bart, telegram to Hal Ashby, Feb. 18, 1971.

Chapter 10

1. William Lucking profile, http://industrycentral.net/content/actors/lucking.html.
2. Letter from orthopedic surgeon Vernon L. Smythe, Feb. 22, 1971.
3. Letter from William Lucking to Hal Ashby, Feb. 29, 1971.
4. Charles Mulvehill, commentary on *Harold and Maude*, 2012 Criterion Collection, Blu Ray release.
5. Hal Ashby, AFI Seminar given at USC, Jan. 11, 1972.
6. Charles Mulvehill, commentary on *Harold and Maude*.
7. "Bud Cort and John Alonzo" interview with James Rogers of the Colin Higgins Trust, Feb. 5, 1997.
8. Charles Mulvehill, commentary on *Harold and Maude*.
9. Hal Ashby, letter to Barry Higgins, April 19, 1971.
10. Jeff Wexler, e-mail interview with the author, August 24, 2014.
11. History of the Santa Cruz Beach Boardwalk, http://www.beachboardwalk.com.
12. Jeff Wexler, e-mail interview with the author, August 24, 2014.
13. Charles Mulvehill, commentary on *Harold and Maude*.
14. Letter from Hal Ashby to Lois Ulrich, Feb. 3, 1971 from Nick Dawson's chapter notes.
15. Peter Bart and Peter Guber, *Shoot Out: Surviving Fame and (Mis)Fortune*

in *Hollywood* (Faber & Faber, London, 2002).
16. Hal Ashby, Jan. 11, 1972, American Film Institute Seminar.
17. *Ibid.*
18. *Ibid.*
19. Letter from Hal Ashby to Peter Bart, May 14, 1971.
20. James Powers, [apost]Dialogue on Film: Hal Ashby,' American Film, May 1980, p.56, from Nick Dawson's chapter notes.
21. Nick Dawson, *Being Hal Ashby: Life of a Hollywood Rebel*, p. 127.
22. James Powers interview with Hal Ashby, October 20, 1976.
23. Ruth Gordon, *My Side*, p. 411.
24. *Ibid.*
25. Interview with James Rogers of the Colin Higgins Trust, "Bud Cort and John Alonzo," Feb. 5, 1997.

Chapter 11

1. Mark Harris, *Pictures at a Revolution: Five Movies and the Birth of the New Hollywood* (New York: The Penguin Press, 2008. p. 360.
2. Letter from Hal Ashby to Robert Evans, Dec. 7, 1970.
3. Yusuf Islam/Cat Stevens biography: http://www.yusufislam.com/.
4. Letter from Hal Ashby to Robert Evans, Dec. 7, 1970.
5. Telegraph from Robert Evans to Hal Ashby, Jan. 15, 1971.
6. Yusuf Islam, interview for the *Harold and Maude* ,Criterion Collection, 2011.
7. *Ibid.*
8. *Ibid.*
9. Charles Mulvehill, commentary on the *Harold and Maude.*
10. Yusuf Islam, interview for the *Harold and Maude.*
11. Charles Mulvehill, memo to Art Ryan, Dec. 16, 1970.
12. Letter from William R. Stinson to Barry Krost, Nov. 29, 1971.
13. Memo from Charles Mulvehill to Art Ryan, Dec. 16, 1970.

Chapter 12

1. Letter from Bud Cort to Hal Ashby, March 20, 1971.
2. Letter from Hal Ashby to Norman Jewison, March 29, 1971.
3. Letter from Skip Nicholson to Hal Ashby, March 18, 1971.
4. Letter from Hal Ashby to Skip Nicholson, March 25, 1971.
5. http://cultureandcommunication.org/deadmedia/index.php/Steenbeck.
6. Jane Fonda, *My Life So Far* (New York: Random House, 2006), p. 374.
7. Hal Ashby, January 11, 1972 American Film Institute Seminar.
8. *Ibid.*
9. Telegram from Peter Bart to Hal Ashby, July 1971.
10. Editing notes, Hal Ashby to Bob Evans, Nov. 1971.
11. *Ibid.*
12. Hal Ashby, January 11, 1972 American Film Institute Seminar.
13. Letter from Attorney Robert R. Lee to Paramount Pictures, Jan. 3, 1972.
14. Hal Ashby, American Film Institute Seminar, Interview by James Powers, Oct. 20, 1976.
15. Colin Higgins, *Harold and Maude*, novel (New York: Lippincott & Sons Publishers, 1971), page 39.
16. *Ibid.*, p. 63.
17. Colin Higgins, "Notes on *Harold and Maude*," Colin Higgins Papers, UCLA Library Special Collections.
18. Nick Dawson, chapter notes on *Being Hal Ashby: Life of a Hollywood Rebel.*
19. Handwritten letter from Hal Ashby to Bob Evans.
20. *Ibid.*
21. Peter Bart and Peter Guber, *Shoot Out: Surviving Fame and (Mis)Fortune in Hollywood*, p. 185.
22. Colin Higgins, notes on a questionnaire filled out for Lippincott Publisher, Sept., 1971, Higgins Papers, UCLA Library Special Collections.
23. *Hollywood Reporter*, Dec. 8, 1971.

Notes—Chapters 13, 14 and 15

Chapter 13

1. Debbie Shapiro, "Deconstructing Harold," *New York Times Magazine*, December 17, 2000.
2. Alex Godfrey, "Bud Cort: 'Harold and Maude' Was a Blessing and a Curse," *The London Guardian*, July 10, 2014.
3. Paramount Publicity Department notes on *Harold and Maude*, 1971.
4. Colin Higgins, Jan., 1979 AFI Masters Film Seminar.
5. *Ibid.*
6. Hal Ashby, Jan. 11, 1972 AFI Masters Film Seminar.
7. Roger Ebert, review of *Harold and Maude*, Jan. 1, 1972, www.rogerebert.com.
8. Vincent Canby, review of *Harold and Maude*, Dec. 21, 1971, www.newyorktimes.com.
9. Nick Dawson, chapter notes for *Being Hal Ashby: Life of a Hollywood Rebel*.
10. Aljean Harmetz, "Harold's Back and Maude's Got Him," *New York Times*, May 26, 1974.
11. Peter Biskind, *Easy Riders, Raging Bulls* (New York: Simon and Schuster, 1998), p. 174.
12. Hal Ashby, Jan. 11, 1972 AFI Masters Film Seminar.
13. Marilyn Beck, "Director Charges Studio Was Afraid of Maude," *The Evening Bulletin*, Jan. 25, 1972.
14. Richard Cuskelly, "A Rip Van Winkle Beard and a Calm Demeanor," *Los Angeles Herald Examiner*, April 2, 1972.
15. Pauline Kael, *I Lost It at the Movies* (London: Marion Boyars Publishers, 1994). Originally published in 1965.
16. http://cinematreasures.org/theaters/10082, The Westgate Theater, Edina, MN.
17. http://www.edinahistoricalsociety.org/uploads/2/0/2/1/2021990/westgate_newsletter.pdf.
18. Harmetz, "Harold's Back and Maude's Got Him."
19. http://www.edinahistoricalsociety.org/uploads/2/0/2/1/2021990/westgate_newsletter.pdf.
20. Harmetz, "Harold's Back and Maude's Got Him."
21. Larry Salvato and Dennis Schaefer, "Hal Ashby Interview," *Millimeter*, October, 1976, pg. 44.
22. Colin Higgins, AFI seminar, moderated by Sam Grogg, August 9, 1979.
23. Letter from George Gelles to Colin Higgins, September 30, 1980, Colin Higgins Papers, UCLA Library Special Collections.
24. Aljean Harmetz, "After 12 Years a Profit for 'Harold and Maude,'" *New York Times*, August 8, 1983.
25. Harmetz, "Harold's Back and Maude's Got Him."

Chapter 14

1. Robert David Crane and Christopher Fryer, "Hal Ashby" 1972. Re-printed in *Hal Ashby: Interviews* (Jackson: University of Mississippi Press, 2011), edited by Nick Dawson, p. 16.
2. Nick Dawson, *Being Hal Ashby, Life of a Hollywood Rebel*, p. 139.
3. Robert David Crane and Christopher Fryer, "Hal Ashby," 1972.
4. Aljean Harmitz, "Gambling on a Film About the Great Depression," *New York Times*, Dec. 5, 1976.
5. Marc Elliot, *Nicholson: A Biography* (New York: Three Rivers Press, 2013), p. 145.
6. Jane Fonda, *My Life So Far*, p. 374.
7. Dawson, *Being Hal Ashby: Life of a Hollywood Rebel*, pp. 333–342.
8. Jeff Wexler, e-mail interview with the author, August 24, 2014.
9. Letter from Norman Jewison to Hal Ashby, November 18, 1970.

Chapter 15

1. Harmetz, "After 12 Years a Profit for 'Harold and Maude.'"
2. Marilyn Beck, "Higgins Eyes Harold's Story," *United Press Syndicate*, August 6, 1978.
3. Scott Saul, *Becoming Richard Pryor* (New York: HarperCollins Publishers, 2014), Pgs. 385–390.

4. Colin Higgins biography, Colin Higgins Foundation website, www.colinhiggins.org.
5. Alex Simon, "Life in the Court of Bud."
6. Ellen Geer, e-mail interview with the author, May 2, 2015.

Chapter 16

1. *Variety* review, Jan. 10, 2005, http://variety.com/2005/legit/reviews/harold-and-maude-the-musical-1200528763/.
2. Review of *Harold and Maude*, http://www.tcm.com/this-month/article/143189|0/Harold-and-Maude.html.
3. "Cameron Crowe on Harold and Maude," YouTube Jan. 7, 2011.
4. "Seth Rogen on Hal Ashby," YouTube, March 20, 2014.
5. "Haskell Wexler on Hal Ashby," YouTube, March 20, 2014.

Bibliography

Ashby, Hal. "Breaking Out of the Cutting Room." *Action* 5.5, 1970.
"Aspect Ratio—Interview with Ann Brebner" by John Morrison, https://vimeo.com/28232852, April, 2011.
Bart, Peter, and Guber, Peter. *Shoot Out: Surviving Fame and (Mis)Fortune in Hollywood*. Faber & Faber, London, 2002.
Beck, Marilyn. "Director Charges Studio was Afraid of Maude." *The Evening Bulletin*, Jan. 25, 1972.
———. "Higgins Eyes Harold's Story." United Press Syndicate, August 6, 1978.
Biskind, Peter. *Easy Riders, Raging Bulls*. New York: Simon & Schuster, 1998.
"Cameron Crowe on Harold and Maude." American Film Institute, https://www.youtube.com/watch?v=8hOV2DsHN4w, Jan. 7, 2011.
Canby, Vincent. Review of *Harold and Maude*, Dec. 21, 1971. http://www.nytimes.com/movie/review?res=990CE7DF1138EF34BC4951DFB467838A669EDE.
City of Colma. www.colma.ca.gov.
Cort, Bud and John Alonzo interview with James Rogers of the Colin Higgins Trust, Feb. 5, 1997. Supplemental materials booklet for *Harold and Maude*, Criterion Collection blu-ray disc, 2012.
Cuskelly, Richard. "A Rip Van Winkle Beard and a Calm Demeanor." *Los Angeles Herald Examiner*, April 2, 1972.
Dawson, Nick. *Being Hal Ashby: Life of a Hollywood Rebel*. Lexington: The University Press of Kentucky, 2009.
———, ed. *Hal Ashby: Interviews*. Jackson: The University Press of Mississippi, 2010.
Ebert, Roger. Review of *Harold and Maude*, Jan. 1, 1972. http://www.rogerebert.com/reviews/harold-and-maude-1972.
———. Review of *The Landlord*, Oct. 21, 1970. http://www.rogerebert.com/reviews/the-landlord-1970.
Elliot, Marc. *Nicholson: A Biography*. New York: Three Rivers Press, 2013.
Evans, Robert. *The Kid Stays in the Picture: A Notorious Life*. New York: HarperCollins Publishers, 2013.
"Expo '67." www.cinemaexpo67.ca.
"Family Feud." *American Journalism Review*, Nov., 1999.
Fonda, Jane. *My Life So Far*. New York: Random House, 2006.
Godfrey, Alex. "Bud Cort: 'Harold and Maude' was a blessing and a curse." *The London Guardian*, July 10, 2014.
Golden Gate National Recreation. http://www.nps.gov/goga/historyculture/sutro-baths.htm.
Gordon, Ruth. *My Side*. New York: Harper & Row, 1976.
Harmetz, Aljean. "After 12 Years a Profit for 'Harold and Maude.'" *New York Times*, August 8, 1983.
———. "Gambling on a Film About the Great Depression." *New York Times*, Dec. 5, 1976.
———. "Harold's Back and Maude's Got Him." *New York Times*, May 26, 1974.
Harold and Maude. Blu-ray edition. Directed by Hal Ashby. New York: Criterion Collection, 2012. Includes "American Film Institute Seminar with Hal

Bibliography

Ashby, Jan. 11, 1972," "American Film Institute Seminar with Colin Higgins, Jan. 10, 1979," "Seeing Songs: Yusuf/Cat Stevens and *Harold and Maude*" (interview with Yusuf/Cat Stevens" and "Commentary" by Charles Mulvehill and Nick Dawson.

Harris, Mark. *Picture at a Revolution: Five Movies and the Birth of the New Hollywood*. New York: The Penguin Press, 2008.

"Haskell Wexler on Hal Ashby." Academy of Motion Picture Arts and Sciences, https://www.youtube.com/watch?v=OMb6pLe9Vdo, March 20, 2014.

Higgins, Colin. *Harold and Maude*. New York: Lippincott & Sons Publishers, 1971.

Hiscock, John. "I Broke Every Rule." London *Daily Telegraph*, Sept. 21, 2002.

"History of UCLA," UCLA website, http://www.tft.ucla.edu/about/history/.

Holy Cross Cemetery. www.holycrosscemeteries.com.

Itzkoff, Dave. *Mad as Hell*. New York: Times Books, 2014.

Jewison, Norman. *This Terrible Business Has Been Good to Me: An Autobiography*. New York: St. Martin's, 2004.

Kael, Pauline. *I Lost it at the Movies*. London: Marion Boyars Publishers, 1994.

Karp, Josh. *Orson Welles's Last Movie: The Making of The Other Side of the Wind*. New York: St. Martin's Press, 2015.

Kent, Leticia. "A Boy of Twenty and a Woman of Eighty," *New York Times*, April 4, 1971.

"Lewis, Edward, biography." http://stanley_kubrick.enacademic.com/126/Lewis,_Edward

Lewis, Jon. *Whom God Wishes to Destroy ... Francis Coppola and the New Hollywood*. Durham and London: Duke University Press, 1995.

"19-Year-Old Weds Woman, 80 ... Says Love Brought Them Together." *National Enquirer*, date and author unknown.

Poppy, John. "Why We Need a New Religion." *Look* Magazine, Jan. 13, 1970.

Powers, James. "Dialogue on Film: Hal Ashby." *American Film*, May, 1980.

Royce, Bill. "The Big Boys Are at Work." *The Daily Cal Arts Magazine*, Feb. 19, 1971.

Ryan, Charles J. "What Is Theosophy? A General View for Inquirers." Section 1. www.theosociety.org.

Saul, Scott. *Becoming Richard Pryor*. New York: HarperCollins Publishers, 2014.

Salvato, Larry, and Schaefer, Dennis. "Hal Ashby Interview." *Millimeter*, October, 1976.

Schatz, Thomas. *The Genius of the System*. New York: Pantheon Books, 1988.

"Seth Rogen on Hal Ashby." Academy of Motion Picture Arts and Sciences, https://www.youtube.com/watch?v=ijmmA6iH7xU, March 20, 2014.

Shapiro, Debbie. "Deconstructing Harold." *New York Times Magazine*, December 17, 2000.

Shedlin, Michael. "Harold and Maude." *Film Quarterly*, fall 1972.

Simon, Alex. "Life in the Court of Bud." *Venice* Magazine, May 2005.

Sir Thomas Aquinos Church. www.paloaltocatholic.org.

Susan, Ed, and Mildred Lewis interview with James Rogers of the Colin Higgins Trust, June 7, 2001. Supplemental materials booklet for *Harold and Maude*, Criterion Collection blu-ray disc, 2012.

Toy, Steve. "Director Hal Ashby's Office is a House with Psychedelic Walls." *Variety*, December 24, 1972.

Variety review of *Harold and Maude: the Musical*, Jan. 10, 2005. http://variety.com/2005/legit/reviews/harold-and-maude-the-musical-1200528763/.

Vivian Pickles Interview. "Being in Harold and Maude." www.criterion.com.

The Westgate Theater, Edina, MN. http://cinematreasures.org/theaters/10082. http://www.edinahistoricalsociety.org/uploads/2/0/2/1/2021990/westgate_newsletter.pdf

Index

Numbers in **bold italics** indicate pages with photographs.

Abe Lincoln in Illinois (movie) 75
Academy of Motion Picture Arts and Sciences 13
Actor's Studio 16
Adam's Rib (movie) 76
The Addams Family (TV show) 88
Adler, Lou 64
Adler, Stella 80
The Admiral Was a Lady (movie) 17
Airport 1975 (movie) 93
Albertson, Jack 46
Aldrich, Robert 184
Alice in Wonderland (TV show) 79
All in the Family (TV show) 80
Almost Famous (movie) 188
Alonzo, John 86, 88, 92, 100, 116–117, 124, 132, 187
Altman, Robert 9, 68–70, 175
American Academy of Dramatic Arts 74
American Film Institute 19
American Hustle (movie) 193
Anderson, Lindsay 184
Anderson, Wes 9, 177, 184, 192
The Ann Brebner Agency 90
Any Which Way You Can (movie) 179
Apatow, Judd 177, 192, 194
Apocalypse Now (movie) 176
Appian Way 64, 65, 81, 87, 168
Arbuckle, Roscoe 74
Arquette, Rosanna 175
Arthur, Jean 46
Ashby, Eileen 50
Ashby, Hal 2, 5, 9, 10, 49, *53*, *62*, 64, 91, 92, 98, 99, 100, 110–113, 116, 117, 118–120, 121, 124, 125, 134, 157, *190*; acquaintance with Jewison 52, 54; biographical background 50–51; casting *Harold and Maude* 68–81; casting the part of Harold 87–89; contention over editing 143–146; decisions made in the finished film 147–152; differences between film and novel 153–154; directing *The Landlord* 55–59; falling behind schedule 126–128; finishing production 130–132; fight over location 65–67; financial participation in *Harold and Maude* 164–165; first day problems 93–94; hiring for *Harold and Maude* 60–63; influence on other filmmakers 192–195; legacy as a director 177–178; Lorimar Pictures 175–176; preproduction dispute with Paramount 82–86; previewing the film 155–156; renting the Rosecourt 107–109; wok on *Coming Home* and *Being There* 173–174; work on *Shampoo* 171–172; work on *The Last Detail* 168–171; working with Cat Stevens 136–141
Ashby, James 50, 51
Ashcroft, Dame Peggy 74
Attenborough, Richard 15

Bacalupi, Bob 48
The Bad News Bears (movie) 185, 187
Bailey, Pearl 58
Balaban, Barney 40, 87
Balaban, Bob 70, 71, 87
Balaban & Katz 40, 41, 87, 162
Ballard, Jack 64, 83, 128
Barrault, Jean-Louis 180
Bart, Peter 85, 117, 127, 128, 144–145, 155, 187, 194
Barton Fink (movie) 193
Beach, Christopher 193
Beach Blanket Babylon (play) 88
Bearden, Jack 70
The Beatles 133
Beatty, Warren 171–172, 176, 177, 178
Bebermeyer, Pamela 93, 99, 104, 123–124
Beck, Marilyn 108, 161, 180
Being Hal Ashby, Life of a Hollywood Rebel (book) 177
Being There (movie) 56, 136, 152, 170, 173–174, 187
Bel Geddes, Barbara 78
Bender, Jack 48
Bergen, Candice 181
Bergner, Elisabeth 73

207

Index

Berkeley, California 95, 96
Berlin, Jeannie 70
The Best Little Whorehouse in Texas (movie) 181, 193
Beverly Hills Buntz (TV show) 175
Big Country (movie) 52
The Big Lebowski (movie) 193
Billy Jack (movie) 85
The Birds (movie) 66
Blake, Robert 174
Blavatsky, Helena Petrovna **23**, 24
Blondell, Kathryn 88
Bloody Mama (movie) 86
Bludhorn, Charles 41–43, 45
Boehm, John 20
Bonnie and Clyde (movie) 35, 41
Borgnine, Ernest 46
Bormann, Martin 129
Born Yesterday (movie) 76
Bound for Glory (movie) 170, 172, 187
Bowen, Roger 46
Bradley, General Omar 27, 101
Brautigan, Richard 176
Breathless (movie) 57
Brebner, Ann 109
Brewster McCloud (movie) 9. 69, 182
Bridges, Beau 58, 178
Bridges, Jeff 46, 175, 176, 178
Bridges, Lloyd 58
Brittania Hospital (movie) 184
Brook, Peter 180
Brown, Jim 58
Brown, Pat 97
Brown, Ross 37
Browne, Jackson 64
Browning, Tod 166
Bryna Productions 18
Buchan, John 15
Bullitt (movie) 66, 90
Burghoff, Gary 10
Burlingame Country Club 106
Burton, Wendell 70

Caan, James 35
Cactus Flower (movie) 42
Cameron, George 105–107, 109, 148
Cameron, Helen 105–107, 109, 148
Canby, Vincent 160
Carnal Knowledge (movie) 168
Carradine, David 172
Catch 22 (movie) 87
Celebrating Laughter: the Life and Films of Colin Higgins (movie) 193
Champlin, Charles 160
Channing, Carol 42
Chaplin, Charlie 76
Chapman, Graham 175

Chase, Chevy 180
Chayefsky, Paddy 76, 161
Chicatelli, Bob 48
China Smith (TV show) 17
Chinatown (movie) 187
Christie, Julie 171
Christmas, Eric 10, 80, 99, 184
The Cincinnati Kid (movie) 52, 118
Cinemobile 96, 126
Clayburgh, Jill 180
The Cliff House restaurant 5, 102
A Clockwork Orange (movie) 161
Close, Glenn 179
Coca-Cola 23
Coen, Ethan 193
Coen, Joel 193
The Coen brothers 177
Colbert, Claudette 74
Coleman, Dabney 181
Collier, Patience 73
Colma, California 97
Columbia Pictures 49, 63, 169
Coming Home (movie) 144, 152, 170, 172, 177, 187, 194
Comingore, Dorothy 73
Connery, Sean 161
Cool Hand Luke (movie) 10, 80
Cooper, Dame Gladys 73,74
Cooper, Sheldon G. 108
Cooper, White and Cooper 107
Coppola, Francis Ford 13, 57, 58, 83, 144, 176
Coppola, Talia 46
Corey, Jeff 118
Corman, Roger 86
The Coronet Theater 158
Cort, Bud 9, 11, **29**, **69**, 71, 78, 103, **104**, **115**, 123–125, 128–129, 132, **140**, 143, 147, 157–158, 160–161, 163, 176, 180–181, **183**, 194, 195; biographical background 69, 70; career after *Harold and Maude* 182–184; casting as Harold 86–88; filming at the Rosecourt 110–116; relationship with Ruth Gordon 91–92
The Cotton Club (movie) 176
The Country Wife (play) 75
Court, Alma M. 69
Cox, Joseph P. 69
Cox, Wally 70
Coyote Ugly (movie) 184
Crawford, Broderick 76
Crawford, Joan 77
Crist, Judith 160
Cronyn, Hume 79
Crosby, David 64
Crosse, Rupert 170
Crowe, Cameron 193, 194

208

Index

Curtis, Tony 76
Cusack, Cyril 10, 81, 124–125, 129
Cuskelly, Richard 161

Daily Cal Arts Magazine (periodical) 114
Daily Variety (periodical) 63, 64
Daniels, William 79
Dare, Michael 129
The Daughter (movie) 63
David, Brad 46
Davis, Bette 77
Davis, Marty 45
Dawn, Hazel 75
Dawson, Nick 2, 50, 57, 58, 101, 130, 177, 189, 193
Death Valley Days (TV show) 128
Decca Records 134
Del Rio, Dolores 74
DeMarco, David 107–108
DeMille, C.B. 40
Democratic Convention of 1968 54
De Mornay, Rebecca 175
Dench, Judi 184
Dern, Bruce 152, 173, 194
The Devil's Daughter (TV movie) 100
de Young, Michael H. 105–106
de Young Museum 105
Diamonds Are Forever (movie) 131, 161
The Diary of Anne Frank (movie) 52
Dieckoff, Henry 107, 108, 113
Dietrich, Marlene 46
DiMaggio, Joe 97
Dirty Harry (movie) 131, 161
Dmytryk, Edward 88
Dmytryk, Michael 88
Dogma (movie) 184
Douglas, Diana 79
Douglas, Kirk 17, 18
Douglas, Michael 171
Dourit, Brad 182
Dowd, Nancy 172
Downey, Robert 148
Dreyfus, Alfred 36, 94, 124
Dreyfuss, Richard 46, 70
Dumbarton Bridge 93, 100, 118
Dunnock, Mildred 46, 77
Durfee, Minta 74
Duvall, Robert 69
Dwight, Reginald 70

Earthquake (1971) 114
Eastman, Charles 174
Eastwood, Clint 179
Easy Rider (movie) 35, 42, 44, 133, 168
Eaton, Marjorie 10, 81, 124
Ebert, Roger 58, 160
Edina, MN 163

Eggar, Samantha 182
Eight Million Ways to Die (movie) 152, 175, 187
Elgin Theater 166
Eliopoulos, Nicholas 193
Ellsberg, Daniel 6
El Topo (movie) 166–167
Emeryville mud flats 94–96, **95**
Engles, Judy 11, 81, 70
Enrietto, Robert 88
EST 23
Evans, Edith **53**, 72–75, 78
Evans, Robert 2, 9, 42, 47, 49, 59, 65, 72, 89, 127, 136, 168, 187; editing Harold and Maude 145–146; hiring of Hal Ashby 60–63; pre-production dispute with Ashby 82–86; previews 155–156; purchase of the *Harold and Maude* script 43–45
Evening Bulletin (periodical) 161
Every Which Way but Loose (movie) 179
The Exorcist (movie) 162
Expo '67 16

Family Plot (movie) 104
Fast, Howard 18
Father Murphy (TV show) 184
The Fay Emerson Show (TV show) 17
The F.B.I. (TV show) 128
Fensch, Thomas 17
Ferro, Pablo 96, 125, 128, 147, 156, 159, 176, 193
Fiddler on the Roof (movie) 54, 56, 58, 74, 161
Fields, W.C. 40
Film Quarterly (periodical) 115
Film ratio 48
Films on Campus (book) 17
Filmways 17
Five Easy Pieces (movie) 168
Flirting with Disaster (movie) 193
Foch, Nina 46
Fonda, Jane 50, 144, 172–173, 177, 178, 193
Footsteps in the Dark, Cat Stevens Greatest Hits 2 (album) 142
Forbes, Bryan 73
Ford, John 42
Forman, Milos 172
Fortas, Danny 87
Foul Play (movie) 164, 180, 188
Fox, Allan 107–108
Frankenheimer, John 39
Frantic (movie) 176
Freaks (movie) 166
Free Fall (play) 70
Free Speech Movement 67

209

Index

The French Connection (movie) 80
Freud, Sigmund 101
Friedkin, William 80
Friends (movie) 71
Fritz the Cat (movie) 185
The Fugitive (TV show) 128

Gaily, Gaily (movie) 54, 58, 80
Gambaccini, Paul 135
Ganja & Hess (movie) 55
Gardens of Stone (movie) 176
Garr, Teri 46
Gaynor, Janet 74, 189
Geer, Ellen 11, 81, 100, 112–113, 185
Geer, Will 11, 81, 185
Gelles, George 165
General Cinema Corp. 163
Georgiou, Steven Demetre 134
Gerber, Ludwig H. 47
Gish, Lilian 46
Gleason, Jackie 42
Glenn, Charles O. 164
God Bless the Child (book) 55
Godard, Jean-Luc 57
The Godfather (movie) 58, 83, 158–159, 162, 176
Godfrey, Ellen 48
Golden Gate Cemetery 5
Golden Gate Park 105
Golden Globe Awards 161
Goodbye, Columbus (movie) 45, 48
Goodfried, Bob 62
Gordon, Ruth 9, **29**, 46, *71*, 72, **73**, 74, 82, 87, 103, ***104***, 114, 117, 121, 123, 124, 129, 130, 132, 139, ***140***, 149, 151, 153, 157–161, 163, 182, ***190***, 195; biographical background 75–78; career after *Harold and Maude* 179; first day of filming *Harold and Maude* 93–94; relationship with Bud Cort 91–92
Gossett, Lou, Jr. 58
Gostelow, Gordon 184
The Graduate (movie) 41, 80, 133
Grant, Lee 58, 171
The Great Escape (movie) 15
The Greatest Story Ever Told (movie) 52
Greensleeves 142, 148
Griffith, D.W. 76
Grusin, David 134
Gulf + Western 41, 42, 45, 61, 157
Gunn, Bill 55
Gunsmoke (TV show) 128

Hackman, Gene 79
Hair (musical) 22
Hal Ashby–A Man Out of Time (movie) 194

Hal Ashby: Interviews (book) 193
Hale, Nathan 27, 101
Half Moon Bay, California 96, 130
Hall, David 86
Haller, Michael 11, 88, 99, 101, 112, 119, 121–122, 176, 187
Hamilton, Murray 79
Hammersmith Art College 134
Hammid, Alexander 16
The Happening (movie) 42
A Hard Day's Night (movie) 133
Harmetz, Aljean 165, 170, 179
Harris, Barbara 79
Harris, Jed 75
Harris, Jones 75
Harris, Mark 52
Harrison, George 6
The Hawkline Monster (novel) 176
Hawks, Howard 42
Hawn, Goldie 171, 178, 180, 194
Hayes, Helen 46, 73
Head (movie) 42
Hearst, William Randolph 105
Heider, Wally 139
Hellman, Jerry 176
Hepburn, Katharine 76
Heraut Concrete Accessories 94
Hickey, William 70
Higgins, Barry 70, 71, 125
Higgins, Colin 2, 9, 13, 14, 38, 41, 61, 68, 79, 85, 87, 91, 101, 109, 112, 115, 117, 123, 125, 130, 148–150, 152, 156, 159, 188, 193; biographical background 14–16; career after *Harold and Maude* 180–182; directorial test 48, 49; enrollment at UCLA 16, 17; financial participation in *Harold and Maude* 164–165; hiring as producer 62–63; novelization of *Harold and Maude* 153–154; sale of the script 44–47; writing the *Harold and Maude* script 18–25, 33–37
Hiller, Arthur 80, 161, 180
Hiscock, John 44
Hitchcock, Alfred 15, 19, 20, 41, 42, 48, 66, 73, 180, 184
Hobart, Lewis Parsons 105
Hodkinson, W.W. 40
Hoffman, Dustin 175
Holden, William 76
Holliday, Judy 76
Hollywood Reporter (periodical) 63, 156
The Hollywood Ten 88
Holm, Celeste 79
Holy Cross Cemetery **96**, 97, 100, 137, 140
The Hospital (movie) 80, 161
Houston Astrodome 69

Index

Hughes, Barnard 79
Hugo, Victor 25
Hunter, Kristen 55
Huntington Hotel 91
Hurst, Mike 134
Huston, John 70

I Capture the Castle (play) 79
I Heart Huckabees (movie) 193
I Love You, Alice B. Toklas (movie) 42
Idiot's Delight (play) 17
The Ik (play) 180
In the Heat of the Night (movie) 52, 54, 55, 58
Inside Daisy Clover (movie) 76
Isadora Duncan, the Biggest Dancer in the World (movie) 79
Isis Unveiled (book) 24
Islam, Yusuf 9, 189
Island Records 135

Jaffe, Howard 45, 63, 85
Jaffe, Stanley 45, 85
Jake's Journey (TV show) 175, 176
Jaws (movie) 162
Jeans, Isabel 73
Jesus Christ, Superstar (movie) 54
Jewison, Norman 52, 54–58, 60, 65, 74, 80, 118, 143, 161, 178, 192
Jodorowsky, Alejandro 166
John, Elton 70, 71, 87, 134
Jolie, Angelina 175
Jones, Hank 48
Jones, Robert C. 171, 173
Jones, Tom 189
Juno (movie) 192

Kael, Pauline 160, 163
Kanin, Garson 17, 71, 72, 75, 76, 91, 114, 132
Katz, Sam 40
Keaton, Diane 46
Kedrova, Lila 74
Kelly, Gregory 75
KEM film editor 144, 145
Kennedy, Robert 54
Kent, Leticia 78
Kent State University 6, 43
The Kid Stays in the Picture (book) 187
Kinfolks (book) 55
King, Carole 64, 135
King, Martin Luther, Jr. 54
King of Hearts (movie) 191
Klavik, Carl 91
Klein, Irving 143
Knocked Up (movie) 192
Korean War 83

Kosberg, Bob 37
Kozinski, Jerzy 173
Krost, Barry 135–137, 141–142, 154
Kubrick, Stanley 74, 161

The Lady Vanishes (movie) 180
The Lakestown Rebellion (book) 55
The Landlord (book) 55–56, 61
The Landlord (movie) 55–59, 83, 86, 101, 144, 160, 168
Lange, Jessica 169
LaRue, Jack, Jr. 48
Lasky, Jesse 40
The Last Detail (movie) 101, 136, 169–171, 187, 194
The Last Picture Show (movie) 170
Latham, Louise 46, 48
Leachman, Cloris 46, 79
Leda and the Swan 150
Lee Daniels' The Butler (movie) 55
LeGalliene, Eva 73
Lemmon, Jack 17
Lennon, John 166
Lenya, Lotte 73
Lester, Richard 112
Let's Spend the Night Together (movie) 175
Lewis, Edward 10, 14, 17, 39, 43, 33, 88, 194
Lewis, Jerry 156
Lewis, Mildred 10, 14, 17, 18, 20, 39, 44, 45, 165, 194
Lewis, Susan 18, 36
Lewis–Higgins Productions, Inc. 44, 63, 64, 78, 94, 165
The Life Aquatic (movie) 184
Lion's Gate 69
Lippincott and Sons 153
The Little Prince (movie) 184
Lockwood, Margaret 74
London, Barry 165
London Guardian (periodical) 158
Long Beach Film Festival 17
The Longest Yard (movie) 184
Look Back in Anger (movie) 73
Lookin' to Get Out (movie) 174–175, 194
Lorimar Pictures 173, 187
Los Angeles Herald Examiner (periodical) 161
Los Prados Motel 90
Love, Bessie 73
Love in a Cold Climate (TV show) 184
Love Story (movie) 72, 156
The Loveable Cheat (movie) 17
The Loved One (movie) 52, 73
Lowell, Sandra 36, 37, 46–48
Lubitsch, Ernst 41

Index

Lucas, George 88
Lucking, William 10, 81, 118–119, 128

MacArthur, General Douglas 101
MacDougall, Roger 210
MacLaine, Shirley 178
Madigan, Susan 93
Malden, Karl 101
Mandel, Johnny 136
Mann, Leslie 192
Manson, Charles 6
Margaret Herrick Library 2
Markson, Morley 16
Marnie (movie) 48
The Marrying Kind (movie) 76
Marshall, Joan 57, 168
Marshall, Penny 46, 48
Martin, Nan 48
Marty (movie) 76
Marx, Groucho 182
The Mary Tyler Moore Show (TV show) 79
MASH (movie) 9, 10, 69, 70, 128, 136
Maxie (movie) 179
May, Elaine 70
Mayco Salvage Co. 94
McAfee, Wes 85
McCormick, Pat 46
McDermott, Keith 189
McGraw, Ali 48, 72
McLaughlin Eastshore State Park *95*, 96
McQueen, Steve 15, 66
Mehta, Zubin 86
Melnitz Hall 14, 17
Menlo Park 15
Meredith, James 16
Merrick, David 72
MGM studios 69
Midnight Cowboy (movie) 42, 44, 87, 133
Milford, Penelope 173
Millimeter (periodical) 164
Milne, Scott 108
Mirisch, Walter 52
Mirisch Company 10, 58, 63, 64
Mission Dolores 97
Mitchell, Joni 64, 135
Mona Bone Jakon (album) 135, 138, 139, 140–141
Montreal, Canada 16
Monty Python 175
Moonstruck (movie) 192
Moore, Roger 79
Mori Point 130
Moriarity, Michael 171
Morrison, Jim 6
Morton, Bob 48
Movieola film editor 144

Multilith machine 51
Mulvehill, Charles "Chuck" 10, 11, 58, 59, 63–65, 71, 79, 81, 82, 85, 88, 90, 93, 103, 108, 114, 119, 125, 126–128, 138, 141, 156, 161, 185, 187, 189
The Munsters (TV show) 168
Murch, Walter 144
Murray, Bill 192
Muse, Margaret 48
My Bodyguard (movie) 179
My Side (book) 72, 91

Nashville (movie) 176
Negri, Pola 74
Neilson, John 87
Nesbitt, Cathleen 73, 74
Network (movie) 76
New York Times (periodical) 6, 60, 61, 160, 164, 167
Nicholas and Alexandria (movie) 109
Nichols, Mike 42, 80, 133, 152
Nicholson, Jack 118, 168–171, 172–173, 187
Nicholson, Skip 143
Night of the Living Dead (movie) 166
Nillson, Harry 133
Nine to Five (movie) 181, 188, 193
Nixon, Richard 6, 43, 101, 171
Nolan, Ann 92
North, Jay 70
North, Sheree 79
North by Northwest (movie) 180
Noumea, New Caledonia 14
The Nun's Story (movie) 73
Nurserymen's Exchange 96
NYU School of Arts 70

O Lucky Man! (movie) 184
Oakland, California 15, 95, 121
O'Connor, Carroll 46, 80
The Odd Couple (movie) 42
Ogden, Utah 40, 50, 51
O'Keefe, Michael 175
Old Vic Theatre 75
Oliver's Story (movie) 181
Once I Was: the Hal Ashby Story (movie) 193
One Flew Over the Cuckoo's Nest (movie) 172, 182
One from the Heart (movie) 176
O'Neal, Ryan 72, 181
Orpheus Descending (play) 80
Owen Butler (movie) 82, 84
Oyster Pt. Boulevard 119, 130

Page, Geraldine 77
Palm Springs, California 155
Palmer, Patrick 64

Index

Palo Alto, California 90, 98, 155
Pan Am Airlines 15
Paramount Studios 5, 10, 39- 42, 43, 44, 49, 60, 61, 62, 64–66, 81, 82, 108, 127, 132, 138, 141, 144, 147, 157–159, 161, 162, 164, 165, 174, 181, 184, 187
Parsons, Estelle 189
Parton, Dolly 181
Pasadena Playhouse 118
The Passenger (movie) 187
Pat and Mike (movie) 76
Patinkin, Mandy 179
Patton (movie) 43, 101
Payne, Julie 48
Pearl Harbor 15
Peckinpah, Sam 161
Peninsula Hospital 119, 125
Penn, Arthur 42, 152
The Pentagon Papers 6
Petulia (movie) 112
Phillips, Michelle 64, 169
The Pianist (movie) 176
Picker, David 56
Pickford, Mary 76
Pickles, Vivian 10, 74, 79, 81, 104, 109–114, *111*, 116, 150, 184
Pink Flamingos (movie) 166, 167
Pirates (movie) 176
Pixar Animation Co. 95
The Player (movie) 176
Plumb, Flora 48
Poitier, Sydney 55
Polanski, Roman 76, 176, 187
Pollack (movie) 184
Ponicsan, Darryl 169
Popeye (movie) 176
Poppy, John 22
Portnoy, Richard 74
The Postman Always Rings Twice (1981 movie) 168–169, 187
Preminger, Otto 42, 108
Priddy, Nancy 48
Prizzi's Honor (movie) 70
Pryor, Richard 180, 181
Psycho (movie) 43

Quaid, Randy 170–171, 178
Quincy, Massachusetts 75, 179
The Quran 186

Rafelson, Bob 169
The Rain People (movie) 35, 144
Random, Bob 46
Ransahoff, Marty 52
Rear Window (movie) 41
Redwood City, California 90, 92, 93, 94, 96, 101

Reefer Madness (movie) 166
Reiner, Carl 77
Reitman, Jason 192
Reynolds, Burt 181
Richardson, Tony 52, 73
Ritter, John 48
Rogan, Seth 194
Rogers, James 39
The Rolling Stones 175
Romeo and Juliet (play) 113
Romero, George 166
Roos, Joanna 73
Rope (movie) 20
The Rosecourt 91, 104–107, ***106***, 108, 109–116
Rosemary's Baby (movie) 9, 42, 72, 73, 76, 77
Roth, Leon 85
Royce, Bill 114
Rubinstein, Arthur 68
Rubinstein, Eva 68
Rubinstein, John 46, 48, 68, 71, 87, 88
Rushmore (movie) 192
Russell, David O. 177, 192–193
Russell, Ken 79
The Russians Are Coming, the Russians Are Coming (movie) 52
Ryan, Ken 83

St. Anthony's College 15
St. Thomas Aquinas Church 98–***99***, 150, 153
Salt, Waldo 172, 173
Salvato, Larry 164
Sammeth, Barbara 37
Samuel Goldwyn Creative Writing Awards 20, 36, 37
Samwell-Smith, Paul 135, 140–141, 154
San Francisco Bay Area 2, 5, 6, 16, 65–67, 82, 85, 90, 195
San Francisco Earthquake of 1906 106
San Francisco International Airport 120
San Mateo, California 117
San Mateo County Hall of Justice 93, 96
Sands, Diana 58
Santa Cruz Beach Boardwalk 126–127
Sassoon, Vidal 171
Savage, John 70
Sawyer, William A. 144
Schaefer, Dennis 164
Schlesinger, John 79, 152, 161, 172
Schlitz Playhouse of Stars (TV show) 17, 18
Schwartzman, Jason 192
Scott, Amy 193
Scott, George C. 43
Sebring, Jay 171

Index

Second Hand Hearts (movie) 79, 174
The Secret Doctrine (book) 24
Segal, George 77
Sellers, Peter 173–174
A Serious Man (movie) 193
Shacove, Gene 171
Shakespeare, William 15
Shampoo (movie) 5, 101, 170, 168, 177
Shedlin, Michael 115
The Sheik (movie) 40
Shire, Talia 46
Signoret, Simone 74
Silicon Valley 90
Silver, Steve 88, 100, 121–122, 132
Silver Linings Playbook (movie) 192
Silver Streak (movie) 164, 180, 181
Simon, Neil 175
Simon, Paul 133, 135
Simon and Garfunkel 133
Skerritt, Tom 11, 93, 128–129, 184
Skidoo (movie) 42
The Slugger's Wife (movie) 175
Sons of Anarchy (TV show) 10
The Sorbonne 16
The Soul Brothers and Sister Lou (book) 55
South San Francisco, California 94, 119, 121, 124, 130
Southern, Terry 52
Southern Pacific Railroad Bayshore Yard 124
Spanking the Monkey (movie) 192
Sparta, Illinois 52
Spartacus (book) 18
Spartacus (movie) 17, 18, 39, 88
Stanford University 16, 66, 99
Stars and Stripes (periodical) 16
Strand, Doug 167
Straw Dogs (movie) 161
Steenbeck (film editor) 144
Stein, Bob 88, 112
The Sterile Cuckoo (movie) 70
Stevens, Cat 9, 61, 120, 124, 132, 145, 147, 151–152, 154, 185–186, 195; biographical background 134–135; completion of music for the film 139–142; hiring for Harold and Maude 136–137; Mona Bone Jakon album 135, 138; Tea for the Tillerman album 136, 138; Teaser and the Firecat album 139; writing original songs 138–139
Stevens, George 51
Stifflemire, Gus 47
Stinson, William 138, 141
Stoumen, Louis C. 20
Sturges, John 15
Sullivan, Mike 191
Summers, Shari 11, 81, 113–114, 185

Sunday, Bloody Sunday (movie) 79, 161
Sunnyvale H.S. Marching Band 99
Sunset Boulevard (movie) 34
Superbad (movie) 192, 194
Susman, Todd 87
Sutro Bath Ruins 5, 101, 102, *103*, 137
Sutro Heights Park 102
Sweet Bird of Youth (play) 80
Swink, Robert 51
Sydney, Australia 15

Tate, Sharon 6
Taylor, James 135
Tea for the Tillerman (album) 136, 138, 139–140, 185
Teaser and the Firecat (album) 139, 185
Tell 'Em I'm Gone (album) 186
Tess (movie) 176
Thalia Theater 164
Thalken, Joseph 189
Theatricum Botanicum 185
Theiss, William 88, 117
Theosophy (philosophy) 23–25, 30, 149
This Is Your Life (TV show) 132, 157
Thomas, Richard 70
The Thomas Crowne Affair (movie) 54
Thompson, Francis 16
Thorndyke, Dame Sybil 74
Three Cornered Circle (movie) 169
THX-1138 (movie) 88
Tick...Tick...Tick... (movie) 58
Tom Jones (movie) 73
Tomlin, Lily 181
Torn Curtain (movie) 74
Toronto, Canada 169
Towers, Constance 46
Towne, Robert 169, 171, 187
Tracy, Spencer 76, 92
Transcendental Meditation 23
Travolta, John 170
The Trip (movie) 42
The Troubadour 71
The Trouble with Angels (movie) 81
Trumbo, Dalton 18, 88
Tucker (movie) 176
Two Faced Woman (movie) 75
Tyner, Charles 10, 80, 101–*104*, 184

Uintah Dairy Co. 50
Ulrich, Lois 127
United Artists 55, 56, 58, 144
Universal Studios 51
University of California, Berkeley 66, 67
University of California, Los Angeles 2, 11, 13, 14, 16, 17, 18, 20, 65, 68, 118, 185
University of California, Santa Cruz 126
University of Southern California 13

Index

Valentino, Rudolph 40
Van Devere, Trish 77
Van Fleet, Jo 73
Vanishing Point (movie) 86
Variety (periodical) 160, 187
Vasgerdsian, Edward 92, 102
Vertigo (movie) 41, 66, 97
The Vietnam War 6, 16, 35, 43
The Village Gate 70
The Virginian (TV show) 128
Voight, Jon 172–175, 178, 193, 194

Walsh, David 86
Walters, Miriam 48
The Waltons (TV show) 70, 81
Warden, Jack 68, 171
Warhol, Andy 166
Warschilka, Edward 144
Washington Township Hospital 119
Waters, John 166
Webster, Diana 46
Weiss, Nat 138
Welles, Orson 177
West, Mae 40
Western Railway Museum 2, 121–*122*
Westgate Theater 163–164, 179
Wexler, Haskell 86, 87, 88, 172–173, 193, 194

Wexler, Jeff 85, 88, 92, 100, 110, 117, 123, 126, 136, 176, 187–188
Whatever Happened to Aunt Alice (movie) 77, 93
Where's Poppa (movie) 77
The Whisperers (movie) 73
Why Shoot the Teacher? (movie) 182
Wilder, Billy 41, 42
Wilder, Gene 180, 194
Williams, Tennessee 80
Willis, Gordon 57, 83, 159
Wings (movie) 40
Wise Child (play) 182
Wood, George 10, 80, 117, 128, 184
Wood, Natalie 76
Wooden, John 13
Woodstock Music Festival 6
Woollcott, Alexander 75
Wyler, William 51

Yoga 23
Young, Neil 64
Young, Otis 170

Zaentz, Saul 172
Zinnemann, Fred 73
Zukor, Adolph 40

215

www.ingramcontent.com/pod-product-compliance
Ingram Content Group UK Ltd.
Pitfield, Milton Keynes, MK11 3LW, UK
UKHW041956140426
5217IPUK00015B/830